PYTHON 3
AND
DATA VISUALIZATION

PYTHON 3
AND
DATA VISUALIZATION

Oswald Campesato

MERCURY LEARNING AND INFORMATION
Dulles, Virginia
Boston, Massachusetts
New Delhi

Publisher: David Pallai
Mercury Learning and Information
121 High Street, 3rd Floor
Boston, MA 02110
info@merclearning.com
www.merclearning.com
800-232-0223

O. Campesato. *Python 3 and Data Visualization.*
ISBN: 978-1-68392-946-8

The publisher recognizes and respects all marks used by companies, manufacturers, and developers as a means to distinguish their products. All brand names and product names mentioned in this book are trademarks or service marks of their respective companies. Any omission or misuse (of any kind) of service marks or trademarks, etc. is not an attempt to infringe on the property of others.

Library of Congress Control Number: 2023944271
232425321   This book is printed on acid-free paper in the United States of America.

Our titles are available for adoption, license, or bulk purchase by institutions, corporations, etc.
For additional information, please contact the Customer Service Dept. at 800-232-0223(toll free).

All of our titles are available in digital format at *academiccourseware.com* and other digital vendors. *Companion files (figures and code listings) for this title are available by contacting info@merclearning.com.* The sole obligation of Mercury Learning and Information to the purchaser is to replace the disc, based on defective materials or faulty workmanship, but not based on the operation or functionality of the product.

*I'd like to dedicate this book to my parents
– may this bring joy and happiness into their lives.*

CONTENTS

*P*REFACE

WHAT IS THE PRIMARY VALUE PROPOSITION FOR THIS BOOK?

This book contains a fast-paced introduction to relevant information about Python-based data visualization. You will learn how to generate graphics using Pandas, Matplotlib, and Seaborn. In addition, an appendix contains SVG-based and D3-based graphics effects, along with links for many additional code samples.

THE TARGET AUDIENCE

This book is intended primarily for those who have worked with Python and are interested in learning about graphics effects with Python libraries. It is also intended to reach an international audience of readers with highly diverse backgrounds in various age groups. Consequently, the book uses standard English rather than colloquial expressions that might be confusing to those readers. It provides a comfortable and meaningful learning experience for the intended readers.

WHAT WILL I LEARN?

The first chapter contains a quick tour of basic Python 3, followed by a chapter that introduces you to NumPy. The third and fourth chapters introduce you to Pandas as well as Pandas with JSON data. MySQL and SQL.

The fifth chapter delves into data visualization with Matplotlib and also working with SweetViz and Skimpy. The final chapter of this book shows you how to create graphics effects with Seaborn, and an example of a rendering graphics effects in Bokeh. In addition, an appendix is included with graphics effects based on SVG and D3.

WHY ARE THE CODE SAMPLES PRIMARILY IN PYTHON?

Most of the code samples are short (usually less than one page and sometimes less than half a page), and if need be, you can easily and quickly copy/paste the code into a new Jupyter notebook. For the Python code samples that reference a CSV file, you do not need any additional code in the corresponding Jupyter notebook to access the CSV file. Moreover, the code samples execute quickly, so you won't need to avail yourself of the free GPU that is provided in Google Colaboratory.

If you do decide to use Google Colaboratory, you can easily copy/paste the Python code into a notebook, and also use the upload feature to upload existing Jupyter notebooks. Keep in mind the following point: if the Python code references a CSV file, make sure that you include the appropriate code snippet (details are available online) to access the CSV file in the corresponding Jupyter notebook in Google Colaboratory.

WHY DOES THIS BOOK INCLUDE SKLEARN MATERIAL?

First, keep in mind that the Sklearn material in this book is minimalistic, because it is not about machine learning. Second, the Sklearn material is located in chapter 6 where you will learn about some of the Sklearn built-in datasets. If you decide to study machine learning, you will have already been introduced to some aspects of Sklearn.

GETTING THE MOST FROM THIS BOOK

Some programmers learn well from prose, others learn well from sample code (and lots of it), which means that there's no single style that can be used for everyone.

Moreover, some programmers want to run the code first, see what it does, and then return to the code to delve into the details (and others use the opposite approach).

Consequently, there are various types of code samples in this book: some are short, some are long, and other code samples "build" from earlier code samples.

WHAT DO I NEED TO KNOW?

Current knowledge of Python 3.x is the most helpful skill. Knowledge of other programming languages (such as Java) can also be helpful because of the exposure to programming concepts and constructs. The less technical knowledge that you have, the more diligence will be required in order to understand the various topics that are covered.

As for the non-technical skills, it's very important to have a strong desire to learn about data visualization, along with the motivation and discipline to read and understand the code samples.

DON'T THE COMPANION FILES OBVIATE THE NEED FOR THIS BOOK?

The companion files contain all the code samples to save you time and effort from the error-prone process of manually typing code into a text file. In addition, there are situations in which you might not have easy access to these files. Furthermore, the code samples in the book provide explanations that are not available in the companion files.

DOES THIS BOOK CONTAIN PRODUCTION-LEVEL CODE SAMPLES?

The primary purpose of the code samples in this book is to show you Python-based libraries for data visualization. Clarity has higher priority than writing more compact code that is more difficult to understand (and possibly more prone to bugs). If you decide to use any of the code in this book in a production website, you ought to subject that code to the same rigorous analysis as the other parts of your code base.

HOW DO I SET UP A COMMAND SHELL?

If you are a Mac user, there are three ways to do so. The first method is to use Finder to navigate to Applications > Utilities and then double click on the Utilities application. Next, if you already have a command shell available, you can launch a new command shell by typing the following command:

```
open /Applications/Utilities/Terminal.app
```

A second method for Mac users is to open a new command shell on a Macbook from a command shell that is already visible simply by clicking command+n in that command shell, and your Mac will launch another command shell.

If you are a PC user, you can install Cygwin (open source *https://cygwin.com/*) that simulates bash commands, or use another toolkit such as MKS (a commercial product). Please read the online documentation that describes the download and installation process. Note that custom aliases are not automatically set if they are defined in a file other than the main start-up file (such as .bash_login).

COMPANION FILES

All the code samples and figures in this book may be obtained by writing to the publisher at *info@merclearning.com*.

WHAT ARE THE "NEXT STEPS" AFTER FINISHING THIS BOOK?

The answer to this question varies widely, mainly because the answer depends heavily on your objectives. If you are interested primarily in NLP, then you can learn more advanced concepts, such as attention, transformers, and the BERT-related models.

If you are primarily interested in machine learning, there are some subfields of machine learning, such as deep learning and reinforcement learning (and deep reinforcement learning) that might appeal to you. Fortunately, there are many resources available, and you can perform an Internet search for those resources. One other point: the aspects of machine learning for you to learn depend on who you are: the needs of a machine learning engineer, data scientist, manager, student or software developer are all different.

Oswald Campesato
September 2023

## CHAPTER 1

INTRODUCTION TO PYTHON 3

This chapter provides an introduction to basic features of `Python`, including examples of working with `Python` strings, arrays, and dictionaries. Please keep in mind that this chapter does not contain details about the `Python` interpreter: you can find that information online in various tutorials.

You will also learn about useful tools for installing `Python` modules, basic `Python` constructs, and how to work with some data types in `Python`.

The first part of this chapter shows you how to work with simple data types, such as numbers, Fractions, and strings. The third part of this chapter discusses exceptions and how to use them in `Python` scripts.

The second part of this chapter introduces you to various ways to perform conditional logic in `Python`, as well as control structures and user-defined functions in `Python`. Virtually every `Python` program that performs useful calculations requires some type of conditional logic or control structure (or both). Although the syntax for these `Python` features is slightly different from other languages, the functionality will be familiar to you.

The third part of this chapter contains examples that involve nested loops and user-defined `Python` functions. The remaining portion of the chapter discusses tuples, sets, and dictionaries.

NOTE   *The* `Python` *scripts in this book are for* `Python` *3.x.*

SOME STANDARD MODULES IN PYTHON

The `Python Standard Library` provides many modules that can simplify your own `Python` scripts. A list of the Standard Library modules is here:

http://www.python.org/doc/

Some of the most important `Python` modules include `cgi`, `math`, `os`, `pickle`, `random`, `re`, `socket`, `sys`, `time`, and `urllib`.

The code samples in this book use the modules `math`, `os`, `random`, and `re`. You need to import these modules in order to use them in your code. For example, the following code block shows you how to import standard `Python` modules:

```
import re
import sys
import time
```

The code samples in this book import one or more of the preceding modules, as well as other `Python` modules. The next section discusses primitive data types in `Python`.

SIMPLE DATA TYPES IN PYTHON

`Python` supports primitive data types, such as numbers (integers, floating point numbers, and exponential numbers), strings, and dates. `Python` also supports more complex data types, such as lists (or arrays), tuples, and dictionaries, all of which are discussed later in this chapter. The next several sections discuss some of the `Python` primitive data types, along with code snippets that show you how to perform various operations on those data types.

WORKING WITH NUMBERS

`Python` provides arithmetic operations for manipulating numbers a straightforward manner that is similar to other programming languages. The following examples involve arithmetic operations on integers:

```
>>> 2+2
4
>>> 4/3
1
>>> 3*8
24
```

The following example assigns numbers to two variables and computes their product:

```
>>> x = 4
>>> y = 7
>>> x * y
28
```

The following examples demonstrate arithmetic operations involving integers:

```
>>> 2+2
4
>>> 4/3
1
>>> 3*8
24
```

Notice that division ("/") of two integers is actually truncation in which only the integer result is retained. The following example converts a floating point number into exponential form:

```
>>> fnum = 0.00012345689000007
>>> "%.14e"%fnum
'1.23456890000070e-04'
```

You can use the int() function and the float() function to convert strings to numbers:

```
word1 = "123"
word2 = "456.78"
var1 = int(word1)
var2 = float(word2)
print("var1: ",var1," var2: ",var2)
```

The output from the preceding code block is here:

```
var1:  123  var2:  456.78
```

Alternatively, you can use the eval() function:

```
word1 = "123"
word2 = "456.78"
var1 = eval(word1)
var2 = eval(word2)
print("var1: ",var1," var2: ",var2)
```

If you attempt to convert a string that is not a valid integer or a floating point number, Python raises an exception, so it's advisable to place your code in a try/except block (discussed later in this chapter).

Working With Other Bases

Numbers in Python are in base 10 (the default), but you can easily convert numbers to other bases. For example, the following code block initializes the variable x with the value 1234, and then displays that number in base 2, 8, and 16, respectively:

```
>>> x = 1234
>>> bin(x) '0b10011010010'
>>> oct(x) '0o2322'
>>> hex(x) '0x4d2' >>>
```

Use the format() function if you want to suppress the 0b, 0o, or 0x prefixes, as shown here:

```
>>> format(x, 'b') '10011010010'
>>> format(x, 'o') '2322'
>>> format(x, 'x') '4d2'
```

Negative integers are displayed with a negative sign:

```
>>> x = -1234
>>> format(x, 'b') '-10011010010'
>>> format(x, 'x') '-4d2'
```

The chr() **Function**

The Python chr() function takes a positive integer as a parameter and converts it to its corresponding alphabetic value (if one exists). The letters A through Z have decimal representation of 65 through 91 (which corresponds to hexadecimal 41 through 5b), and the lowercase letters a through z have decimal representation 97 through 122 (hexadecimal 61 through 7b).

Here is an example of using the chr() function to print uppercase A:

```
>>> x=chr(65)
>>> x
'A'
```

The following code block prints the ASCII values for a range of integers:

```
result = ""
for x in range(65,91):
  print(x, chr(x))
  result = result+chr(x)+' '
print("result: ",result)
```

NOTE   Python 2 *uses* ASCII *strings whereas* Python 3 *uses* UTF-8.

You can represent a range of characters with the following line:

```
for x in range(65,91):
```

However, the following equivalent code snippet is more intuitive:

```
for x in range(ord('A'), ord('Z')):
```

If you want to display the result for lowercase letters, change the preceding range from (65,91) to either of the following statements:

```
for x in range(65,91):
for x in range(ord('a'), ord('z')):
```

The round() **Function in Python**

The Python round() function enables you to round decimal values to the nearest precision:

```
>>> round(1.23, 1)
1.2
>>> round(-3.42,1)
-3.4
```

Before delving into Python code samples that work with strings, the next section briefly discusses Unicode and UTF-8, both of which are character encodings.

UNICODE AND UTF-8

A Unicode string consists of a sequence of numbers that are between 0 and 0x10ffff, where each number represents a group of bytes. An encoding is the manner in which a Unicode string is translated into a sequence of bytes. Among the various encodings, UTF-8 ("Unicode Transformation Format") is perhaps the most common, and it's also the default encoding for many systems. The digit 8 in UTF-8 indicates that the encoding uses 8-bit numbers, whereas UTF-16 uses 16-bit numbers (but this encoding is less common).

The ASCII character set is a subset of UTF-8, so a valid ASCII string can be read as a UTF-8 string without any re-encoding required. In addition, a Unicode string can be converted into a UTF-8 string.

WORKING WITH UNICODE

Python supports Unicode, which means that you can render characters in different languages. Unicode data can be stored and manipulated in the same way as strings. Create a Unicode string by prepending the letter 'u', as shown here:

```
>>> u'Hello from Python!'
u'Hello from Python!'
```

Special characters can be included in a string by specifying their Unicode value. For example, the following Unicode string embeds a space (which has the Unicode value 0x0020) in a string:

```
>>> u'Hello\u0020from Python!'
u'Hello from Python!'
```

Listing 1.1 displays the contents of Unicode1.py that illustrates how to display a string of characters in Japanese and another string of characters in Chinese (Mandarin).

LISTING 1.1 Unicode1.py

```
chinese1 = u'\u5c07\u63a2\u8a0e HTML5 \u53ca\u5176\u4ed6'
hiragana = u'D3 \u306F \u304B\u3063\u3053\u3043\u3043 \u3067\u3059!'

print('Chinese:',chinese1)
print('Hiragana:',hiragana)
```

The output of Listing 1.1 is here:

```
Chinese: 將探討 HTML5 及其他
Hiragana: D3 は かっこいい です!
```

The next portion of this chapter shows you how to "slice and dice" text strings with built-in Python functions.

WORKING WITH STRINGS

Literal strings in Python 3 are Unicode by default. You can concatenate two strings using the '+' operator. The following example prints a string and then concatenates two single-letter strings:

```
>>> 'abc'
'abc'
```

```
>>> 'a' + 'b'
'ab'
```

You can use '+' or '*' *to* concatenate identical strings, as shown here:

```
>>> 'a' + 'a' + 'a'
'aaa'
>>> 'a' * 3
'aaa'
```

You can assign strings to variables and print them using the `print()` statement:

```
>>> print('abc')
abc
>>> x = 'abc'
>>> print(x)
abc
>>> y = 'def'
>>> print(x + y)
abcdef
```

You can "unpack" the letters of a string and assign them to variables, as shown here:

```
>>> str = "World"
>>> x1,x2,x3,x4,x5 = str
>>> x1
'W'
>>> x2
'o'
>>> x3
'r'
>>> x4
'l'
>>> x5
'd'
```

The preceding code snippets shows you how easy it is to extract the letters in a text string. You can also extract substrings of a string as shown in the following examples:

```
>>> x = "abcdef"
>>> x[0]
'a'
>>> x[-1]
'f'
>>> x[1:3]
'bc'
>>> x[0:2] + x[5:]
'abf'
```

However, you will cause an error if you attempt to subtract two strings, as you probably expect:

```
>>> 'a' - 'b'
Traceback (most recent call last):
```

```
    File "<stdin>", line 1, in <module>
TypeError: unsupported operand type(s) for -: 'str' and 'str'
```

The `try/except` construct in `Python` (discussed later in this chapter) enables you to handle the preceding type of exception more gracefully.

Comparing Strings

You can use the methods `lower()` and `upper()` to convert a string to lowercase and uppercase, respectively, as shown here:

```
>>> 'Python'.lower()
'python'
>>> 'Python'.upper()
'PYTHON'
>>>
```

The methods `lower()` and `upper()` are useful for performing a case insensitive comparison of two ASCII strings. Listing 1.2 displays the contents of `Compare.py` that uses the `lower()` function in order to compare two ASCII strings.

LISTING 1.2 Compare.py

```
x = 'Abc'
y = 'abc'

if(x == y):
  print('x and y: identical')
elif (x.lower() == y.lower()):
  print('x and y: case insensitive match')
else:
  print('x and y: different')
```

Since x contains mixed case letters and y contains lowercase letters, Listing 1.2 displays the following output:

```
x and y: different
```

Uninitialized Variables and the Value None in Python

`Python` distinguishes between an uninitialized variable and the value `None`. The former is a variable that has not been assigned a value, whereas the value `None` is a value that indicates "no value." Collections and methods often return the value `None`, and you can test for the value `None` in conditional logic (shown later in this chapter).

The next portion of this chapter shows you how to "slice and dice" text strings with built-in `Python` functions.

SLICING AND SPLICING STRINGS

`Python` enables you to extract substrings of a string (called "slicing") using array notation. Slice notation is `start:stop:step`, where the start, stop, and step values are integers that specify the start value, end value, and the increment value. The interesting part about slicing in Python is that you can use the value -1, which operates from the right-side instead of the left-side of a string. Some examples of slicing a string are here:

```
text1 = "this is a string"
print('First 7 characters:',text1[0:7])
print('Characters 2-4:',text1[2:4])
print('Right-most character:',text1[-1])
print('Right-most 2 characters:',text1[-3:-1])
```

The output from the preceding code block is here:

```
First 7 characters: this is
Characters 2-4: is
Right-most character: g
Right-most 2 characters: in
```

Later in this chapter you will see how to insert a string in the middle of another string.

Testing for Digits and Alphabetic Characters

Python enables you to examine each character in a string and then test whether that character is a bona fide digit or an alphabetic character. This section provides a precursor to regular expressions that are discussed in Chapter 8.

Listing 1.3 displays the contents of CharTypes.py that illustrates how to determine if a string contains digits or characters. In case you are unfamiliar with the conditional "if" statement in Listing 1.3, more detailed information is available later in this chapter.

LISTING 1.3 CharTypes.py

```
str1 = "4"
str2 = "4234"
str3 = "b"
str4 = "abc"
str5 = "a1b2c3"

if(str1.isdigit()):
  print("this is a digit:",str1)

if(str2.isdigit()):
  print("this is a digit:",str2)

if(str3.isalpha()):
  print("this is alphabetic:",str3)

if(str4.isalpha()):
  print("this is alphabetic:",str4)

if(not str5.isalpha()):
  print("this is not pure alphabetic:",str5)
```

```
print("capitalized first letter:",str5.title())
```

Listing 1.3 initializes some variables, followed by two conditional tests that check whether or not str1 and str2 are digits using the isdigit() function. The next portion of Listing 1.3 checks if str3, str4, and str5 are alphabetic strings using the isalpha() function. The output of Listing 1.3 is here:

```
this is a digit: 4
this is a digit: 4234
this is alphabetic: b
this is alphabetic: abc
this is not pure alphabetic: a1b2c3
capitalized first letter: A1B2C3
```

SEARCH AND REPLACE A STRING IN OTHER STRINGS

Python provides methods for searching and also for replacing a string in a second text string. Listing 1.4 displays the contents of FindPos1.py that shows you how to use the find() function to search for the occurrence of one string in another string.

LISTING 1.4 FindPos1.py

```
item1 = 'abc'
item2 = 'Abc'
text = 'This is a text string with abc'

pos1 = text.find(item1)
pos2 = text.find(item2)

print('pos1=',pos1)
print('pos2=',pos2)
```

Listing 1.4 initializes the variables item1, item2, and text, and then searches for the index of the contents of item1 and item2 in the string text. The Python find() function returns the column number where the first successful match occurs; otherwise, the find() function returns a –1 if a match is unsuccessful. The output from launching Listing 1.4 is here:

```
pos1= 27
pos2= -1
```

In addition to the find() method, you can use the in operator when you want to test for the presence of an element, as shown here:

```
>>> lst = [1,2,3]
>>> 1 in lst
True
```

Listing 1.5 displays the contents of Replace1.py that shows you how to replace one string with another string.

LISTING 1.5: Replace1.py

```
text = 'This is a text string with abc'
print('text:',text)
text = text.replace('is a', 'was a')
print('text:',text)
```

Listing 1.5 starts by initializing the variable text and then printing its contents. The next portion of Listing 1.5 replaces the occurrence of "is a" with "was a" in the string text, and then prints the modified string. The output from launching Listing 1.5 is here:

```
text: This is a text string with abc
text: This was a text string with abc
```

PRECEDENCE OF OPERATORS IN PYTHON

When you have an expression involving numbers, you might remember that multiplication ("*") and division ("/") have higher precedence than addition ("+") or subtraction ("−"). Exponentiation has even higher precedence than these four arithmetic operators.

However, instead of relying on precedence rules, it's simpler (as well as safer) to use parentheses. For example, `(x/y)+10` is clearer than `x/y+10`, even though they are equivalent expressions.

As another example, the following two arithmetic expressions are the equivalent, but the second is less error prone than the first:

```
x/y+3*z/8+x*y/z-3*x
(x/y)+(3*z)/8+(x*y)/z-(3*x)
```

In any case, the following website contains precedence rules for operators in Python:

http://www.mathcs.emory.edu/~valerie/courses/fall10/155/resources/op_precedence.html

PYTHON RESERVED WORDS

Every programming language has a set of reserved words, which is a set of words that cannot be used as identifiers, and Python is no exception. The Python reserved words are: and, exec, not, assert, finally, or, break, for, pass, class, from, print, continue, global, raise, def, if, return, del, import, try, elif, in, while, else, is, with, except, lambda, and yield.

If you inadvertently use a reserved word as a variable, you will see an "invalid syntax" error message instead of a "reserved word" error message. For example, suppose you create a Python script test1.py with the following code:

```
break = 2
print('break =', break)
```

If you run the preceding Python code you will see the following output:

```
File "test1.py", line 2
  break = 2
```

```
                  ^
SyntaxError: invalid syntax
```

However, a quick inspection of the `Python` code reveals the fact that you are attempting to use the reserved word `break` as a variable.

WORKING WITH LOOPS IN PYTHON

`Python` supports `for` loops, `while` loops, and `range()` statements. The following subsections illustrate how you can use each of these constructs.

Python `for` Loops

`Python` supports the `for` loop whose syntax is slightly different from other languages (such as `JavaScript` and `Java`). The following code block shows you how to use a `for` loop in `Python` in order to iterate through the elements in a list:

```
>>> x = ['a', 'b', 'c']
>>> for w in x:
...     print(w)
...
a
b
c
```

The preceding code snippet prints three letters on three separate lines. You can force the output to be displayed on the same line (which will "wrap" if you specify a large enough number of characters) by appending a comma "," in the `print()` statement, as shown here:

```
>>> x = ['a', 'b', 'c']
>>> for w in x:
...     print(w, end=' ')
...
a b c
```

You can use this type of code when you want to display the contents of a text file in a single line instead of multiple lines.

`Python` also provides the built-in `reversed()` function that reverses the direction of the loop, as shown here:

```
>>> a = [1, 2, 3, 4, 5]
>>> for x in reversed(a):
... print(x)
5
4
3
2
1
```

Note that reversed iteration only works if the size of the current object can be determined or if the object implements a __reversed__() special method.

Numeric Exponents in Python

Listing 1.6 displays the contents of `Nth_exponent.py` that illustrates how to calculate intermediate powers of a set of integers.

LISTING 1.6: Nth_exponent.py

```
maxPower = 4
maxCount = 4

def pwr(num):
  prod = 1
  for n in range(1,maxPower+1):
    prod = prod*num
    print(num,'to the power',n, 'equals',prod)
  print('-----------')

for num in range(1,maxCount+1):
    pwr(num)
```

Listing 1.6 contains a function called `pwr()` that accepts a numeric value. This function contains a loop that prints the value of that number raised to the power n, where n ranges between 1 and `maxPower+1`.

The second part of Listing 1.6 contains a `for` loop that invokes the function `pwr()` with the numbers between 1 and `maxPower+1`. The output from Listing 1.16 is here:

```
1 to the power 1 equals 1
1 to the power 2 equals 1
1 to the power 3 equals 1
1 to the power 4 equals 1
-----------
2 to the power 1 equals 2
2 to the power 2 equals 4
2 to the power 3 equals 8
2 to the power 4 equals 16
-----------
3 to the power 1 equals 3
3 to the power 2 equals 9
3 to the power 3 equals 27
3 to the power 4 equals 81
-----------
4 to the power 1 equals 4
4 to the power 2 equals 16
4 to the power 3 equals 64
4 to the power 4 equals 256
-----------
```

NESTED LOOPS

Listing 1.7 displays the contents of `Triangular1.py` that illustrates how to print a row of consecutive integers (starting from 1), where the length of each row is one greater than the previous row.

LISTING 1.7: Triangular1.py

```
max = 8
for x in range(1,max+1):
  for y in range(1,x+1):
    print(y, '', end='')
  print()
```

Listing 1.7 initializes the variable `max` with the value 8, followed by an outer `for` loop whose loop variable x ranges from 1 to max+1. The inner loop has a loop variable y that ranges from 1 to x+1, and the inner loop prints the value of y. The output of Listing 1.7 is here:

```
1
1 2
1 2 3
1 2 3 4
1 2 3 4 5
1 2 3 4 5 6
1 2 3 4 5 6 7
1 2 3 4 5 6 7 8
```

THE `split()` FUNCTION WITH FOR LOOPS

`Python` supports various useful string-related functions, including the `split()` function and the `join()` function. The `split()` function is useful when you want to tokenize ("split") a line of text into words and then use a `for` loop to iterate through those words and process them accordingly.

The `join()` function does the opposite of `split()`: it "joins" two or more words into a single line. You can easily remove extra spaces in a sentence by using the `split()` function and then invoking the `join()` function, thereby creating a line of text with one white space between any two words.

USING THE `split()` FUNCTION TO COMPARE WORDS

Listing 1.8 displays the contents of `Compare2.py` that illustrates how to use the split function to compare each word in a text string with another word.

LISTING 1.8: Compare2.py

```
x = 'This is a string that contains abc and Abc'
y = 'abc'
identical = 0
casematch = 0

for w in x.split():
  if(w == y):
    identical = identical + 1
  elif (w.lower() == y.lower()):
    casematch = casematch + 1
```

```
if(identical > 0):
 print('found identical matches:', identical)

if(casematch > 0):
 print('found case matches:', casematch)

if(casematch == 0 and identical == 0):
 print('no matches found')
```

Listing 1.8 uses the `split()` function in order to compare each word in the string x with the word abc. If there is an exact match, the variable `identical` is incremented. If a match does not occur, a case-insensitive match of the current word is performed with the string abc, and the variable `casematch` is incremented if the match is successful. The output from Listing 1.8 is here:

```
found identical matches: 1
found case matches: 1
```

PYTHON while LOOPS

You can define a `while` loop to iterate through a set of numbers, as shown in the following examples:

```
>>> x = 0
>>> while x < 5:
...     print(x)
...     x = x + 1
...
0
1
2
3
4
5
```

`Python` uses indentation instead of curly braces that are used in other languages such as `JavaScript` and `Java`. Although the `Python list` data structure is not discussed until later in this chapter, you can probably understand the following simple code block that contains a variant of the preceding `while` loop that you can use when working with lists:

```
lst  = [1,2,3,4]

while lst:
  print('list:',lst)
  print('item:',lst.pop())
```

The preceding `while` loop terminates when the lst variable is empty, and there is no need to explicitly test for an empty list. The output from the preceding code is here:

```
list: [1, 2, 3, 4]
item: 4
```

```
list: [1, 2, 3]
item: 3
list: [1, 2]
item: 2
list: [1]
item: 1
```

This concludes the examples that use the `split()` function in order to process words and characters in a text string. The next part of this chapter shows you examples of using conditional logic in `Python` code.

CONDITIONAL LOGIC IN PYTHON

If you have written code in other programming languages, you have undoubtedly seen `if/then/else` (or `if-elseif-else`) conditional statements. Although the syntax varies between languages, the logic is essentially the same. The following example shows you how to use `if/elif` statements in `Python`:

```
>>> x = 25
>>> if x < 0:
...     print('negative')
... elif x < 25:
...     print('under 25')
... elif x == 25:
...     print('exactly 25')
... else:
...   print('over 25')
...
exactly 25
```

The preceding code block illustrates how to use multiple conditional statements, and the output is exactly what you expected.

THE `break/continue/pass` STATEMENTS

The `break` statement in `Python` enables you to perform an "early exit" from a loop, whereas the `continue` statement essentially returns to the top of the loop and continues with the next value of the loop variable. The `pass` statement is essentially a "do nothing" statement.

Listing 1.9 displays the contents of `BreakContinuePass.py` that illustrates the use of these three statements.

LISTING 1.9: *BreakContinuePass.py*

```
print('first loop')
for x in range(1,4):
  if(x == 2):
    break
  print(x)
```

```
print('second loop')
for x in range(1,4):
  if(x == 2):
    continue
  print(x)

print('third loop')
for x in range(1,4):
  if(x == 2):
    pass
  print(x)
```

The output of Listing 1.9 is here:

```
first loop
1
second loop
1
3
third loop
1
2
3
```

COMPARISON AND Boolean OPERATORS

Python supports a variety of Boolean operators, such as in, not in, is, is not, and, or, and not. The next several sections discuss these operators and provide some examples of how to use them.

The in/not in/is/is not Comparison Operators

The in and not in operators are used with sequences to check whether a value occurs or does not occur in a sequence. The operators is and is not determine whether or not two objects are the same object, which is important only matters for mutable objects such as lists. All comparison operators have the same priority, which is lower than that of all numerical operators. Comparisons can also be chained. For example, a < b == c tests whether a is less than b and moreover b equals c.

The and, or, and not Boolean Operators

The Boolean operators and, or, and not have lower priority than comparison operators. The Boolean and and or are binary operators whereas the Boolean or operator is a unary operator. Here are some examples:

- A and B can only be true if both A and B are true
- A or B is true if either A or B is true
- not(A) is true if and only if A is false

You can also assign the result of a comparison or other Boolean expression to a variable, as shown here:

```
>>> string1, string2, string3 = '', 'b', 'cd'
>>> str4 = string1 or string2 or string3
>>> str4
'b'
```

The preceding code block initializes the variables `string1`, `string2`, and `string3`, where `string1` is an empty string. Next, `str4` is initialized via the `or` operator, and since the first non-null value is `string2`, the value of `str4` is equal to `string2`.

LOCAL AND GLOBAL VARIABLES

`Python` variables can be local or global. A `Python` variable is local to a function if the following are true:

- a parameter of the function
- on the left side of a statement in the function
- bound to a control structure (such as for, with, and except)

A variable that is referenced in a function but is not local (according to the previous list) is a nonlocal variable. You can specify a variable as nonlocal with this snippet:

```
nonlocal z
```

A variable can be explicitly declared as global with this statement:

```
global z
```

The following code block illustrates the behavior of a global versus a local variable:

```
global z
z = 3

def changeVar(z):
  z = 4
  print('z in function:',z)

print('first global z:',z)

if __name__ == '__main__':
  changeVar(z)
  print('second global z:',z)
```

The output from the preceding code block is here:

```
first global z: 3
z in function: 4
second global z: 3
```

SCOPE OF VARIABLES

The accessibility or scope of a variable depends on where that variable has been defined. Python provides two scopes: global and local, with the added "twist" that global is actually module-level scope (i.e., the current file), and therefore you can have a variable with the same name in different files and they will be treated differently.

Local variables are straightforward: they are defined inside a function, and they can only be accessed inside the function where they are defined. Any variables that are not local variables have global scope, which means that those variables are "global" *only* with respect to the file where it has been defined, and they can be accessed anywhere in a file.

There are two scenarios to consider regarding variables. First, suppose two files (aka modules) file1.py and file2.py have a variable called x, and file1.py also imports file2.py. The question now is how to disambiguate between the x in the two different modules. As an example, suppose that file2.py contains the following two lines of code:

```
x = 3
print('unscoped x in file2:',x)
```

Suppose that file1.py contains the following code:

```
import file2 as file2

x = 5
print('unscoped x in file1:',x)
print('scoped x from file2:',file2.x)
```

Launch file1.py from the command line, and you will see the following output:

```
unscoped x in file2: 3
unscoped x in file1: 5
scoped x from file2: 3
```

The second scenario involves a program containing a local variable and a global variable with the same name. According to the earlier rule, the local variable is used in the function where it is defined, and the global variable is used outside of that function.

The following code block illustrates the use of a global and local variable with the same name:

```
#!/usr/bin/python
# a global variable:
total = 0;

def sum(x1, x2):
    # this total is local:
    total = x1+x2;

    print("Local total : ", total)
    return total

# invoke the sum function
sum(2,3);
print("Global total : ", total)
```

When the above code is executed, it produces following result:

```
Local total :    5
Global total :   0
```

What about unscoped variables, such as specifying the variable x without a module prefix? The answer consists of the following sequence of steps that Python will perform:

1. Check the local scope for the name.
2. Ascend the enclosing scopes and check for the name.
3. Perform Step 2 until the global scope (i.e., module level).
4. If x still hasn't been found, Python checks __builtins__</nl>

```
Python 3.9.1 (v3.9.1:1e5d33e9b9, Dec  7 2020, 12:44:01)
[Clang 12.0.0 (clang-1200.0.32.27)] on darwin
Type "help", "copyright", "credits" or "license" for more information.
>>> x = 1
>>> g = globals()
>>> g
{'g': {...}, '__builtins__': <module '__builtin__' (built-in)>, '__package__': None, 'x': 1, '__name__': '__main__', '__doc__': None}
>>> g.pop('x')
1
>>> x
Traceback (most recent call last):
  File "<stdin>", line 1, in <module>
NameError: name 'x' is not defined
```

NOTE *You can access the* dicts *that* Python *uses to track local and global scope by invoking* locals() *and* globals() *respectively.*

PASS BY REFERENCE VERSUS VALUE

All parameters (arguments) in the Python language are passed by reference. Thus, if you change what a parameter refers to within a function, the change is reflected in the calling function. For example:

```
def changeme(mylist):
   #This changes a passed list into this function
   mylist.append([1,2,3,4])
   print("Values inside the function: ", mylist)
   return

# Now you can call changeme function
mylist = [10,20,30]
changeme(mylist)
print("Values outside the function: ", mylist)
```

Here we are maintaining reference of the passed object and appending values in the same object, and the result is shown here:

```
Values inside the function:  [10, 20, 30, [1, 2, 3, 4]]
Values outside the function:  [10, 20, 30, [1, 2, 3, 4]]
```

The fact that values are passed by reference gives rise to the notion of mutability versus immutability that is discussed in Chapter 3.

ARGUMENTS AND PARAMETERS

`Python` differentiates between arguments to functions and parameter declarations in functions: a positional (mandatory) and keyword (optional/default value). This concept is important because `Python` has operators for packing and unpacking these kinds of arguments. `Python` unpacks positional arguments from an iterable, as shown here:

```
>>> def foo(x, y):
...    return x - y
...
>>> data = 4,5
>>> foo(data) # only passed one arg
Traceback (most recent call last):
  File "<stdin>", line 1, in <module>
TypeError: foo() takes exactly 2 arguments (1 given)
>>> foo(*data) # passed however many args are in tuple
-1
```

USER-DEFINED FUNCTIONS IN PYTHON

`Python` provides built-in functions and also enables you to define your own functions. You can define functions to provide the required functionality. Here are simple rules to define a function in `Python`:

- Function blocks begin with the keyword `def` followed by the function name and parentheses.
- Any input arguments should be placed within these parentheses.
- The first statement of a function can be an optional statement—the documentation string of the function or docstring.
- The code block within every function starts with a colon (:) and is indented.
- The statement return [expression] exits a function, optionally passing back an expression to the caller. A return statement with no arguments is the same as return None.
- If a function does not specify return statement, the function automatically returns None, which is a special type of value in `Python`.

A very simple custom `Python` function is here:

```
>>> def func():
...    print 3
...
>>> func()
3
```

The preceding function is trivial, but it does illustrate the syntax for defining custom functions in `Python`. The following example is slightly more useful:

```
>>> def func(x):
...     for i in range(0,x):
...         print(i)
...
>>> func(5)
0
1
2
3
4
```

SPECIFYING DEFAULT VALUES IN A FUNCTION

Listing 1.10 displays the contents of `DefaultValues.py` that illustrates how to specify default values in a function.

LISTING 1.10: DefaultValues.py

```
def numberFunc(a, b=10):
  print (a,b)

def stringFunc(a, b='xyz'):
  print (a,b)

def collectionFunc(a, b=None):
  if(b is None):
      print('No value assigned to b')

numberFunc(3)
stringFunc('one')
collectionFunc([1,2,3])
```

Listing 1.10 defines three functions, followed by an invocation of each of those functions. The functions `numberFunc()` and `stringFunc()` print a list containing the values of their two parameters, and `collectionFunc()` displays a message if the second parameter is `None`. The output from Listing 1.10 is here:

```
(3, 10)
('one', 'xyz')
No value assigned to b
```

Returning Multiple Values From a Function

This task is accomplished by the code in Listing 1.11, which displays the contents of `MultipleValues.py`.

LISTING 1.11: MultipleValues.py

```
def MultipleValues():
    return 'a', 'b', 'c'

x, y, z = MultipleValues()

print('x:',x)
print('y:',y)
print('z:',z)
```

The output from Listing 1.11 is here:

```
x:  a
y:  b
z:  c
```

LAMBDA EXPRESSIONS

Listing 1.12 displays the contents of Lambda1.py that illustrates how to create a simple lambda function in Python.

LISTING 1.12: Lambda1.py

```
add = lambda x, y: x + y

x1 = add(5,7)
x2 = add('Hello', 'Python')

print(x1)
print(x2)
```

Listing 1.12 defines the lambda expression add that accepts two input parameters and then returns their sum (for numbers) or their concatenation (for strings).

The output from Listing 1.12 is here:

```
12
HelloPython
```

The next portion of this chapter discusses Python collections, such as lists (or arrays), sets, tuples, and dictionaries. You will see many short code blocks that will help you rapidly learn how to work with these data structures in Python. After you have finished reading this chapter, you will be in a better position to create more complex Python modules using one or more of these data structures.

WORKING WITH LISTS

Python supports a list data type, along with a rich set of list-related functions. Since lists are not typed, you can create a list of different data types, as well as multidimensional lists. The next several sections show you how to manipulate list structures in Python.

Lists and Basic Operations

A `Python` list consists of comma-separated values enclosed in a pair of square brackets. The following examples illustrate the syntax for defining a list in `Python`, and also show how to perform various operations on a `Python` list:

```
>>> list = [1, 2, 3, 4, 5]
>>> list
[1, 2, 3, 4, 5]
>>> list[2]
3
>>> list2 = list + [1, 2, 3, 4, 5]
>>> list2
[1, 2, 3, 4, 5, 1, 2, 3, 4, 5]
>>> list2.append(6)
>>> list2
[1, 2, 3, 4, 5, 1, 2, 3, 4, 5, 6]
>>> len(list)
5
>>> x = ['a', 'b', 'c']
>>> y = [1, 2, 3]
>>> z = [x, y]
>>> z[0]
['a', 'b', 'c']
>>> len(x)
3
```

You can assign multiple variables to a list, provided that the number and type of the variables match the structure. Here is an example:

```
>>> point = [7,8]
>>> x,y = point
>>> x
7
>>> y
8
```

The following example shows you how to assign values to variables from a more complex data structure:

```
>>> line = ['a', 10, 20, (2023,01,31)]
>>> x1,x2,x3,date1 = line
>>> x1
'a'
>>> x2
10
>>> x3
20
>>> date1
(2023, 1, 31)
```

If you want to access the year/month/date components of the `date1` element in the preceding code block, you can do so with the following code block:

```
>>> line = ['a', 10, 20, (2023,01,31)]
>>> x1,x2,x3,(year,month,day) = line
>>> x1
'a'
>>> x2
10
>>> x3
20
>>> year
2023
>>> month
1
>>> day
31
```

If the number and/or structure of the variables do not match the data, an error message is displayed, as shown here:

```
>>> point = (1,2)
>>> x,y,z = point
Traceback (most recent call last):
  File "<stdin>", line 1, in <module>
ValueError: need more than 2 values to unpack
```

If the number of variables that you specify is less than the number of data items, you will see an error message, as shown here:

```
>>> line = ['a', 10, 20, (2014,01,31)]
>>> x1,x2 = line
Traceback (most recent call last):
  File "<stdin>", line 1, in <module>
ValueError: too many values to unpack
```

Lists and Arithmetic Operations

The minimum value of a list of numbers is the first number in the sorted list of numbers. If you reverse the sorted list, the first number is the maximum value. There are several ways to reverse a list, starting with the technique shown in the following code:

```
x = [3,1,2,4]
maxList = x.sort()
minList = x.sort(x.reverse())

min1 = min(x)
max1 = max(x)
print min1
print max1
```

The output of the preceding code block is here:

```
1
4
```

A second (and better) way to sort a list is shown here:

```
minList = x.sort(reverse=True)
```

A third way to sort a list involves the built-in functional version of the `sort()` method, as shown here:

```
sorted(x, reverse=True)
```

The preceding code snippet is useful when you do not want to modify the original order of the list or you want to compose multiple list operations on a single line.

Lists and Filter-Related Operations

Python enables you to filter a list (also called *list comprehension*) as shown here:

```
mylist = [1, -2, 3, -5, 6, -7, 8]
pos = [n for n in mylist if n > 0]
neg = [n for n in mylist if n < 0]

print pos
print neg
```

You can also specify `if/else` logic in a filter, as shown here:

```
mylist = [1, -2, 3, -5, 6, -7, 8]
negativeList = [n if n < 0 else 0 for n in mylist]
positiveList = [n if n > 0 else 0 for n in mylist]

print positiveList
print negativeList
```

The output of the preceding code block is here:

```
[1, 3, 6, 8]
[-2, -5, -7]
[1, 0, 3, 0, 6, 0, 8]
[0, -2, 0, -5, 0, -7, 0]
```

THE JOIN(), RANGE(), AND SPLIT() FUNCTIONS

Python provides the `join()` method for concatenating text strings, as shown here:

```
>>> parts = ['Is', 'SF', 'In', 'California?']
>>> ' '.join(parts)
'Is SF In California?'
>>> ','.join(parts)
'Is,SF,In,California?'
>>> ''.join(parts) 'IsSFInCalifornia?'
```

There are several ways to concatenate a set of strings and then print the result. The following is the most inefficient way to do so:

```
print "This" + " is" + " a" + " sentence"
```

Either of the following is preferred:

```
print "%s %s %s %s" % ("This", "is", "a", "sentence")
print " ".join(["This","is","a","sentence"])
```

The next code block illustrates the `Python range()` function that you can use to iterate through a list, as shown here:

```
>>> for i in range(0,5):
...     print i
...
0
1
2
3
4
```

You can use a `for` loop to iterate through a list of strings, as shown here:

```
>>> x
['a', 'b', 'c']
>>> for w in x:
...     print w
...
a
b
c
```

You can use a `for` loop to iterate through a list of strings and provide additional details, as shown here:

```
>>> x
['a', 'b', 'c']
>>> for w in x:
...     print len(w), w
...
1 a
1 b
1 c
```

The preceding output displays the length of each word in the list x, followed by the word itself.

You can use the `Python split()` function to split the words in a text string and populate a list with those words. An example is here:

```
>>> x = "this is a string"
>>> list = x.split()
>>> list
['this', 'is', 'a', 'string']
```

A simple way to print the list of words in a text string is shown here:

```
>>> x = "this is a string"
```

```
>>> for w in x.split():
...     print w
...
this
is
a
string
```

You can search for a word in a string as follows:

```
>>> x = "this is a string"
>>> for w in x.split():
...     if(w == 'this'):
...         print "x contains this"
...
x contains this
...
```

ARRAYS AND THE APPEND() FUNCTION

Although Python does have an array type (import array), which is essentially a heterogeneous list, the array type has no advantages over the list type other than a slight saving in memory use. You can also define heterogeneous arrays:

```
a = [10, 'hello', [5, '77']]
```

You can append a new element to an element inside a list:

```
>>> a = [10, 'hello', [5, '77']]
>>> a[2].append('abc')
>>> a
[10, 'hello', [5, '77', 'abc']]
```

You can assign simple variables to the elements of a list, as shown here:

```
myList = [ 'a', 'b', 91.1, (2014, 01, 31) ]
x1, x2, x3, x4 = myList
print 'x1:',x1
print 'x2:',x2
print 'x3:',x3
print 'x4:',x4
```

The output of the preceding code block is here:

```
x1: a
x2: b
x3: 91.1
x4: (2014, 1, 31)
```

The Python split() function is more convenient (especially when the number of elements is unknown or variable) than the preceding sample, and you will see examples of the split() function in the next section.

OTHER LIST-RELATED FUNCTIONS

Python provides additional functions that you can use with lists, such as append(), insert(), delete(), pop(), and extend(). Python also supports the functions index(), count(), sort(), and reverse(). Examples of these functions are illustrated in the following code block.

Define a Python list (notice that duplicates are allowed):

```
>>> a = [1, 2, 3, 2, 4, 2, 5]
```

Display the number of occurrences of 1 and 2:

```
>>> print a.count(1), a.count(2)
1 3
```

Insert -8 in position 3:

```
>>> a.insert(3,-8)
>>> a
[1, 2, 3, -8, 2, 4, 2, 5]
```

Remove occurrences of 3:

```
>>> a.remove(3)
>>> a
[1, 2, -8, 2, 4, 2, 5]
```

Remove occurrences of 1:

```
>>> a.remove(1)
>>> a
[2, -8, 2, 4, 2, 5]
```

Append 19 to the list:

```
>>> a.append(19)
>>> a
[2, -8, 2, 4, 2, 5, 19]
```

Print the index of 19 in the list:

```
>>> a.index(19)
6
```

Reverse the list:

```
>>> a.reverse()
>>> a
[19, 5, 2, 4, 2, -8, 2]
```

Sort the list:

```
>>> a.sort()
>>> a
[-8, 2, 2, 2, 4, 5, 19]
```

Extend list a with list b:

```
>>> b = [100,200,300]
>>> a.extend(b)
>>> a
[-8, 2, 2, 2, 4, 5, 19, 100, 200, 300]
```

Remove the first occurrence of 2:

```
>>> a.pop(2)
2
>>> a
[-8, 2, 2, 4, 5, 19, 100, 200, 300]
```

Remove the last item of the list:

```
>>> a.pop()
300
>>> a
[-8, 2, 2, 4, 5, 19, 100, 200]
```

WORKING WITH LIST COMPREHENSIONS

A list comprehension is a powerful construct in `Python` that enables you to create a list of values in one line of code. Here is a simple example:

```
letters = [w for w in "Chicago Pizza"]
print(letters)
```

If you launch the preceding code snippet you will see the following output:

```
['C', 'h', 'i', 'c', 'a', 'g', 'o', ' ', 'P', 'i', 'z', 'z', 'a']
```

Another example is shown in the following two lines of code:

```
names1 = ["Sara","Dave","Jane","Bill","Elly","Dawn"]
names2 = [name for name in names1 if name.startswith("D")]AA
print("names2:",names2)
```

If you launch the preceding code snippet you will see the following output:

```
names2: ['Dave', 'Dawn']
```

Another example involves a "for … for …" construct, as shown here:

```
names3 = ["Sara","Dave"]
names4 = [char for name in names3 for char in name]
```

If you launch the preceding code snippet you will see the following output:

```
names3: ['Sara', 'Dave']
names4: ['S', 'a', 'r', 'a', 'D', 'a', 'v', 'e']
```

The following example illustrates a list comprehension that is an alternative to the `map()` function:

```
squared = [a*a for a in range(1,10)]
print("squared:",squared)
```

If you launch the preceding code snippet you will see the following output:

```
squared: [1, 4, 9, 16, 25, 36, 49, 64, 81]
```

The following example illustrates a list comprehension that is an alternative to the `filter()` function:

```
evens = [a for a in range(1,10) if a%2 == 0]
print("evens:",evens)
```

If you launch the preceding code snippet you will see the following output:

```
evens: [2, 4, 6, 8]
```

You can also use list comprehensions with two-dimensional arrays, as shown here:

```
import numpy as np
arr1 = np.random.rand(3,3)
maxs = [max(row) for row in arr1]

print("arr1:")
print(arr1)
print("maxs:")
print(maxs)
```

If you launch the preceding code snippet you will see the following output:

```
arr1:
[[0.8341748  0.16772064 0.79493066]
 [0.876434   0.9884486  0.86085496]
 [0.16727298 0.13095968 0.75362753]]
maxs:
[0.8341747956062362, 0.9884485986312492, 0.7536275263907967]
```

The complete code sample is `list_comprehensions.py` that is available in the companion files for this chapter.

Now that you understand how to use list comprehensions, the next section shows you how to work with vectors in `Python`.

WORKING WITH VECTORS

A vector is a one-dimensional array of values, and you can perform vector-based operations, such as addition, subtraction, and inner product. Listing 1.13 displays the contents of `MyVectors.py` that illustrates how to perform vector-based operations.

LISTING 1.13: MyVectors.py

```
v1 = [1,2,3]
v2 = [1,2,3]
v3 = [5,5,5]

s1 = [0,0,0]
d1 = [0,0,0]
p1 = 0

print("Initial Vectors"
print('v1:',v1)
print('v2:',v2)
print('v3:',v3)

for i in range(len(v1)):
    d1[i] = v3[i] - v2[i]
    s1[i] = v3[i] + v2[i]
    p1    = v3[i] * v2[i] + p1

print("After operations")
print('d1:',d1)
print('s1:',s1)
print('p1:',p1)
```

Listing 1.13 starts with the definition of three lists in `Python`, each of which represents a vector. The lists `d1` and `s1` represent the difference of v2 and the sum v2, respectively. The number `p1` represents the "inner product" (also called the "dot product") of v3 and v2. The output from Listing 1.13 is here:

```
Initial Vectors
v1: [1, 2, 3]
v2: [1, 2, 3]
v3: [5, 5, 5]
After operations
d1: [4, 3, 2]
s1: [6, 7, 8]
p1: 30
```

WORKING WITH MATRICES

A two-dimensional matrix is a two-dimensional array of values, and you can easily create such a matrix. For example, the following code block illustrates how to access different elements in a 2D matrix:

```
mm = [["a","b","c"],["d","e","f"],["g","h","i"]];
print 'mm:       ',mm
print 'mm[0]:    ',mm[0]
print 'mm[0][1]:',mm[0][1]
```

The output from the preceding code block is here:

```
mm:          [['a', 'b', 'c'], ['d', 'e', 'f'], ['g', 'h', 'i']]
mm[0]:       ['a', 'b', 'c']
mm[0][1]: b
```

Listing 1.14 displays the contents of My2DMatrix.py that illustrates how to create and populate 2 two-dimensional matrix.

LISTING 1.14: My2DMatrix.py

```
rows = 3
cols = 3

my2DMatrix = [[0 for i in range(rows)] for j in range(rows)]
print('Before:',my2DMatrix)

for row in range(rows):
  for col in range(cols):
    my2DMatrix[row][col] = row*row+col*col
print('After: ',my2DMatrix)
```

Listing 1.14 initializes the variables rows x cols and then uses them to create the rows x cols matrix my2DMatrix whose values are initially 0. The next part of Listing 1.14 contains a nested loop that initializes the element of my2DMatrix whose position is (row,col) with the value row*row+col*col. The last line of code in Listing 1.14 prints the contents of my2DArray. The output from Listing 1.14 is here:

```
Before: [[0, 0, 0], [0, 0, 0], [0, 0, 0]]
After:  [[0, 1, 4], [1, 2, 5], [4, 5, 8]]
```

QUEUES

A queue is a FIFO ("First In First Out") data structure. Thus, the oldest item in a queue is removed when a new item is added to a queue that is already full.

Earlier in the chapter you learned how to use a Python list to emulate a queue. However, there is also a queue object in Python. The following code snippets illustrate how to use a queue in Python.

```
>>> from collections import deque
>>> q = deque('',maxlen=10)
>>> for i in range(10,20):
...     q.append(i)
...
>>> print q
deque([10, 11, 12, 13, 14, 15, 16, 17, 18, 19], maxlen=10)
```

The next section shows you how to use tuples in Python.

TUPLES (IMMUTABLE LISTS)

`Python` supports a data type called a *tuple* that consists of comma-separated values without brackets (square brackets are for lists, round brackets are for arrays, and curly braces are for dictionaries). Various examples of `Python` tuples are here:

https://docs.python.org/3.6/tutorial/datastructures.html#tuples-and-sequences

The following code block illustrates how to create a tuple and create new tuples from an existing type in `Python`.

Define a `Python` tuple t as follows:

```
>>> t = 1,'a', 2,'hello',3
>>> t
(1, 'a', 2, 'hello', 3)
```

Display the first element of t:

```
>>> t[0]
1
```

Create a tuple v containing 10, 11, and t:

```
>>> v = 10,11,t
>>> v
(10, 11, (1, 'a', 2, 'hello', 3))
```

Try modifying an element of t (which is immutable):

```
>>> t[0] = 1000
Traceback (most recent call last):
  File "<stdin>", line 1, in <module>
TypeError: 'tuple' object does not support item assignment
```

`Python` "deduplication" is useful because you can remove duplicates from a set and obtain a list, as shown here:
```
>>> lst = list(set(lst))
```

NOTE *The "in" operator on a list to search is O(n) whereas the "in" operator on set is O(1).*

The next section discusses `Python` sets.

SETS

A `Python` *set* is an unordered collection that does not contain duplicate elements. Use curly braces or the `set()` function to create sets. Set objects support set-theoretic operations such as union, intersection, and difference.

NOTE `set()` *is required in order to create an empty set because* {} *creates an empty dictionary.*

The following code block illustrates how to work with a `Python` set. Create a list of elements:

```
>>> l = ['a', 'b', 'a', 'c']
```

Create a set from the preceding list:

```
>>> s = set(l)
>>> s
set(['a', 'c', 'b'])
```

Test if an element is in the set:

```
>>> 'a' in s
True
>>> 'd' in s
False
>>>
```

Create a set from a string:

```
>>> n = set('abacad')
>>> n
set(['a', 'c', 'b', 'd'])
>>>
```

Subtract n from s:

```
>>> s - n
set([])
```

Subtract s from n:

```
>>> n - s
set(['d'])
>>>
```

The union of s and n:

```
>>> s | n
set(['a', 'c', 'b', 'd'])
```

The intersection of s and n:

```
>>> s & n
set(['a', 'c', 'b'])
```

The exclusive-or of s and n:

```
>>> s ^ n
set(['d'])
```

The next section shows you how to work with `Python` dictionaries.

DICTIONARIES

`Python` has a key/value structure called a "dict" that is a hash table. A `Python` dictionary (and hash tables in general) can retrieve the value of a key in constant time, regardless of the number of entries in the dictionary (and the same is true for sets). You can think of a set as essentially just the keys (not the values) of a `dict` implementation.

The contents of a `dict` can be written as a series of `key:value` pairs, as shown here:

```
dict1 = {key1:value1, key2:value2, ... }
```

The "empty dict" is just an empty pair of curly braces `{}`.

Creating a Dictionary

A `Python` dictionary (or hash table) contains of colon-separated key/value bindings inside a pair of curly braces, as shown here:

```
dict1 = {}
dict1 = {'x' : 1, 'y' : 2}
```

The preceding code snippet defines `dict1` as an empty dictionary, and then adds two key/value bindings.

Displaying the Contents of a Dictionary

You can display the contents of `dict1` with the following code:

```
>>> dict1 = {'x':1,'y':2}
>>> dict1
{'y': 2, 'x': 1}
>>> dict1['x']
1
>>> dict1['y']
2
>>> dict1['z']
Traceback (most recent call last):
  File "<stdin>", line 1, in <module>
KeyError: 'z'
```

NOTE *key/value bindings for a `dict` and a set are not necessarily stored in the same order that you defined them.*

`Python` dictionaries also provide the `get` method in order to retrieve key values:

```
>>> dict1.get('x')
1
>>> dict1.get('y')
2
>>> dict1.get('z')
```

As you can see, the `Python` `get` method returns `None` (which is displayed as an empty string) instead of an error when referencing a key that is not defined in a dictionary.

You can also use `dict` comprehensions to create dictionaries from expressions, as shown here:

```
>>> {x: x**3 for x in (1, 2, 3)}
{1: 1, 2: 8, 3: 37}
```

Checking for Keys in a Dictionary

You can easily check for the presence of a key in a `Python` dictionary as follows:

```
>>> 'x' in dict1
True
>>> 'z' in dict1
False
```

Use square brackets for finding or setting a value in a dictionary. For example, `dict['abc']` finds the value associated with the key `'abc'`. You can use strings, numbers, and tuples as key values, and you can use any type as the value.

If you access a value that is not in the `dict`, `Python` throws a `KeyError`. Consequently, use the "in" operator to check if the key is in the dict. Alternatively, use `dict.get(key)` which returns the value or `None` if the key is not present. You can even use the expression `get(key, not-found-string)` to specify the value to return if a key is not found.

Deleting Keys From a Dictionary

Launch the `Python` interpreter and enter the following statements:

```
>>> MyDict = {'x' : 5,  'y' : 7}
>>> MyDict['z'] = 13
>>> MyDict
{'y': 7, 'x': 5, 'z': 13}
>>> del MyDict['x']
>>> MyDict
{'y': 7, 'z': 13}
>>> MyDict.keys()
['y', 'z']
>>> MyDict.values()
[13, 7]
>>> 'z' in MyDict
True
```

Iterating Through a Dictionary

The following code snippet shows you how to iterate through a dictionary:

```
MyDict = {'x' : 5,  'y' : 7, 'z' : 13}

for key, value in MyDict.iteritems():
    print key, value
```

The output from the preceding code block is here:

```
y 7
x 5
z 13
```

Interpolating Data From a Dictionary

The % operator substitutes values from a `Python` dictionary into a string by name. An example is shown in Listing 1.15.

LISTING 1.15: InterpolateDict1.py

```
hash = {}
hash['beverage'] = 'coffee'
hash['count'] = 3

# %d for int, %s for string
s = 'Today I drank %(count)d cups of %(beverage)s' % hash
print('s:', s)
```

The output from the preceding code block is here:

```
Today I drank 3 cups of coffee
```

DICTIONARY FUNCTIONS AND METHODS

`Python` provides various functions and methods for a `Python` dictionary, such as `cmp()`, `len()`, and `str()` that compare two dictionaries, return the length of a dictionary, and display a string representation of a dictionary, respectively.

You can also manipulate the contents of a `Python` dictionary using the functions `clear()` to remove all elements, `copy()` to return a shall copy, `get()` to retrieve the value of a key, `items()` to display the `(key, value)` pairs of a dictionary, `keys()` to displays the keys of a dictionary, and `values()` to return the list of values of a dictionary.

The next section discusses other `Python` sequence types that have not been discussed in previous sections of this chapter.

OTHER SEQUENCE TYPES IN PYTHON

`Python` supports 7 sequence types: `str`, `unicode`, `list`, `tuple`, `bytearray`, `buffer`, and `xrange`.

You can iterate through a sequence and retrieve the position index and corresponding value at the same time using the `enumerate()` function.

```
>>> for i, v in enumerate(['x', 'y', 'z']):
...     print i, v
...
0 x
1 y
2 z
```

`Bytearray` objects are created with the built-in function `bytearray()`. Although buffer objects are not directly supported by `Python` syntax, you can create them via the built-in `buffer()` function.

Objects of type `xrange` are created with the `xrange()` function. An `xrange` object is similar to a buffer in the sense that there is no specific syntax to create them. Moreover, `xrange` objects do not support operations such as slicing, concatenation or repetition.

At this point you have seen all the `Python` type that you will encounter in the remaining chapters of this book, so it makes sense to discuss mutable and immutable types in `Python`, which is the topic of the next section.

MUTABLE AND IMMUTABLE TYPES IN PYTHON

`Python` represents its data as objects. Some of these objects (such as lists and dictionaries) are mutable, which means you can change their content without changing their identity. Objects such as integers, floats, strings and tuples are objects that cannot be changed. The key point to understand is the difference between changing the value versus assigning a new value to an object; you cannot change a string but you can assign it a different value. This detail can be verified by checking the `id` value of an object, as shown in Listing 1.16.

LISTING 1.16: Mutability.py

```
s = "abc"
print('id #1:', id(s))
print('first char:', s[0])

try:
  s[0] = "o"
except:
  print('Cannot perform reassignment')

s = "xyz"
print('id #2:',id(s))
s += "uvw"
print('id #3:',id(s))
```

The output of Listing 1.16 is here:

```
id #1: 4297972672
first char: a
Cannot perform reassignment
id #2: 4299809336
id #3: 4299777872
```

Thus, a `Python` type is immutable if its value cannot be changed (even though it's possible to assign a new value to such a type), otherwise a `Python` type is mutable. The `Python` immutable objects are of type `bytes`, `complex`, `float`, `int`, `str`, or `tuple`. On the other hand, dictionaries, lists, and sets are mutable. The key in a hash table must be an immutable type.

Since strings are immutable in `Python`, you cannot insert a string in the "middle" of a given text string unless you construct a second-string using concatenation. For example, suppose you have the string:

```
"this is a string"
```

and you want to create the following string:

```
"this is a longer string"
```

The following `Python` code block illustrates how to perform this task:

```
text1 = "this is a string"
text2 = text1[0:10] + "longer" + text1[9:]
print 'text1:',text1
print 'text2:',text2
```

The output of the preceding code block is here:

```
text1: this is a string
text2: this is a longer string
```

SUMMARY

This chapter showed you how to work with numbers and perform arithmetic operations on numbers, and then you learned how to work with strings and use string operations. The next chapter shows you how to work with conditional statements, loops, and user-defined functions in `Python`.

Next, you learned about condition logic, such as `if/elif` statements. You also learned how to work with loops in `Python`, including `for` loops and `while` loops. In addition, you saw how to compute various values, such as the

In addition, you saw how to work with various `Python` data types. In particular, you learned about tuples, sets, and dictionaries. Then you learned how to work with lists and how to use list-related operations to extract sublists.

## CHAPTER 2

NumPy and Data Visualization

This chapter provides a quick introduction to the `Python NumPy` package, which provides very useful functionality, not only for "regular" `Python` scripts, but also for `Python`-based scripts with TensorFlow. For instance, you will see `NumPy` code samples containing loops, arrays, and lists. You will also learn about dot products, the `reshape()` method (very useful!), how to plot with `Matplotlib` (discussed in more detail in Chapter 4), and examples of linear regression.

The first part of this chapter briefly discusses `NumPy` and some of its useful features. The second part contains examples of working arrays in `NumPy`, and contrasts some of the APIs for lists with the same APIs for arrays. In addition, you will see how easy it is to compute the exponent-related values (square, cube, and so forth) of elements in an array.

The second part of the chapter introduces subranges, which are very useful (and frequently used) for extracting portions of datasets in machine learning tasks. In particular, you will see code samples that handle negative (−1) subranges for vectors as well as for arrays, because they are interpreted one way for vectors and a different way for arrays.

The third part of this chapter delves into other `NumPy` methods, including the `reshape()` method, which is extremely useful (and very common) when working with images files: some `TensorFlow` APIs require converting a 2D array of `(R, G, B)` values into a corresponding one-dimensional vector.

The fourth part of this chapter delves into linear regression, the mean squared error (MSE), and how to calculate MSE with the `NumPy linspace()` API.

WHAT IS NUMPY?

`NumPy` is a `Python` library that provides many convenient methods and also better performance. `NumPy` provides a core library for scientific computing in `Python`, with performant multidimensional arrays and good vectorized math functions, along with support for linear algebra and random numbers.

`NumPy` is modeled after MatLab, with support for lists, arrays, and so forth. `NumPy` is easier to use than Matlab, and it's very common in TensorFlow code as well as `Python` code.

Useful NumPy Features

The NumPy package provides the *ndarray* object that encapsulates multi-dimensional arrays of homogeneous data types. Many ndarray operations are performed in compiled code in order to improve performance.

Keep in mind the following important differences between NumPy arrays and the standard Python sequences. First, NumPy arrays have a fixed size, whereas Python lists can expand dynamically. Second, NumPy arrays are homogeneous, which means that the elements in a NumPy array must have the same data type. Third, NumPy arrays support more efficient execution (and require less code) of various types of operations on large numbers of data.

Now that you have a general idea about NumPy, let's delve into some examples that illustrate how to work with NumPy arrays, which is the topic of the next section.

WHAT ARE NUMPY ARRAYS?

An *array* is a set of consecutive memory locations used to store data. Each item in the array is called an *element*. The number of elements in an array is called the *dimension* of the array. A typical array declaration is shown here:

```
arr1 = np.array([1,2,3,4,5])
```

The preceding code snippet declares arr1 as an array of five elements, which you can access via arr1[0] through arr1[4]. Notice that the first element has an index value of 0, the second element has an index value of 1, and so forth. Thus, if you declare an array of 100 elements, then the 100th element has an index value of 99.

NOTE *The first position in a NumPy array has index 0.*

NumPy treats arrays as vectors. Math ops are performed element-by-element. Remember the following difference: "doubling" an array *multiplies* each element by 2, whereas "doubling" a list *appends* a list to itself.

Listing 2.1 displays the contents of nparray1.py that illustrates some operations on a NumPy array.

LISTING 2.1: nparray1.py

```
import numpy as np

list1 = [1,2,3,4,5]
print(list1)

arr1  = np.array([1,2,3,4,5])
print(arr1)

list2 = [(1,2,3),(4,5,6)]
print(list2)

arr2  = np.array([(1,2,3),(4,5,6)])
print(arr2)
```

Listing 2.1 defines the variables `list1` and `list2` (which are `Python` lists), as well as the variables `arr1` and `arr2` (which are arrays), and prints their values. The output from launching Listing 2.1 is here:

```
[1, 2, 3, 4, 5]
[1 2 3 4 5]
[(1, 2, 3), (4, 5, 6)]
[[1 2 3]
 [4 5 6]]
```

As you can see, `Python` lists and arrays are very easy to define, and now we're ready to look at some loop operations for lists and arrays.

WORKING WITH LOOPS

Listing 2.2 displays the contents of `loop1.py` that illustrates how to iterate through the elements of a `NumPy` array and a `Python` list.

LISTING 2.2: loop1.py

```
import numpy as np

list = [1,2,3]
arr1 = np.array([1,2,3])

for e in list:
  print(e)

for e in arr1:
  print(e)

list1 = [1,2,3,4,5]
```

Listing 2.2 initializes the variable `list`, which is a `Python` list, and also the variable `arr1`, which is a `NumPy` array. The next portion of Listing 2.2 contains two loops, each of which iterates through the elements in `list` and `arr1`. As you can see, the syntax is identical in both loops. The output from launching Listing 2.2 is here:

```
1
2
3
1
2
3
```

APPENDING ELEMENTS TO ARRAYS (1)

Listing 2.3 displays the contents of `append1.py` that illustrates how to append elements to a `NumPy` array and a `Python` list.

LISTING 2.3: append1.py

```
import numpy as np

arr1 = np.array([1,2,3])

# these do not work:
#arr1.append(4)
#arr1 = arr1 + [5]

arr1 = np.append(arr1,4)
arr1 = np.append(arr1,[5])

for e in arr1:
  print(e)

arr2 = arr1 + arr1

for e in arr2:
  print(e)
```

Listing 2.3 initializes the variable arr1, which is a NumPy array. The output from launching Listing 2.3 is here:

```
1
2
3
4
5
2
4
6
8
10
```

APPENDING ELEMENTS TO ARRAYS (2)

Listing 2.4 displays the contents of append2.py that illustrates how to append elements to a NumPy array.

LISTING 2.4: append2.py

```
import numpy as np

arr1 = np.array([1,2,3])
arr1 = np.append(arr1,4)

for e in arr1:
  print(e)

arr1 = np.array([1,2,3])
arr1 = np.append(arr1,4)
```

```
arr2 = arr1 + arr1

for e in arr2:
  print(e)
```

Listing 2.4 initializes the variable `arr1`, which is a `NumPy` array. Notice that `NumPy` arrays do not have an "append" method: this method is available through `NumPy` itself. Recall the previously mentioned difference between `Python` lists and `NumPy` arrays: the "+" operator *concatenates* `Python` lists, whereas this operator *doubles* the elements in a `NumPy` array. The output from launching Listing 2.4 is here:

```
1
2
3
4
2
4
6
8
```

MULTIPLYING LISTS AND ARRAYS

Listing 2.5 displays the contents of `multiply1.py` that illustrates how to multiply elements in a `Python` list and a `NumPy` array.

LISTING 2.5: multiply1.py

```
import numpy as np

list1 = [1,2,3]
arr1  = np.array([1,2,3])
print('list:  ',list1)
print('arr1:  ',arr1)
print('2*list:',2*list)
print('2*arr1:',2*arr1)
```

Listing 2.5 contains a `Python` list called list and a `NumPy` array called `arr1`. The `print()` statements display the contents of `list1` and `arr1` as well as the result of doubling `list1` and `arr1`. Recall that "doubling" a `Python` list is different from doubling a `Python` array, which you can see in the output from launching Listing 2.5:

```
('list:  ', [1, 2, 3])
('arr1:  ', array([1, 2, 3]))
('2*list:', [1, 2, 3, 1, 2, 3])
('2*arr1:', array([2, 4, 6]))
```

DOUBLING THE ELEMENTS IN A LIST

Listing 2.6 displays the contents of `double_list1.py` that illustrates how to double the elements in a `Python` list.

LISTING 2.6: double_list1.py

```
import numpy as np

list1 = [1,2,3]
list2 = []

for e in list1:
  list2.append(2*e)

print('list1:',list1)
print('list2:',list2)
```

Listing 2.6 contains a Python list called list1 and an empty Python list called list2. The next code snippet iterates through the elements of list1 and appends them to the variable list2. The pair of print() statements display the contents of list1 and list2 to show you that they are the same. The output from launching Listing 2.6 is here:

```
('list: ', [1, 2, 3])
('list2:', [2, 4, 6])
```

LISTS AND EXPONENTS

Listing 2.7 displays the contents of exponent_list1.py that illustrates how to compute exponents of the elements in a Python list.

LISTING 2.7: exponent_list1.py

```
import numpy as np

list1 = [1,2,3]
list2 = []

for e in list1:
  list2.append(e*e) # e*e = squared

print('list1:',list1)
print('list2:',list2)
```

Listing 2.7 contains a Python list called list1 and an empty Python list called list2. The next code snippet iterates through the elements of list1 and appends the square of each element to the variable list2. The pair of print() statements display the contents of list1 and list2. The output from launching Listing 2.7 is here:

```
('list1:', [1, 2, 3])
('list2:', [1, 4, 9])
```

ARRAYS AND EXPONENTS

Listing 2.8 displays the contents of exponent_array1.py that illustrates how to compute exponents of the elements in a NumPy array.

LISTING 2.8: exponent_array1.py

```
import numpy as np

arr1 = np.array([1,2,3])
arr2 = arr1**2
arr3 = arr1**3

print('arr1:',arr1)
print('arr2:',arr2)
print('arr3:',arr3)
```

Listing 2.8 contains a NumPy array called arr1 followed by two NumPy arrays called arr2 and arr3. Notice the compact manner in which the NumPy arr2 is initialized with the square of the elements in in arr1, followed by the initialization of the NumPy array arr3 with the cube of the elements in arr1. The three print() statements display the contents of arr1, arr2, and arr3. The output from launching Listing 2.8 is here:

```
('arr1:', array([1, 2, 3]))
('arr2:', array([1, 4, 9]))
('arr3:', array([1, 8, 27]))
```

MATH OPERATIONS AND ARRAYS

Listing 2.9 displays the contents of mathops_array1.py that illustrates how to compute exponents of the elements in a NumPy array.

LISTING 2.9: mathops_array1.py

```
import numpy as np

arr1 = np.array([1,2,3])
sqrt = np.sqrt(arr1)
log1 = np.log(arr1)
exp1 = np.exp(arr1)

print('sqrt:',sqrt)
print('log1:',log1)
print('exp1:',exp1)
```

Listing 2.9 contains a NumPy array called arr1 followed by three NumPy arrays called sqrt, log1, and exp1 that are initialized with the square root, the log, and the exponential value of the elements in arr1, respectively. The three print() statements display the contents of sqrt, log1, and exp1. The output from launching Listing 2.9 is here:

```
('sqrt:', array([1.        , 1.41421356, 1.73205081]))
('log1:', array([0.        , 0.69314718, 1.09861229]))
('exp1:', array([2.71828183, 7.3890561 ,  20.08553692]))
```

WORKING WITH "–1" SUBRANGES WITH VECTORS

Listing 2.10 displays the contents of npsubarray2.py that illustrates how to compute exponents of the elements in a NumPy array.

LISTING 2.10: npsubarray2.py

```
import numpy as np

# -1 => "all except the last element in …" (row or col)

arr1  = np.array([1,2,3,4,5])
print('arr1:',arr1)
print('arr1[0:-1]:',arr1[0:-1])
print('arr1[1:-1]:',arr1[1:-1])
print('arr1[::-1]:', arr1[::-1]) # reverse!
```

Listing 2.10 contains a NumPy array called arr1 followed by four print statements, each of which displays a different subrange of values in arr1. The output from launching Listing 2.10 is here:

```
('arr1:',        array([1, 2, 3, 4, 5]))
('arr1[0:-1]:', array([1, 2, 3, 4]))
('arr1[1:-1]:', array([2, 3, 4]))
('arr1[::-1]:', array([5, 4, 3, 2, 1]))
```

WORKING WITH "–1" SUBRANGES WITH ARRAYS

Listing 2.11 displays the contents of np2darray2.py that illustrates several ways of using "-1" in a two-dimensional NumPy array.

LISTING 2.11: np2darray2.py

```
import numpy as np

# -1 => "the last element in …" (row or col)

arr1  = np.array([(1,2,3),(4,5,6),(7,8,9),(10,11,12)])
print('arr1:',         arr1)
print('arr1[-1,:]:',   arr1[-1,:])
print('arr1[:,-1]:',   arr1[:,-1])
print('arr1[-1:,-1]:',arr1[-1:,-1])
```

Listing 2.11 contains a NumPy array called arr1 followed by four print statements, each of which displays a different subrange of values in arr1. The output from launching Listing 2.11 is here:

```
(arr1:', array([[1,   2,   3],
                [4,   5,   6],
                [7,   8,   9],
                [10,  11,  12]]))
(arr1[-1,:]]', array([10, 11, 12]))
(arr1[:,-1]:', array([3,  6,  9, 12]))
(arr1[-1:,-1]]', array([12]))
```

OTHER USEFUL NUMPY METHODS

In addition to the NumPy methods that you saw in the code samples prior to this section, the following (often intuitively named) NumPy methods are also very useful.

- The method np.zeros() initializes an array with 0 values.
- The method np.ones() initializes an array with 1 values.
- The method np.empty()initializes an array with 0 values.
- The method np.arange() provides a range of numbers.
- The method np.shape() displays the shape of an object.
- The method np.reshape() changes the shape of an object
- The method np.linspace() partitions an interval into subintervals
- The method np.mean() computes the mean of a set of numbers.
- The method np.std() computes the standard deviation of a set of numbers.

Although the np.zeros() and np.empty() both initialize a 2D array with 0, np.zeros() requires less execution time. You could also use np.full(size, 0), but this method is the slowest of all three methods.

The reshape() method and the linspace() method are very useful for changing the dimensions of an array and generating a list of numeric values, respectively. The reshape() method often appears in TensorFlow code, and the linspace() method is useful for generating a set of numbers in linear regression.

The mean() and std() methods are useful for calculating the mean and the standard deviation of a set of numbers. For example, you can use these two methods in order to resize the values in a Gaussian distribution so that their mean is 0 and the standard deviation is 1. This process is called *standardizing* a Gaussian distribution.

ARRAYS AND VECTOR OPERATIONS

Listing 2.12 displays the contents of array_vector.py that illustrates how to perform vector operations on the elements in a NumPy array.

LISTING 2.12: array_vector.py

```
import numpy as np

a = np.array([[1,2], [3, 4]])
b = np.array([[5,6], [7,8]])

print('a:          ', a)
print('b:          ', b)
print('a + b:      ', a+b)
print('a - b:      ', a-b)
print('a * b:      ', a*b)
print('a / b:      ', a/b)
print('b / a:      ', b/a)
print('a.dot(b):',a.dot(b))
```

Listing 2.12 contains two NumPy arrays called a and b followed by eight print statements, each of which displays the result of "applying" a different arithmetic operation to the NumPy arrays a and b. The output from launching Listing 2.12 is here:

```
('a      :    ', array([[1, 2], [3, 4]]))
('b      :    ', array([[5, 6], [7, 8]]))
('a + b:    ', array([[6,  8], [10, 12]]))
('a - b:    ', array([[-4, -4], [-4, -4]]))
('a * b:    ', array([[5, 12], [21, 32]]))
('a / b:    ', array([[0, 0], [0, 0]]))
('b / a:    ', array([[5, 3], [2, 2]]))
('a.dot(b):', array([[19, 22], [43, 50]]))
```

NUMPY AND DOT PRODUCTS (1)

Listing 2.13 displays the contents of dotproduct1.py that illustrates how to perform the dot product on the elements in a NumPy array.

LISTING 2.13: dotproduct1.py

```
import numpy as np

a = np.array([1,2])
b = np.array([2,3])

dot2 = 0
for e,f in zip(a,b):
  dot2 += e*f

print('a:     ',a)
print('b:     ',b)
print('a*b:  ',a*b)
print('dot1:',a.dot(b))
print('dot2:',dot2)
```

Listing 2.13 contains two NumPy arrays called a and b followed by a simple loop that computes the dot product of a and b. The next section contains five print statements that display the contents of a and b, their inner product that's calculated in three different ways. The output from launching Listing 2.13 is here:

```
('a:     ', array([1, 2]))
('b:     ', array([2, 3]))
('a*b:  ', array([2, 6]))
('dot1:', 8)
('dot2:', 8)
```

NUMPY AND DOT PRODUCTS (2)

NumPy arrays support a "dot" method for calculating the inner product of an array of numbers, which uses the same formula that you use for calculating the inner product of a pair of vectors. Listing 2.14 displays the contents of `dotproduct2.py` that illustrates how to calculate the dot product of two `NumPy` arrays.

LISTING 2.14: dotproduct2.py

```
import numpy as np

a = np.array([1,2])
b = np.array([2,3])

print('a:            ',a)
print('b:            ',b)
print('a.dot(b):     ',a.dot(b))
print('b.dot(a):     ',b.dot(a))
print('np.dot(a,b):',np.dot(a,b))
print('np.dot(b,a):',np.dot(b,a))
```

Listing 2.14 contains two `NumPy` arrays called `a` and `b` followed by six `print` statements that display the contents of `a` and `b`, and also their inner product that's calculated in three different ways. The output from launching Listing 2.14 is here:

```
('a:            ', array([1, 2]))
('b:            ', array([2, 3]))
('a.dot(b):     ', 8)
('b.dot(a):     ', 8)
('np.dot(a,b):', 8)
('np.dot(b,a):', 8)
```

NUMPY AND THE LENGTH OF VECTORS

The *norm* of a vector (or an array of numbers) is the length of a vector, which is the square root of the dot product of a vector with itself. `NumPy` also provides the "sum" and "square" functions that you can use to calculate the norm of a vector.

Listing 2.15 displays the contents of `array_norm.py` that illustrates how to calculate the magnitude ("norm") of a `NumPy` array of numbers.

LISTING 2.15: array_norm.py

```
import numpy as np

a = np.array([2,3])
asquare = np.square(a)
asqsum  = np.sum(np.square(a))
anorm1  = np.sqrt(np.sum(a*a))
anorm2  = np.sqrt(np.sum(np.square(a)))
anorm3  = np.linalg.norm(a)

print('a:       ',a)
print('asquare:',asquare)
print('asqsum: ',asqsum)
```

```
print('anorm1: ',anorm1)
print('anorm2: ',anorm2)
print('anorm3: ',anorm3)
```

Listing 2.15 contains an initial `NumPy` array called a, followed by the `NumPy` array `asquare` and the numeric values `asqsum, anorm1, anorm2,` and `anorm3`. The `NumPy` array `asquare` contains the square of the elements in the `NumPy` array a, and the numeric value `asqsum` contains the sum of the elements in the `NumPy` array `asquare`.

Next, the numeric value `anorm1` equals the square root of the sum of the square of the elements in a. The numeric value `anorm2` is the same as `anorm1`, computed in a slightly different fashion. Finally, the numeric value `anorm3` is equal to `anorm2`, but as you can see, `anorm3` is calculated via a single `NumPy` method, whereas `anorm2` requires a succession of `NumPy` methods.

The last portion of Listing 2.15 consists of six `print()` statements, each of which displays the computed values. The output from launching Listing 2.15 is here:

```
('a:        ', array([2, 3]))
('asquare:', array([4, 9]))
('asqsum: ', 13)
('anorm1: ', 3.605551275463989)
('anorm2: ', 3.605551275463989)
('anorm3: ', 3.605551275463989)
```

NUMPY AND OTHER OPERATIONS

`NumPy` provides the "*" operator to multiply the components of two vectors to produce a third vector whose components are the products of the corresponding components of the initial pair of vectors. This operation is called a "Hadamard" product, which is the name of a famous mathematician. If you then add the components of the third vector, the sum is equal to the inner product of the initial pair of vectors.

Listing 2.16 displays the contents of `otherops.py` that illustrates how to perform other operations on a `NumPy` array.

LISTING 2.16: otherops.py

```
import numpy as np

a = np.array([1,2])
b = np.array([3,4])

print('a:            ',a)
print('b:            ',b)
print('a*b:          ',a*b)
print('np.sum(a*b): ',np.sum(a*b))
print('(a*b.sum()): ',(a*b).sum())
```

Listing 2.16 contains two `NumPy` arrays called a and b followed five `print` statements that display the contents of a and b, their Hadamard product, and also their inner product that's calculated in two different ways. The output from launching Listing 2.16 is here:

```
('a:             ', array([1, 2]))
('b:             ', array([3, 4]))
('a*b:           ', array([3, 8]))
('np.sum(a*b): ', 11)
('(a*b.sum()): ', 11)
```

NUMPY AND THE reshape() METHOD

NumPy arrays support the "reshape" method that enables you to restructure the dimensions of an array of numbers. In general, if a NumPy array contains m elements, where m is a positive integer, then that array can be restructured as an m1 x m2 NumPy array, where m1 and m2 are positive integers such that m1*m2 = m.

Listing 2.17 displays the contents of numpy_reshape.py that illustrates how to use the reshape() method on a NumPy array.

LISTING 2.17: numpy_reshape.py

```
import numpy as np

x = np.array([[2, 3], [4, 5], [6, 7]])
print(x.shape) # (3, 2)

x = x.reshape((2, 3))
print(x.shape) # (2, 3)
print('x1:',x)

x = x.reshape((-1))
print(x.shape) # (6,)
print('x2:',x)

x = x.reshape((6, -1))
print(x.shape) # (6, 1)
print('x3:',x)

x = x.reshape((-1, 6))
print(x.shape) # (1, 6)
print('x4:',x)
```

Listing 2.17 contains a NumPy array called x whose dimensions are 3x2, followed by a set of invocations of the reshape() method that reshape the contents of x. The first invocation of the reshape() method changes the shape of x from 3x2 to 2x3. The second invocation changes the shape of x from 2x3 to 6x1. The third invocation changes the shape of x from 1x6 to 6x1. The final invocation changes the shape of x from 6x1 to 1x6 again.

Each invocation of the reshape() method is followed by a print() statement so that you can see the effect of the invocation. The output from launching Listing 2.17 is here:

```
(3, 2)
(2, 3)
('x1:', array([[2, 3, 4],
```

```
            [5, 6, 7]]))
(6,)
('x2:', array([2, 3, 4, 5, 6, 7]))
(6, 1)
('x3:', array([[2],
        [3],
        [4],
        [5],
        [6],
        [7]]))
(1, 6)
```

CALCULATING THE MEAN AND STANDARD DEVIATION

If you need to review these concepts from statistics (and perhaps also the mean, median, and mode as well), please read the appropriate on-line tutorials.

NumPy provides various built-in functions that perform statistical calculations, such as the following list of methods:

```
np.linspace() <= useful for regression
np.mean()
np.std()
```

The np.linspace() method generates a set of equally spaced numbers between a lower bound and an upper bound. The np.mean() and np.std() methods calculate the mean and standard deviation, respectively, of a set of numbers. Listing 2.18 displays the contents of sample_mean_std.py that illustrates how to calculate statistical values from a NumPy array.

LISTING 2.18: sample_mean_std.py

```
import numpy as np

x2 = np.arange(8)
print('mean = ',x2.mean())
print('std  = ',x2.std())

x3 = (x2 - x2.mean())/x2.std()
print('x3 mean = ',x3.mean())
print('x3 std  = ',x3.std())
```

Listing 2.18 contains a NumPy array x2 that consists of the first eight integers. Next, the mean() and std() that are "associated" with x2 are invoked in order to calculate the mean and standard deviation, respectively, of the elements of x2. The output from launching Listing 2.18 is here:

```
('a:           ', array([1, 2]))
('b:           ', array([3, 4]))
```

CODE SAMPLE WITH MEAN AND STANDARD DEVIATION

The code sample in this section extends the code sample in the previous section with additional statistical values, and the code in Listing 2.19 can be used for any data distribution. Keep in mind that the code sample uses random numbers simply for the purposes of illustration: after you have launched the code sample, replace those numbers with values from a CSV file or some other dataset containing meaningful values.

Moreover, this section does not provide details regarding the meaning of quartiles, but you can learn about quartiles here:

https://en.wikipedia.org/wiki/Quartile

Listing 2.19 displays the contents of stat_values.py that illustrates how to display various statistical values from a NumPy array of random numbers.

LISTING 2.19: stat_values.py

```
import numpy as np

from numpy import percentile
from numpy.random import rand

# generate data sample
data = np.random.rand(1000)

# calculate quartiles, min, and max
quartiles = percentile(data, [25, 50, 75])
data_min, data_max = data.min(), data.max()

# print summary information
print('Minimum:   %.3f' % data_min)
print('Q1 value: %.3f' % quartiles[0])
print('Median:    %.3f' % quartiles[1])
print('Mean Val: %.3f' % data.mean())
print('Std Dev:  %.3f' % data.std())
print('Q3 value: %.3f' % quartiles[2])
print('Maximum:   %.3f' % data_max)
```

The data sample (shown in bold) in Listing 2.19 is from a uniform distribution between 0 and 1. The NumPy percentile() function calculates a linear interpolation (average) between observations, which is needed to calculate the median on a sample with an even number of values. As you can surmise, the NumPy functions min() and max() calculate the smallest and largest values in the data sample. The output from launching Listing 2.19 is here:

```
Minimum:   0.000
Q1 value: 0.237
Median:    0.500
Mean Val: 0.495
Std Dev:  0.295
Q3 value: 0.747
Maximum:   0.999
```

Trimmed Mean and Weighted Mean

In addition to the arithmetic mean, there are variants that are known as weighted mean and a trimmed mean (also called a truncated mean).

A *trimmed mean* is a robust estimate (i.e., a metric that is not sensitive to outliers). As a simple example of a trimmed mean, suppose that you have five scores for the evaluation of a product: simply drop the highest and lowest scores and then compute the average of the remaining three scores. If you have multiple sets of five scores, repeat the preceding process and then compute the average of the set of trimmed mean values.

A *weighted mean* is useful when sample data does not represent different groups in a dataset. Assigning a larger weight to groups that are underrepresented yields a weighted mean that more accurate represents the various groups in the dataset. However, keep in mind that outliers can affect the mean as well as the weighted mean.

The weighted mean is the same as the expected value. In case you are unfamiliar with the notion of an expected value, suppose that the set P = {p1,p2,...,pn} is a probability distribution, which means that the numeric values in the set P must be nonnegative and have a sum equal to 1. In addition, suppose that V = {v1,v2,...,vn} is a set of numeric scores that are assigned to n features of a product M. The values in the set V are probably positive integers in some range (e.g., between 1 and 10).

Then the *expected value* E for that product is computed as follows:

```
E = p1*v1 + p2*v2 + ... + pn*vn
```

The Python code samples in the next several sections contain some rudimentary APIs from matplotlib. The code samples start with simple examples of line segments, followed by an introduction to linear regression.

WORKING WITH LINES IN THE PLANE (OPTIONAL)

This section contains a short review of lines in the Euclidean plane, so you can skip this section if you are comfortable with this topic. A minor point that's often overlooked is that lines in the Euclidean plane have infinite length. If you select two distinct points of a line, then all the points between those two selected points is a *line segment*. A *ray* is a "half infinite" line: when you select one point as an endpoint, then all the points on one side of the line constitute a ray.

For example, the points in the plane whose y-coordinate is 0 are a line and also the x-axis, whereas the points between (0,0) and (1,0) on the x-axis form a line segment. In addition, the points on the x-axis that are to the right of (0,0) form a ray, and the points on the x-axis that are to the left of (0,0) also form a ray.

For simplicity and convenience, in this book we'll use the terms "line" and "line segment" interchangeably, and now let's delve into the details of lines in the Euclidean plane. Just in case you're a bit fuzzy on the details, here is the equation of a (nonvertical) line in the Euclidean plane:

```
y = m*x + b
```

The value of m is the slope of the line and the value of b is the y-intercept (i.e., the place where the nonvertical line intersects the y-axis). In case you're wondering, the following form for a line in the plane is a more general equation that includes vertical lines:

```
a*x + b*y + c = 0
```

However, we won't be working with vertical lines, so we'll stick with the first formula. Figure 2.1 displays three horizontal lines whose equations (from top to bottom) are $y = 3$, $y = 0$, and $y = -3$, respectively.

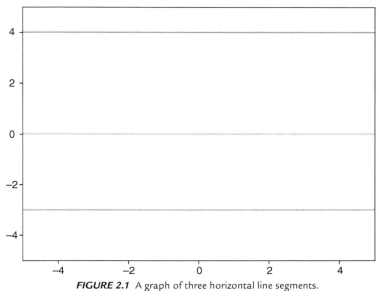

FIGURE 2.1 A graph of three horizontal line segments.

Figure 2.2 displays two slanted lines whose equations are y = x and y = –x, respectively.

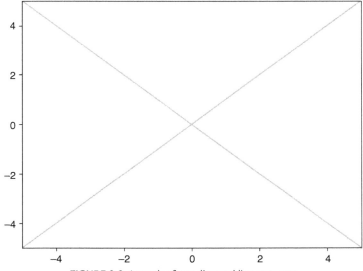

FIGURE 2.2 A graph of two diagonal line segments.

Figure 2.3 displays two slanted parallel lines whose equations are y = 2*x and y = 2*x+3, respectively.

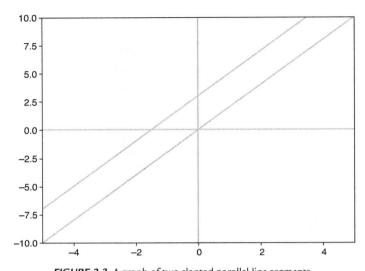

FIGURE 2.3 A graph of two slanted parallel line segments.

Figure 2.4 displays a piece-wise linear graph consisting of connected line segments.

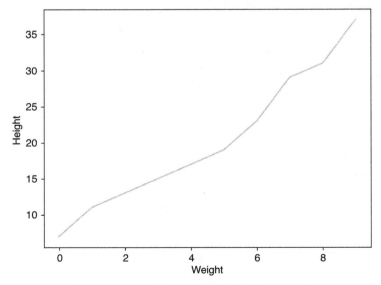

FIGURE 2.4 A piece-wise linear graph of line segments.

Now that you have seen some basic examples of lines in the Euclidean plane, let's look at some code samples that use NumPy and Matplotlib to display scatter plots of points in the plane.

PLOTTING RANDOMIZED POINTS WITH NumPy AND MATPLOTLIB

The previous section contains simple examples of line segments, but the code is deferred until Chapter 7. This section and the next section contain code samples with Matplotlib APIs that are not discussed; however, the code is straightforward, so you can infer its purpose. In addition, you can learn more about Matplotlib in Chapter 7 (which focuses on data visualization) or read a short online tutorial for more details.

Listing 2.20 displays the contents of np_plot.py and illustrates how to plot multiple points on a line in the plane.

LISTING 2.20: np_plot.py

```
import numpy as np
import matplotlib.pyplot as plt

x = np.random.randn(15,1)
y = 2.5*x + 5 + 0.2*np.random.randn(15,1)

plt.scatter(x,y)
plt.show()
```

Listing 2.20 starts with two import statements, followed by the initialization of x as a set of random values via the NumPy randn() API. Next, y is assigned a range of values that consist of two parts: a linear equation with input values from the x values, which is combined with a randomization factor. Figure 2.5 displays the output generated by the code in Listing 2.20.

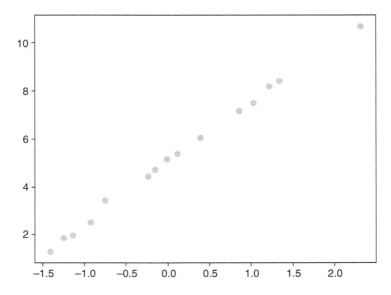

FIGURE 2.5 Datasets with potential linear regression.

PLOTTING A QUADRATIC WITH NUMPY AND MATPLOTLIB

Listing 2.21 displays the contents of np_plot_quadratic.py that illustrates how to plot a quadratic function in the plane.

LISTING 2.21: np_plot_quadratic.py

```
import numpy as np
import matplotlib.pyplot as plt

x = np.linspace(-5,5,num=100)[:,None]
y = -0.5 + 2.2*x +0.3*x**3+ 2*np.random.randn(100,1)

plt.plot(x,y)
plt.show()
```

Listing 2.21 starts with two import statements, followed by the initialization of x as a range of values via the NumPy linspace() API. Next, y is assigned a range of values that fit a quadratic equation, which are based on the values for the variable x. Figure 2.6 displays the output generated by the code in Listing 2.21.

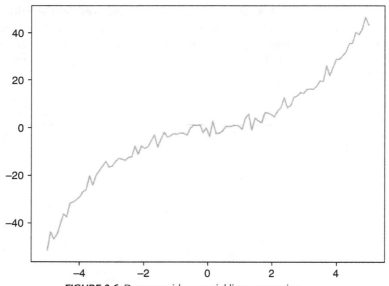

FIGURE 2.6 Datasets with potential linear regression.

Now that you have seen an assortment of line graphs and scatterplots, let's delve into linear regression, which is the topic of the next section.

WHAT IS LINEAR REGRESSION?

Linear regression was created in 1805 (more than two hundred years ago), and it's a very important algorithm in statistical analysis and in machine learning. Any decent statistical package supports linear regression and invariably supports polynomial regression. Just to make sure: linear regression involves lines, which are polynomials with degree one, whereas polynomial regression involves fitting polynomials of degree greater than one to a dataset.

In general terms, linear regression finds the equation of the best fitting hyperplane that approximates a dataset, where a hyperplane has degree one less than the dimensionality of the dataset. In particular, if the dataset is in the Euclidean plane, the hyperplane is simply a line; if the dataset is in 3D the hyperplane is a "regular" plane.

Linear regression is suitable when the points in a dataset are distributed in such a way that they can reasonably be approximated by a hyperplane. If not, then you can try to fit other types of multivariable polynomial surfaces to the points in the dataset.

Keep in mind two other details. First, the best fitting hyperplane does not necessarily intersect all (or even most of) the points in the dataset. In fact, the best fitting hyperplane might not intersect *any* points in the dataset. The purpose of a best fitting hyperplane is to *approximate* the points in dataset as closely as possible. Second, linear regression is *not* the same as curve fitting, which attempts to find a polynomial that passes through a set of points.

Some details about curve fitting: given n points in the plane (no two of which have the same x value), there is a polynomial of degree less than or equal to n-1 that passes through those points. Thus, a line (which has degree one) will pass through any pair of nonvertical points in the plane. For any triple of points in the plane, there is a quadratic equation or a line that passes through those points.

In some cases, a lower degree polynomial is available. For instance, consider the set of 100 points in which the x value equals the y value: clearly the line y = x (a polynomial of degree one) passes through all of those points.

However, keep in mind that the extent to which a line "represents" a set of points in the plane depends on how closely those points can be approximated by a line.

What Is Multivariate Analysis?

Multivariate analysis generalizes the equation of a line in the Euclidean plane, and it has the following form:

```
y = w1*x1 + w2*x2 + . . . + wn*xn + b
```

As you can see, the preceding equation contains a linear combination of the variables x1, x2, . . ., xn. In this book we will usually work with datasets that involve lines in the Euclidean plane.

What About Nonlinear Datasets?

Simple linear regression finds the best fitting line that fits a dataset, but what happens if the dataset does not fit a line in the plane? This is an excellent question! In such a scenario, we look for other curves to approximate the dataset, such as quadratic, cubic, or higher-degree polynomials. However, these alternatives involve trade-offs, as we'll discuss later.

Another possibility is to use a continuous piece-wise linear function, which is a function that comprises a set of line segments, where adjacent line segments are connected. If one or more pairs of adjacent line segments are not connected, then it's a piece-wise linear function (i.e., the function is discontinuous). In either case, line segments have degree one, which involves lower computational complexity than higher order polynomials.

Thus, given a set of points in the plane, try to find the "best fitting" line that fits those points, after addressing the following questions:

1. How do we know that a line "fits" the data?
2. What if a different type of curve is a better fit?
3. What does "best fit" mean?

One way to check if a line fits the data well is through a simple visual check: display the data in a graph and if the data conforms to the shape of a line reasonably well, then a line might be a good fit. However, this is a subjective decision, and a sample dataset that does not fit a line is displayed in Figure 2.7.

Figure 2.7 displays a line with very few points intersecting the line.

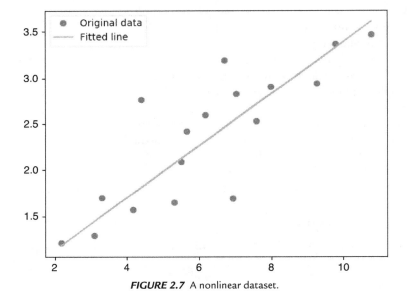

FIGURE 2.7 A nonlinear dataset.

On the other hand, if a line does not appear to be a good fit for the data, then perhaps a quadratic or cubic (or even higher degree) polynomial has the potential of being a better fit. Let's defer the nonlinear scenario and let's make the assumption that a line would be a good fit for the data. There is a well-known technique for finding the "best fitting" line for such a dataset, and it's called mean squared error (MSE).

THE MSE (MEAN SQUARED ERROR) FORMULA

Figure 2.8 displays the formula for the MSE. Translated into English: the MSE is the sum of the squares of the difference between an *actual* y value and the *predicted* y value, divided by the number of points. Note that the predicted y value is the y value that each data point would have if that data point were actually on the best-fitting line.

In general, the goal is to minimize the error, which determines the best fitting line in the case of linear regression. However, you might be satisfied with a "good enough" value when the time and/or cost for any additional reduction in the error is deemed prohibitive, which means that this decision is not a purely programmatic decision.

Figure 2.8 displays the formula for MSE for calculating the best-fitting line for a set of points in the plane.

$$\text{MSE} = \frac{1}{n} \sum_{i=1}^{n} (Y_i - \hat{Y}_i)^2$$

FIGURE 2.8 The MSE formula.

Other Error Types

Although we will only discuss MSE for linear regression in this book, there are other types of formulas for errors that you can use for linear regression, some of which are listed here:

- MSE
- RMSE
- RMSPROP
- MAE

The MSE is the basis for the preceding error types. For example, RMSE is "root mean squared error", which is the square root of MSE.

On the other hand, MAE is "mean absolute error," which is *the sum of the absolute value of the differences of the y terms* (not the square of the differences of the y terms).

The RMSProp optimizer utilizes the magnitude of recent gradients to normalize the gradients. Maintain a moving average over the RMS ("root mean squared," which is the square root of the MSE) gradients, and then divide that term by the current gradient.

Although it's easier to compute the derivative of MSE (because it's a differentiable function), it's also true that MSE is more susceptible to outliers, more so than MAE. The reason is simple: a squared term can be significantly larger than adding the absolute value of a term. For example, if a difference term is 10, then the squared term 100 is added to MSE, whereas only 10 is added to MAE. Similarly, if a difference term is –20, then the squared term 400 is added to MSE, whereas only 20 (which is the absolute value of –20) is added to MAE.

Nonlinear Least Squares

When predicting housing prices, where the dataset contains a wide range of values, techniques such as linear regression or random forests can cause the model to "overfit" the samples with the highest values in order to reduce quantities such as mean absolute error.

In this scenario, you probably want an error metric, such as relative error, that reduces the importance of fitting the samples with the largest values. This technique is called nonlinear least squares, which may use a log-based transformation of labels and predicted values.

CALCULATING THE MSE MANUALLY

Let's look at two simple graphs, each of which contains a line that approximates a set of points in a scatter plot. Notice that the line segment is the same for both sets of points, but the datasets are slightly different. We will manually calculate the MSE for both datasets and determine which value of MSE is smaller.

Figure 2.9 displays a set of points and a line that is a potential candidate for best-fitting line for the data.

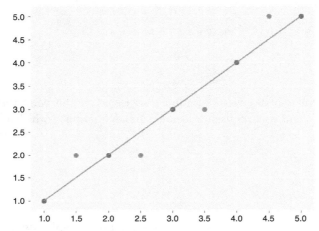

FIGURE 2.9 A line graph that approximates points of a scatter plot.

The MSE for the line in Figure 2.9 is computed as follows:

```
MSE = [1*1 + (-1)*(-1) + (-1)*(-1) + 1*1]/9 = 4/9
```

Now look at Figure 2.10 that also displays a set of points and a line that is a potential candidate for best-fitting line for the data.

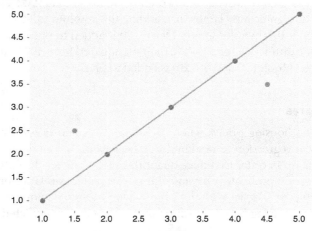

FIGURE 2.10 A line graph that approximates points of a scatter plot.

The MSE for the line in Figure 2.10 is computed as follows:

```
MSE = [(-2)*(-2) + 2*2]/7 = 8/7
```

Thus, the line in Figure 2.9 has a smaller MSE than the line in Figure 2.10, which might have surprised you (or did you guess correctly)?

In these two figures we calculated the MSE easily and quickly, but in general it's significantly more difficult. For instance, if we plot 10 points in the Euclidean plane that do not closely fit a line, with individual terms that involve noninteger values, we would probably need a calculator. A better solution involves NumPy functions, as discussed in the next section.

FIND THE BEST-FITTING LINE IN NUMPY

Earlier in this chapter you saw examples of lines in the plane, including horizontal, slanted, and parallel lines. Most of those lines have a positive slope and a nonzero value for their y-intercept. Although there are scatterplots of data points in the plane where the best-fitting line has a negative slope, the examples in this book involve scatterplots whose best-fitting line has a positive slope.

Listing 2.22 displays the contents of find_best_fit.py that illustrates how to determine the best fitting line for a set of points in the Euclidean plane. The solution is based on so-called "closed form" formulas that are available from statistics.

LISTING 2.22: find_best_fit.py

```
import numpy as np

xs = np.array([1,2,3,4,5], dtype=np.float64)
ys = np.array([1,2,3,4,5], dtype=np.float64)

def best_fit_slope(xs,ys):
  m = (((np.mean(xs)*np.mean(ys))-np.mean(xs*ys)) /
       ((np.mean(xs)**2) - np.mean(xs**2)))
  b = np.mean(ys) - m * np.mean(xs)

  return m, b

m,b = best_fit_slope(xs,ys)
print('m:',m,'b:',b)
```

Listing 2.22 starts with two NumPy arrays xs and ys that are initialized with the first five positive integers. The Python function best_fit_slope() calculate the optimal values of m (the slope) and b (the y-intercept) of a set of numbers. The output from Listing 2.22 is here:

```
m: 1.0 b: 0.0
```

Notice that the NumPy arrays xs and ys are identical, which means that these points lie on the identity function whose slope is 1. By simple extrapolation, the point (0,0) is also a point on the same line. Hence, the y-intercept of this line must equal 0.

If you are interested, you can search online to find the derivation for the values of m and b. In this chapter, we're going to skip the derivation and proceed with examples of calculating the MSE. The first example involves calculating the MSE manually, followed by an example that uses NumPy formulas to perform the calculations.

CALCULATING MSE BY SUCCESSIVE APPROXIMATION (1)

This section contains a code sample that uses a simple technique for successively determining better approximations for the slope and y-intercept of a best-fitting line. Recall that an approximation of a derivative is the ratio of "delta y" divided by "delta x." The "delta" values calculate the difference of the y values and the difference of the x values, respectively, of two nearby points (x1,y1) and (x2,y2) on a function. Hence, the delta-based approximation ratio is (y2-y1)/(x2-x1).

The technique in this section involves a simplified approximation for the "delta" values: we assume that the denominators are equal to 1. As a result, we need only calculate the numerators of the "delta" values: in this code sample, those numerators are the variables dw and db.

Listing 2.23 displays the contents of plain_linreg1.py that illustrates how to compute the MSE with simulated data.

LISTING 2.23: plain_linreg1.py

```
import numpy as np
import matplotlib.pyplot as plt

X = [0,0.12,0.25,0.27,0.38,0.42,0.44,0.55,0.92,1.0]
Y = [0,0.15,0.54,0.51,0.34,0.1, 0.19,0.53,1.0,0.58]

losses = []
#Step 1: Parameter initialization
W = 0.45 # the initial slope
b = 0.75 # the initial y-intercept

for i in range(1, 100):
  #Step 2: Calculate Cost
  Y_pred = np.multiply(W, X) + b
  loss_error = 0.5 * (Y_pred - Y)**2
  cost = np.sum(loss_error)/10

  #Step 3: Calculate dw and db
  db = np.sum((Y_pred - Y))
  dw = np.dot((Y_pred - Y), X)
  losses.append(cost)

  #Step 4: Update parameters:
  W = W - 0.01*dw
  b = b - 0.01*db
```

```
  if i%10 == 0:
    print("Loss at", i,"iteration = ", loss)

#Step 5: Repeat via a for loop with 1000 iterations
#Plot loss versus # of iterations
print("W = ", W,"& b = ",  b)
plt.plot(losses)
plt.ylabel('loss')
plt.xlabel('iterations (per tens)')
plt.show()
```

Listing 2.23 defines the variables X and Y that are simple arrays of numbers (this is our dataset). Next, the losses array is initialized as an empty array, and we will append successive loss approximations to this array. The variables W and b correspond to the slope and y-intercept, and they are initialized with the values 0.45 and 0.75, respectively (feel free to experiment with these values).

The next portion of Listing 2.23 is a for loop that executes 100 times. During each iteration, the variables Y_pred, loss_error, and loss are computed, and they correspond to the predicted value, the error, and the loss, respectively (remember: we are performing linear regression). The value of loss (which is the error for the current iteration) is then appended to the losses array.

Next, the variables dw and db are calculated: these correspond to "delta w" and "delta b" that we'll use to update the values of W and b, respectively. The code is reproduced here:

```
#Step 4: Update parameters:
W = W - 0.01*dw
b = b - 0.01*db
```

Notice that dw and db are both multiplied by the value 0.01, which is the value of our "learning rate" (experiment with this value as well).

The next code snippet displays the current loss, which is performed every tenth iteration through the loop. When the loop finishes execution, the values of W and b are displayed, and a plot is displayed that shows the loss values on the vertical axis and the loop iterations on the horizontal axis. The output from Listing 2.23 is here:

```
Loss at 10 iteration =  0.04114630674619491
Loss at 20 iteration =  0.026706242729839395
Loss at 30 iteration =  0.024738889446900423
Loss at 40 iteration =  0.023850565034634254
Loss at 50 iteration =  0.0231499048706651
Loss at 60 iteration =  0.02255361434242207
Loss at 70 iteration =  0.0220425055291673
Loss at 80 iteration =  0.021604128492245713
Loss at 90 iteration =  0.021228111750568435
W =  0.47256473531193927 & b =  0.19578262688662174
```

Figure 2.11 displays the plot of loss-versus-iterations for Listing 2.23.

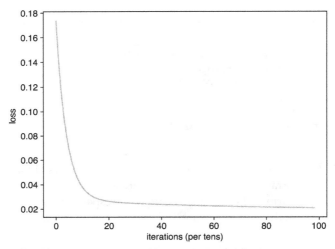

FIGURE 2.11 A Plot of loss-versus-iterations.

CALCULATING MSE BY SUCCESSIVE APPROXIMATION (2)

In the previous section, you saw how to calculate "delta" approximations in order to determine the equation of a best-fitting line for a set of points in a 2D plane. The example in this section generalizes the code in the previous section by adding an outer loop that represents the number of epochs. In case you don't already know, the number of epochs specifies the number of times that an inner loop is executed.

Listing 2.24 displays the contents of `plain_linreg2.py` that illustrates how to compute the MSE with simulated data.

LISTING 2.24: plain_linreg2.py

```
import numpy as np
import matplotlib.pyplot as plt

# %matplotlib inline
X = [0,0.12,0.25,0.27,0.38,0.42,0.44,0.55,0.92,1.0]
Y = [0,0.15,0.54,0.51, 0.34,0.1,0.19,0.53,1.0,0.58]

#uncomment to see a plot of X versus Y values
#plt.plot(X,Y)
#plt.show()

costs = []
#Step 1: Parameter initialization
W = 0.45
b = 0.75

epochs = 100
lr = 0.001
```

```
for j in range(1, epochs):
  for i in range(1, 100):
    #Step 2: Calculate Loss
    Y_pred = np.multiply(W, X) + b
    Loss_error = 0.5 * (Y_pred - Y)**2
    loss = np.sum(Loss_error)/10

    #Step 3: Calculate dW and db
    db = np.sum((Y_pred - Y))
    dw = np.dot((Y_pred - Y), X)
    losses.append(loss)

    #Step 4: Update parameters:
    W = W - lr*dw
    b = b - lr*db

    if i%50 == 0:
      print("Loss at epoch", j,"= ", loss)

#Plot loss versus # of iterations
print("W = ", W,"& b = ",  b)
plt.plot(losses)
plt.ylabel('loss')
plt.xlabel('iterations (per tens)')
plt.show()
```

Compare the new contents of Listing 2.24 (shown in bold) with the contents of Listing 2.23: the changes are minimal, and the main difference is to execute the inner loop 100 times for each iteration of the outer loop, which also executes 100 times. The output from Listing 2.24 is here:

```
('Loss at epoch', 1, '= ', 0.07161762489862147)
('Loss at epoch', 2, '= ', 0.030073922512586938)
('Loss at epoch', 3, '= ', 0.025415528992988472)
('Loss at epoch', 4, '= ', 0.0242278263736677794)
('Loss at epoch', 5, '= ', 0.023462419670711181)
('Loss at epoch', 6, '= ', 0.022827707922883803)
('Loss at epoch', 7, '= ', 0.022284262669854064)
('Loss at epoch', 8, '= ', 0.02181735173716673)
('Loss at epoch', 9, '= ', 0.0214160501797776294)
('Loss at epoch', 10, '= ', 0.02107112540934384)
// details omitted for brevity
('Loss at epoch', 90, '= ', 0.018960749188638278)
('Loss at epoch', 91, '= ', 0.018960747557776306)
('Loss at epoch', 92, '= ', 0.018960746155994725)
('Loss at epoch', 93, '= ', 0.018960744951148113)
('Loss at epoch', 94, '= ', 0.018960743915559485)
('Loss at epoch', 95, '= ', 0.018960743025451313)
('Loss at epoch', 96, '= ', 0.018960742260386375)
('Loss at epoch', 97, '= ', 0.018960741602798474)
('Loss at epoch', 98, '= ', 0.018960741037589136)
('Loss at epoch', 99, '= ', 0.018960740551780944)
('W = ', 0.6764145874436108, '& b = ', 0.09976839618922698)
```

Figure 2.12 displays the plot of loss-versus-iterations for Listing 2.24.

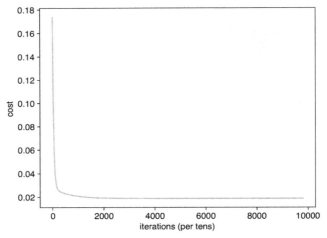

FIGURE 2.12 A Plot of loss-versus-iterations.

Notice that Figure 2.12 has 10,000 iterations on the horizontal axis, whereas Figure 2.11 has only 100 iterations on the horizontal axis.

GOOGLE COLABORATORY

Fortunately, Google Colaboratory is a cloud-based environment that provides free GPU support, and also runs as a `Jupyter` notebook environment. In addition, Google Colaboratory executes your code in the cloud and involves zero configuration, and it's available here:

https://colab.research.google.com/notebooks/welcome.ipynb

This `Jupyter` notebook is suitable for training simple models and testing ideas quickly. Google Colaboratory makes it easy to upload local files, install software in `Jupyter` notebooks, and even connect Google Colaboratory to a `Jupyter` runtime on your local machine.

Some of the supported features of Colaboratory include TF 2 execution with GPUs, visualization using Matplotlib, and the ability to save a copy of your Google Colaboratory notebook to Github by using `File > Save a copy to GitHub`.

Moreover, you can load any `.ipynb` on GitHub by just adding the path to the URL `colab. research.google.com/github/` (see the Colaboratory website for details).

Google Colaboratory has support for other technologies such as HTML and SVG, enabling you o render SVG-based graphics in notebooks that are in Google Colaboratory. One point to keep in mind: any software that you install in a Google Colaboratory notebook is only available on a per-session basis: if you log out and log in again, you need to perform the same installation steps that you performed during your earlier Google Colaboratory session.

As mentioned earlier, there is one other *very* nice feature of Google Colaboratory: you can execute code on a GPU for up to twelve hours per day for free. This free GPU support is extremely useful for people who don't have a suitable GPU on their local machine (which is probably the majority of users), and now they launch TF 2 code to train neural networks in less than 20 or 30 minutes that would otherwise require multiple hours of CPU-based execution time.

Keep in mind the following details about Google Colaboratory. First, whenever you connect to a server in Google Colaboratory, you start what's known as a *session*. You can execute the code in a session with a CPU (the default), a GPU, or a TPU (which is available for free), and you can execute your code without any time limit for your session. However, if you select the GPU option for your session, *only the first 12 hours of GPU execution time are free*. Any additional GPU time during that same session incurs a small charge (see the website for those details).

The other point to keep in mind is that any software that you install in a Jupyter notebook during a given session will *not* be saved when you exit that session. For example, the following code snippet installs TFLearn in a Jupyter notebook:
```
!pip install tflearn
```
When you exit the current session and at some point later you start a new session, you need to install TFLearn again, as well as any other software (such as Github repositories) that you also installed in any previous session.

Uploading CSV Files in Google Colaboratory

Listing 2.25 displays the contents upload_csv_file.ipynb that illustrates how to upload a CSV file in a Google Colaboratory notebook.

LISTING 2.25: upload_csv_file.ipynb

```
import pandas as pd

from google.colab import files
uploaded = files.upload()

df = pd.read_csv("weather_data.csv")
print("dataframe df:")
df
```

Listing 2.25 uploads the CSV file weather_data.csv whose contents are not shown because they are not important for this example. The code shown in bold is the Colaboratory-specific code that is required to upload the CSV file. When you launch this code, you will see a small button labeled "Browse," which you must click and then select the CSV file that is listed in the code snippet. After doing so, the rest of the code is executed and you will see the contents of the CSV file displayed in your browser session.

———
NOTE *You must supply the CSV file weather_data.csv if you want to launch this Jupyter notebook successfully in Google Colaboratory.*

SUMMARY

This chapter introduced you to the NumPy library for Python. You learned how to write Python scripts containing loops, arrays, and lists. You also saw how to work with dot products, the `reshape()` method, plotting with `Matplotlib` (discussed in more detail in Chapter 6), and examples of linear regression.

Then you learned how to work with subranges of arrays, and also negative subranges of vectors and arrays, both of which are very useful for extracting portions of datasets in machine learning tasks. You also saw various other `NumPy` operations, such as the `reshape()` method that is extremely useful (and very common) when working with images files.

Next, you learned how to use `NumPy` for linear regression, the mean squared error (`MSE`), and how to calculate `MSE` with the `NumPy linspace()` method. Finally, you got an introduction Google Colaboratory where you can take advantage of the free GPU time when you launch Jupyter notebooks.

## CHAPTER 3

PANDAS AND DATA VISUALIZATION

This chapter introduces the `Pandas` library and contains various code samples that illustrate some useful `Pandas` features. As you will see, the title of each section clearly indicates its contents, so you can easily scan this chapter for those sections that contain material that is new to you. This approach will help you make efficient use of your time when you read the contents of this chapter.

The first part of this chapter contains a brief introduction to `Pandas`, followed by code samples that illustrate how to define `Pandas DataFrames` and also display their attributes. Please keep in mind that this chapter is devoted to `Pandas DataFrames`. There is one code block that illustrates how to define a `Pandas Series`, and if you want to learn more about this `Pandas Series`, you can search online for more information.

The second part of this chapter discusses various types of `DataFrames` that you can create, such as numeric and Boolean `DataFrames`. In addition, you will see examples of creating `DataFrames` with `NumPy` functions and random numbers. You will also see examples of converting between `Python` dictionaries and `JSON`-based data, and also how to create a `Pandas DataFrame` from `JSON`-based data.

WHAT IS PANDAS?

`Pandas` is a `Python` library that is compatible with other `Python` libraries, such as `NumPy`, `Matplotlib`, and so forth. Install `Pandas` by opening a command shell and invoking this command for Python 3.x:

```
pip3 install pandas
```

In many ways the `Pandas` library has the semantics of a spreadsheet, and it also works with various file types, such as `xsl`, `xml`, `html`, `csv` files. `Pandas` provides a data type called a `DataFrame` (similar to a `Python` dictionary) with extremely powerful functionality (similar to the functionality of a spreadsheet).

Pandas DataFrames

In simplified terms, a `Pandas DataFrame` is a two-dimensional data structure, and it's convenient to think of the data structure in terms of rows and columns. `DataFrames` can be labeled (rows as well as columns), and the columns can contain different data types. The source of the dataset can be a data file, database tables, Web service, and so forth. `Pandas DataFrame` features include:

- data frame methods
- data frame statistics
- grouping, pivoting, and reshaping
- handle missing data
- join data frames

Dataframes and Data Cleaning Tasks

The specific tasks that you need to perform depend on the structure and contents of a dataset. In general, you will perform a workflow with the following steps (not necessarily always in this order), all of which can be performed with a `Pandas DataFrame`:

- read data into a DataFrame
- display top of DataFrame
- display column data types
- display non-missing values
- replace NA with a value
- iterate through the columns
- statistics for each column
- find missing values
- total missing values
- percentage of missing values
- sort table values
- print summary information
- columns with > 50% missing values
- rename columns

A PANDAS DATAFRAME EXAMPLE

Listing 3.1 displays the contents of `pandas_df.py` that illustrates how to define several `Pandas DataFrames` and display their contents.

LISTING 3.1: pandas_df.py

```
import pandas as pd
import numpy as np

myvector1 = np.array([1,2,3,4,5])
print("myvector1:")
print(myvector1)
print()
mydf1 = pd.DataFrame(myvector1)
print("mydf1:")
```

```
print(mydf1)
print()

myvector2 = np.array([i for i in range(1,6)])
print("myvector2:")
print(myvector2)
print()

mydf2 = pd.DataFrame(myvector2)
print("mydf2:")
print(mydf2)
print()

myarray = np.array([[10,30,20], [50,40,60],[1000,2000,3000]])
print("myarray:")
print(myarray)
print()

mydf3 = pd.DataFrame(myarray)
print("mydf3:")
print(mydf3)
print()
```

Listing 3.1 starts with a standard import statement for Pandas and NumPy, followed by the definition of two one-dimensional NumPy arrays and a two-dimensional NumPy array. The NumPy syntax ought to be familiar to you (many basic tutorials are available online). Each NumPy variable is followed by a corresponding Pandas DataFrame mydf1, mydf2, and mydf3. Now launch the code in Listing 3.1 and you will see the following output, and you can compare the NumPy arrays with the Pandas DataFrames:

```
myvector1:
[1 2 3 4 5]

mydf1:
   0
0  1
1  2
2  3
3  4
4  5


myvector2:
[1 2 3 4 5]

mydf2:
   0
0  1
1  2
2  3
3  4
4  5
```

```
myarray:
[[10    30    20]
 [50    40    60]
 [1000 2000 3000]]

mydf3:
      0     1     2
0    10    30    20
1    50    40    60
2  1000  2000  3000
```

By contrast, the following code block illustrates how to define a `Pandas Series`:

```
names = pd.Series(['SF', 'San Jose', 'Sacramento'])
sizes = pd.Series([852469, 1015785, 485199])
df = pd.DataFrame({'Cities': names, 'Size': sizes})
print(df)
```

Create a `Python` file with the preceding code (along with the required `import` statement) and when you launch that code you will see the following output:

```
   City name     sizes
0         SF    852469
1   San Jose   1015785
2 Sacramento    485199
```

DESCRIBING A PANDAS DATAFRAME

Listing 3.2 displays the contents of `pandas_df_describe.py` that illustrates how to define a `Pandas DataFrame` that contains a 3x3 `NumPy` array of integer values, where the rows and columns of the DataFrame are labeled. Various other aspects of the DataFrame are also displayed.

LISTING 3.2: pandas_df_describe.py

```
import numpy as np
import pandas as pd

myarray = np.array([[10,30,20], [50,40,60],[1000,2000,3000]])

rownames = ['apples', 'oranges', 'beer']
colnames = ['January', 'February', 'March']

mydf = pd.DataFrame(myarray, index=rownames, columns=colnames)
print("contents of df:")
print(mydf)
print()

print("contents of January:")
print(mydf['January'])
print()

print("Number of Rows:")
print(mydf.shape[0])
print()
```

```
print("Number of Columns:")
print(mydf.shape[1])
print()

print("Number of Rows and Columns:")
print(mydf.shape)
print()

print("Column Names:")
print(mydf.columns)
print()

print("Column types:")
print(mydf.dtypes)
print()

print("Description:")
print(mydf.describe())
print()
```

Listing 3.2 starts with two standard `import` statements followed by the variable `myarray`, which is a 3x3 `NumPy` array of numbers. The variables `rownames` and `colnames` provide names for the rows and columns, respectively, of the `Pandas DataFrame mydf`, which is initialized as a `Pandas DataFrame` with the specified datasource (i.e., `myarray`).

The first portion of the output below requires a single `print` statement (which simply displays the contents of `mydf`). The second portion of the output is generated by invoking the `describe()` method that is available for any `NumPy DataFrame`. The `describe()` method is very useful: you will see various statistical quantities, such as the mean, standard deviation minimum, and maximum performed column wise (not row wise), along with values for the 25th, 50th, and 75th percentiles. The output of Listing 3.2 is here:

```
contents of df:
        January  February  March
apples       10        30     20
oranges      50        40     60
beer       1000      2000   3000

contents of January:
apples        10
oranges       50
beer        1000
Name: January, dtype: int64

Number of Rows:
3

Number of Columns:
3
Number of Rows and Columns:
(3, 3)
```

```
Column Names:
Index(['January', 'February', 'March'], dtype='object')

Column types:
January      int64
February     int64
March        int64
dtype: object

Description:
            January      February        March
count      3.000000      3.000000     3.000000
mean     353.333333    690.000000  1026.666667
std      560.386771   1134.504297  1709.073823
min       10.000000     30.000000    20.000000
25%       30.000000     35.000000    40.000000
50%       50.000000     40.000000    60.000000
75%      525.000000   1020.000000  1530.000000
max     1000.000000   2000.000000  3000.000000
```

PANDAS BOOLEAN DataFrame**s**

Pandas supports Boolean operations on DataFrames, such as the logical or, the logical and, and the logical negation of a pair of DataFrames. Listing 3.3 displays the contents of pandas_boolean_df.py that illustrates how to define a Pandas DataFrame whose rows and columns are Boolean values.

LISTING 3.3: pandas_boolean_df.py

```
import pandas as pd

df1 = pd.DataFrame({'a': [1, 0, 1], 'b': [0, 1, 1] }, dtype=bool)
df2 = pd.DataFrame({'a': [0, 1, 1], 'b': [1, 1, 0] }, dtype=bool)

print("df1 & df2:")
print(df1 & df2)

print("df1 | df2:")
print(df1 | df2)

print("df1 ^ df2:")
print(df1 ^ df2)
```

Listing 3.3 initializes the DataFrames df1 and df2, and then computes df1 & df2, df1 | df2, df1 ^ df2, which represent the logical AND, the logical OR, and the logical negation, respectively, of df1 and df2. The output from launching the code in Listing 3.3 is here:

```
df1 & df2:
       a       b
0  False   False
1  False    True
2   True   False
df1 | df2:
```

```
       a     b
0   True  True
1   True  True
2   True  True
df1 ^ df2:
       a      b
0   True   True
1   True  False
2  False   True
```

Transposing a Pandas DataFrame

The T attribute (as well as the transpose function) enables you to generate the transpose of a Pandas DataFrame, similar to a NumPy ndarray.

For example, the following code snippet defines a Pandas DataFrame df1 and then displays the transpose of df1:

```
df1 = pd.DataFrame({'a': [1, 0, 1], 'b': [0, 1, 1]}, dtype=int)

print("df1.T:")
print(df1.T)
```

The output is here:

```
df1.T:
   0  1  2
a  1  0  1
b  0  1  1
```

The following code snippet defines Pandas DataFrames df1 and df2 and then displays their sum:

```
df1 = pd.DataFrame({'a' : [1, 0, 1], 'b' : [0, 1, 1]}, dtype=int)
df2 = pd.DataFrame({'a' : [3, 3, 3], 'b' : [5, 5, 5]}, dtype=int)

print("df1 + df2:")
print(df1 + df2)
```

The output is here:

```
df1 + df2:
   a  b
0  4  5
1  3  6
2  4  6
```

PANDAS DATAFRAMES AND RANDOM NUMBERS

Listing 3.4 displays the contents of pandas_random_df.py that illustrates how to create a Pandas DataFrame with random numbers.

LISTING 3.4: pandas_random_df.py

```
import pandas as pd
import numpy as np
```

```
df = pd.DataFrame(np.random.randint(1, 5, size=(5, 2)),
columns=['a','b'])
df = df.append(df.agg(['sum', 'mean']))

print("Contents of data frame:")
print(df)
```

Listing 3.4 defines the `Pandas DataFrame df` that consists of 5 rows and 2 columns of random integers between 1 and 5. Notice that the columns of `df` are labeled "a" and "b." In addition, the next code snippet appends two rows consisting of the sum and the mean of the numbers in both columns. The output of Listing 3.4 is here:

```
a      b
0      1.0  2.0
1      1.0  1.0
2      4.0  3.0
3      3.0  1.0
4      1.0  2.0
sum   10.0  9.0
mean   2.0  1.8
```

Listing 3.5 displays the contents of `pandas_combine_df.py` that illustrates how to define a `Pandas DataFrame` that is based on two `NumPy` arrays of numbers.

LISTING 3.5: pandas_combine_df.py

```
import pandas as pd
import numpy as np

df = pd.DataFrame({'foo1' : np.random.randn(5),
                   'foo2' : np.random.randn(5)})

print("contents of df:")
print(df)

print("contents of foo1:")
print(df.foo1)

print("contents of foo2:")
print(df.foo2)
```

Listing 3.5 defines the `Pandas DataFrame df` that consists of 5 rows and 2 columns (labeled "foo1" and "foo2") of random real numbers between 0 and 5. The next portion of Listing 3.5 displays the contents of `df` and `foo1`. The output of Listing 3.5 is here:

```
contents of df:
        foo1      foo2
0   0.274680 _0.848669
1 _0.399771 _0.814679
2  0.454443 _0.363392
3  0.473753  0.550849
4 _0.211783 _0.015014
```

```
contents of foo1:
0     0.256773
1     1.204322
2     1.040515
3    _0.518414
4     0.634141
Name: foo1, dtype: float64
contents of foo2:
0    _2.506550
1    _0.896516
2    _0.222923
3     0.934574
4     0.527033
Name: foo2, dtype: float64
```

CONVERTING CATEGORICAL DATA TO NUMERIC DATA

One common task in machine learning involves converting a feature containing character data into a feature that contains numeric data.

Listing 3.6 displays the contents of `sometext.tsv` that contains labeled data (spam or ham), which is used in the code sample displayed in Listing 3.7 (displayed after Listing 3.6).

LISTING 3.6: *sometext.tsv*

```
type      text
ham       I'm telling the truth
spam      What a deal such a deal!
spam      Free vacation for your family
ham       Thank you for your help
spam      Spring break next week!
ham       I received the documents
spam      One million dollars for you
ham       My wife got covid19
spam      You might have won the prize
ham       Everyone is in good health
```

Listing 3.7 displays the contents of `cat2numeric.py` that illustrates how to replace a text field with a corresponding numeric field.

LISTING 3.7: *cat2numeric.py*

```python
import pandas as pd
import numpy as np

df = pd.read_csv('sometext.tsv', delimiter='\t')

print("=> First five rows (before):")
print(df.head(5))
print("------------------------")

# map ham/spam to 0/1 values:
df['type'] = df['type'].map( {'ham':0 , 'spam':1} )
```

```
print("=> First five rows (after):")
print(df.head(5))
print("------------------------")
```

Listing 3.7 initializes the `DataFrame` `df` with the contents of the CSV file `sometext.tsv`, and then displays the contents of the first five rows by invoking `df.head(5)`, which is also the default number of rows to display. The next code snippet in Listing 3.7 invokes the `map()` method to replace occurrences of `ham` with 0 and replace occurrences of `spam` with 1 in the column labeled type, as shown here:

```
df['type'] = df['type'].map( {'ham':0 , 'spam':1} )
```

The last portion of Listing 3.7 invokes the `head()` method again to display the first five rows of the dataset after having renamed the contents of the column type. Launch the code in Listing 3.7 and you will see the following output:

```
=> First five rows (before):
    type                       text
0   ham        Available only for today
1   ham              I'm joking with you
2   spam    Free entry in 2 a wkly comp
3   ham            U dun say so early hor
4   ham    I don't think he goes to usf
------------------------
=> First five rows (after):
    type                       text
0    0         Available only for today
1    0               I'm joking with you
2    1     Free entry in 2 a wkly comp
3    0             U dun say so early hor
4    0     I don't think he goes to usf
------------------------
```

As another example, Listing 3.8 displays the contents of `shirts.csv` and Listing 3.9 displays the contents of `shirts.py` that illustrates four techniques for converting categorical data to numeric data.

LISTING 3.8: *shirts.csv*

```
type,ssize
shirt,xxlarge
shirt,xxlarge
shirt,xlarge
shirt,xlarge
shirt,xlarge
shirt,large
shirt,medium
shirt,small
shirt,small
shirt,xsmall
shirt,xsmall
shirt,xsmall
```

LISTING 3.9: shirts.py

```
import pandas as pd

shirts = pd.read_csv("shirts.csv")
print("shirts before:")
print(shirts)
print()

# TECHNIQUE #1:
#shirts.loc[shirts['ssize']=='xxlarge','size'] = 4
#shirts.loc[shirts['ssize']=='xlarge', 'size'] = 4
#shirts.loc[shirts['ssize']=='large',  'size'] = 3
#shirts.loc[shirts['ssize']=='medium', 'size'] = 2
#shirts.loc[shirts['ssize']=='small',  'size'] = 1
#shirts.loc[shirts['ssize']=='xsmall', 'size'] = 1

# TECHNIQUE #2:
#shirts['ssize'].replace('xxlarge', 4, inplace=True)
#shirts['ssize'].replace('xlarge',  4, inplace=True)
#shirts['ssize'].replace('large',   3, inplace=True)
#shirts['ssize'].replace('medium',  2, inplace=True)
#shirts['ssize'].replace('small',   1, inplace=True)
#shirts['ssize'].replace('xsmall',  1, inplace=True)

# TECHNIQUE #3:
#shirts['ssize'] = shirts['ssize'].apply({'xxlarge':4, 'xlarge':4,
'large':3, 'medium':2, 'small':1, 'xsmall':1}.get)

# TECHNIQUE #4:
shirts['ssize'] = shirts['ssize'].replace(regex='xlarge', value=4)
shirts['ssize'] = shirts['ssize'].replace(regex='large',  value=3)
shirts['ssize'] = shirts['ssize'].replace(regex='medium', value=2)
shirts['ssize'] = shirts['ssize'].replace(regex='small',  value=1)

print("shirts after:")
print(shirts)
```

Listing 3.9 starts with a code block of six statements that uses direct comparison with strings to make numeric replacements. For example, the following code snippet replaces all occurrences of the string xxlarge with the value 4:

```
shirts.loc[shirts['ssize']=='xxlarge','size'] = 4
```

The second code block consists of six statements that use the replace() method to perform the same updates, an example of which is shown here:

```
shirts['ssize'].replace('xxlarge', 4, inplace=True)
```

The third code block consists of a single statement that use the apply() method to perform the same updates, as shown here:

```
shirts['ssize'] = shirts['ssize'].apply({'xxlarge':4, 'xlarge':4,
'large':3, 'medium':2, 'small':1, 'xsmall':1}.get)
```

The fourth code block consists of four statements that use regular expressions to perform the same updates, an example of which is shown here:

```
shirts['ssize'] = shirts['ssize'].replace(regex='xlarge', value=4)
```

Since the preceding code snippet matches xxlarge as well as xlarge, we only need four statements instead of six statements. If you are unfamiliar with regular expressions, you can find online articles that can introduce you to regular expressions. Now launch the code in Listing 3.9 and you will see the following output:

```
shirts before
      type     size
0    shirt   xxlarge
1    shirt   xxlarge
2    shirt    xlarge
3    shirt    xlarge
4    shirt    xlarge
5    shirt     large
6    shirt    medium
7    shirt     small
8    shirt     small
9    shirt    xsmall
10   shirt    xsmall
11   shirt    xsmall

shirts after:
      type    size
0    shirt      4
1    shirt      4
2    shirt      4
3    shirt      4
4    shirt      4
5    shirt      3
6    shirt      2
7    shirt      1
8    shirt      1
9    shirt      1
10   shirt      1
11   shirt      1
```

MATCHING AND SPLITTING STRINGS IN PANDAS

Listing 3.10 displays the contents of shirts_str.py that illustrates how to match a column value with an initial string and also how to split a column value based on a letter.

LISTING 3.10: shirts_str.py

```
import pandas as pd

shirts = pd.read_csv("shirts.csv")
print("shirts:")
```

```
print(shirts)
print()

print("shirts starting with xl:")
print(shirts[shirts.ssize.str.startswith('xl')])
print()

print("Exclude 'xlarge' shirts:")
print(shirts[shirts['ssize'] != 'xlarge'])
print()

print("first three letters:")
shirts['sub1'] = shirts['ssize'].str[:3]
print(shirts)
print()

print("split ssize on letter 'a':")
shirts['sub2'] = shirts['ssize'].str.split('a')
print(shirts)
print()

print("Rows 3 through 5 and column 2:")
print(shirts.iloc[2:5, 2])
print()
```

Listing 3.10 initializes the `DataFrame` df with the contents of the CSV file `shirts.csv`, and then displays the contents of the `DataFrame`. The next code snippet in Listing 3.10 uses the `startswith()` method to match the shirt types that start with the letters `xl`, followed by a code snippet that displays the shorts whose size does not equal the string `xlarge`.

The next code snippet uses the construct `str[:3]` to display the first three letters of the shirt types, followed by a code snippet that uses the `split()` method to split the shirt types based on the letter "a." The final code snippet invokes `iloc[2:5,2]` to display the contents of rows 3 through 5 inclusive, and only the second column. The output of Listing 3.10 is here:

```
shirts:
      type    ssize
0    shirt  xxlarge
1    shirt  xxlarge
2    shirt   xlarge
3    shirt   xlarge
4    shirt   xlarge
5    shirt    large
6    shirt   medium
7    shirt    small
8    shirt    small
9    shirt   xsmall
10   shirt   xsmall
11   shirt   xsmall
```

```
shirts starting with xl:
    type   ssize
2  shirt  xlarge
3  shirt  xlarge
4  shirt  xlarge

Exclude 'xlarge' shirts:
     type    ssize
0   shirt  xxlarge
1   shirt  xxlarge
5   shirt    large
6   shirt   medium
7   shirt    small
8   shirt    small
9   shirt   xsmall
10  shirt   xsmall
11  shirt   xsmall

first three letters:
     type    ssize sub1
0   shirt  xxlarge  xxl
1   shirt  xxlarge  xxl
2   shirt   xlarge  xla
3   shirt   xlarge  xla
4   shirt   xlarge  xla
5   shirt    large  lar
6   shirt   medium  med
7   shirt    small  sma
8   shirt    small  sma
9   shirt   xsmall  xsm
10  shirt   xsmall  xsm
11  shirt   xsmall  xsm

split ssize on letter 'a':
     type    ssize sub1         sub2
0   shirt  xxlarge  xxl   [xxl, rge]
1   shirt  xxlarge  xxl   [xxl, rge]
2   shirt   xlarge  xla    [xl, rge]
3   shirt   xlarge  xla    [xl, rge]
4   shirt   xlarge  xla    [xl, rge]
5   shirt    large  lar     [l, rge]
6   shirt   medium  med     [medium]
7   shirt    small  sma      [sm, ll]
8   shirt    small  sma      [sm, ll]
9   shirt   xsmall  xsm     [xsm, ll]
10  shirt   xsmall  xsm     [xsm, ll]
11  shirt   xsmall  xsm     [xsm, ll]

Rows 3 through 5 and column 2:
2    xlarge
3    xlarge
4    xlarge
Name: ssize, dtype: object
```

MERGING AND SPLITTING COLUMNS IN PANDAS

Listing 3.11 displays the contents of `employees.csv` and Listing 3.12 displays the contents of `emp_merge_split.py` that illustrates how to merge columns and split columns of a CSV file.

LISTING 3.11: employees.csv

```
name,year,month
Jane-Smith,2015,Aug
Dave-Smith,2020,Jan
Jane-Jones,2018,Dec
Jane-Stone,2017,Feb
Dave-Stone,2014,Apr
Mark-Aster,,Oct
Jane-Jones,NaN,Jun
```

LISTING 3.12: emp_merge_split.py

```
import pandas as pd

emps = pd.read_csv("employees.csv")
print("emps:")
print(emps)
print()

emps['year']  = emps['year'].astype(str)
emps['month'] = emps['month'].astype(str)

# separate column for first name and for last name:
emps['fname'],emps['lname'] = emps['name'].str.split("-",1).str

# concatenate year and month with a "#" symbol:
emps['hdate1'] = emps['year'].astype(str)+"#"+emps['month'].astype(str)

# concatenate year and month with a "-" symbol:
emps['hdate2'] = emps[['year','month']].agg('-'.join, axis=1)

print(emps)
print()
```

Listing 3.12 initializes the `DataFrame` `df` with the contents of the CSV file `employees.csv`, and then displays the contents of the `DataFrame`. The next pair of code snippets invoke the `astype()` method to convert the contents of the `year` and `month` columns to strings.

The next code snippet in Listing 3.12 uses the `split()` method to split the name column into the columns `fname` and `lname` that contain the first name and last name, respectively, of each employee's name:

```
emps['fname'],emps['lname'] = emps['name'].str.split("-",1).str
```

The next code snippet concatenates the contents of the year and month string with a "#" character to create a new column called `hdate1`, as shown here:

```
emps['hdate1'] = emps['year'].astype(str)+"#"+emps['month'].astype(str)
```

The final code snippet concatenates the contents of the year and month string with a "-" to create a new column called `hdate2`, as shown here:

```
emps['hdate2'] = emps[['year','month']].agg('-'.join, axis=1)
```

Now launch the code in Listing 3.12 and you will see the following output:

```
emps:
        name      year month
0  Jane-Smith  2015.0   Aug
1  Dave-Smith  2020.0   Jan
2  Jane-Jones  2018.0   Dec
3  Jane-Stone  2017.0   Feb
4  Dave-Stone  2014.0   Apr
5  Mark-Aster     NaN   Oct
6  Jane-Jones     NaN   Jun

        name      year month fname  lname      hdate1      hdate2
0  Jane-Smith  2015.0   Aug  Jane  Smith  2015.0#Aug  2015.0-Aug
1  Dave-Smith  2020.0   Jan  Dave  Smith  2020.0#Jan  2020.0-Jan
2  Jane-Jones  2018.0   Dec  Jane  Jones  2018.0#Dec  2018.0-Dec
3  Jane-Stone  2017.0   Feb  Jane  Stone  2017.0#Feb  2017.0-Feb
4  Dave-Stone  2014.0   Apr  Dave  Stone  2014.0#Apr  2014.0-Apr
5  Mark-Aster     nan   Oct  Mark  Aster    nan#Oct    nan-Oct
6  Jane-Jones     nan   Jun  Jane  Jones    nan#Jun    nan-Jun
```

One other detail regarding the following code snippet:

```
#emps['fname'],emps['lname'] = emps['name'].str.split("-",1).str
```

The following deprecation message is displayed:

```
#FutureWarning: Columnar iteration over characters
#will be deprecated in future releases.
```

COMBINING PANDAS DATAFRAMES

Pandas supports the "concat" method in DataFrames in order to concatenate DataFrames. Listing 3.13 displays the contents of `concat_frames.py` that illustrates how to combine two Pandas DataFrames.

LISTING 3.13: concat_frames.py

```
import pandas as pd

can_weather = pd.DataFrame({
    "city": ["Vancouver","Toronto","Montreal"],
```

```
        "temperature": [72,65,50],
        "humidity": [40, 20, 25]
})

us_weather = pd.DataFrame({
    "city": ["SF","Chicago","LA"],
    "temperature": [60,40,85],
    "humidity": [30, 15, 55]
})

df = pd.concat([can_weather, us_weather])
print(df)
```

The first line in Listing 3.13 is an `import` statement, followed by the definition of the `Pandas DataFrames` `can_weather` and `us_weather` that contain weather-related information for cities in Canada and the United States, respectively. The `Pandas DataFrame` df is the concatenation of `can_weather` and `us_weather`. The output from Listing 3.13 is here:

```
0   Vancouver        40          72
1     Toronto        20          65
2    Montreal        25          50
0          SF        30          60
1     Chicago        15          40
2          LA        55          85
```

DATA MANIPULATION WITH PANDAS DATAFRAMES

As a simple example, suppose that we have a two-person company that keeps track of income and expenses on a quarterly basis, and we want to calculate the profit/loss for each quarter, and also the overall profit/loss.

Listing 3.14 displays the contents of `pandas_quarterly_df1.py` that illustrates how to define a `Pandas DataFrame` consisting of income-related values.

LISTING 3.14: pandas_quarterly_df1.py

```
import pandas as pd

summary = {
    'Quarter': ['Q1', 'Q2', 'Q3', 'Q4'],
    'Cost':    [23500, 34000, 57000, 32000],
    'Revenue': [40000, 40000, 40000, 40000]
}

df = pd.DataFrame(summary)

print("Entire Dataset:\n",df)
print("Quarter:\n",df.Quarter)
print("Cost:\n",df.Cost)
print("Revenue:\n",df.Revenue)
```

Listing 3.14 defines the variable `summary` that contains hard-coded quarterly information about cost and revenue for our two-person company. In general, these hard-coded values would be replaced by data from another source (such as a CSV file), so think of this code sample as a simple way to illustrate some of the functionality that is available in `Pandas DataFrame`s.

The variable `df` is a `Pandas DataFrame` based on the data in the `summary` variable. The three `print()` statements display the quarters, the cost per quarter, and the revenue per quarter. The output from Listing 3.14 is here:

```
Entire Dataset:
      Cost Quarter   Revenue
0   23500      Q1     40000
1   34000      Q2     60000
2   57000      Q3     50000
3   32000      Q4     30000
Quarter:
0    Q1
1    Q2
2    Q3
3    Q4
Name: Quarter, dtype: object
Cost:
0    23500
1    34000
2    57000
3    32000
Name: Cost, dtype: int64
Revenue:
0    40000
1    60000
2    50000
3    30000
Name: Revenue, dtype: int64
```

DATA MANIPULATION WITH PANDAS DATAFRAMES (2)

In this section, let's suppose that we have a two-person company that keeps track of income and expenses on a quarterly basis, and we want to calculate the profit/loss for each quarter, and also the overall profit/loss.

Listing 3.15 displays the contents of `pandas_quarterly_df1.py` that illustrates how to define a `Pandas DataFrame` consisting of income-related values.

LISTING 3.15: pandas_quarterly_df2.py

```
import pandas as pd

summary = {
    'Quarter': ['Q1', 'Q2', 'Q3', 'Q4'],
    'Cost':    [-23500, -34000, -57000, -32000],
    'Revenue': [40000, 40000, 40000, 40000]
}
```

```
df = pd.DataFrame(summary)
print("First Dataset:\n",df)

df['Total'] = df.sum(axis=1)
print("Second Dataset:\n",df)
```

Listing 3.15 defines the variable `summary` that contains quarterly information about cost and revenue for our two-person company. The variable `df` is a Pandas `DataFrame` based on the data in the `summary` variable. The three `print` statements display the quarters, the cost per quarter, and the revenue per quarter. The output from Listing 3.15 is here:

```
First Dataset:
      Cost Quarter   Revenue
0 -23500       Q1     40000
1 -34000       Q2     60000
2 -57000       Q3     50000
3 -32000       Q4     30000
Second Dataset:
      Cost Quarter   Revenue   Total
0 -23500       Q1     40000   16500
1 -34000       Q2     60000   26000
2 -57000       Q3     50000   -7000
3 -32000       Q4     30000   -2000
```

DATA MANIPULATION WITH PANDAS DATAFRAMES (3)

Let's start with the same assumption as the previous section: we have a two-person company that keeps track of income and expenses on a quarterly basis, and we want to calculate the profit/loss for each quarter, and also the overall profit/loss. In addition, we want to compute column totals and row totals.

Listing 3.16 displays the contents of `pandas_quarterly_df1.py` that illustrates how to define a Pandas `DataFrame` consisting of income-related values.

LISTING 3.16: pandas_quarterly_df3.py

```
import pandas as pd

summary = {
    'Quarter': ['Q1', 'Q2', 'Q3', 'Q4'],
    'Cost':    [_23500, _34000, _57000, _32000],
    'Revenue': [40000, 40000, 40000, 40000]
}

df = pd.DataFrame(summary)
print("First Dataset:\n",df)

df['Total'] = df.sum(axis=1)
df.loc['Sum'] = df.sum()
print("Second Dataset:\n",df)
```

```
# or df.loc['avg'] / 3
#df.loc['avg'] = df[:3].mean()
#print("Third Dataset:\n",df)
```

Listing 3.16 defines the variable `summary` that contains quarterly information about cost and revenue for our two-person company. The variable `df` is a `Pandas DataFrame` based on the data in the `summary` variable. The three `print` statements display the quarters, the cost per quarter, and the revenue per quarter. The output from Listing 3.16 is here:

```
First Dataset:
      Cost Quarter  Revenue
0 -23500      Q1     40000
1 -34000      Q2     60000
2 -57000      Q3     50000
3 -32000      Q4     30000
Second Dataset:
         Cost   Quarter  Revenue  Total
0      -23500       Q1     40000  16500
1      -34000       Q2     60000  26000
2      -57000       Q3     50000  -7000
3      -32000       Q4     30000  -2000
Sum  -146500  Q1Q2Q3Q4   180000  33500
```

PANDAS DATAFRAMES AND CSV FILES

The code samples in several earlier sections contain hard-coded data inside the `Python` scripts. However, it's also very common to read data from a CSV file. You can use the `Python` `csv.reader()` function, the `NumPy loadtxt()` function, or the `Pandas` function `read_csv()` function (shown in this section) to read the contents of CSV files.

Listing 3.17 displays the contents of the CSV file `weather_data.csv` and Listing 3.18 displays the contents of `weather_data.py` that illustrates how to read the CSV `weather_data.csv`.

LISTING 3.17: weather_data.csv

```
day,temperature,windspeed,event
7/1/2018,42,16,Rain
7/2/2018,45,3,Sunny
7/3/2018,78,12,Snow
7/4/2018,74,9,Snow
7/5/2018,42,24,Rain
7/6/2018,51,32,Sunny
```

LISTING 3.18: weather_data.py

```
import pandas as pd

df = pd.read_csv("weather_data.csv")

print(df)
print(df.shape)   # rows, columns
```

```
print(df.head()) # df.head(3)
print(df.tail())
print(df[1:3])
print(df.columns)
print(type(df['day']))
print(df[['day','temperature']])
print(df['temperature'].max())
```

Listing 3.18 invokes the Pandas read_csv() function to read the contents of the CSV file weather_data.csv, followed by a set of Python print() statements that display various portions of the CSV file. The output from Listing 3.18 is here:

```
        day  temperature  windspeed      event
0  7/1/2018           42         16    Rain
1  7/2/2018           45          3    Sunny
2  7/3/2018           78         12    Snow
3  7/4/2018           74          9   Snow
4  7/5/2018           42         24    Rain
5  7/6/2018           51         32      Sunny
(6, 4)
        day  temperature  windspeed      event
0  7/1/2018           42         16    Rain
1  7/2/2018           45          3    Sunny
2  7/3/2018           78         12    Snow
3  7/4/2018           74          9   Snow
4  7/5/2018           42         24    Rain
        day  temperature  windspeed      event
1  7/2/2018           45          3    Sunny
2  7/3/2018           78         12    Snow
3  7/4/2018           74          9   Snow
4  7/5/2018           42         24    Rain
5  7/6/2018           51         32      Sunny
        day  temperature  windspeed      event
1  7/2/2018           45          3    Sunny
2  7/3/2018           78         12    Snow
Index(['day', 'temperature', 'windspeed', 'event'], dtype='object')
<class 'pandas.core.series.Series'>
        day  temperature
0  7/1/2018           42
1  7/2/2018           45
2  7/3/2018           78
3  7/4/2018           74
4  7/5/2018           42
5  7/6/2018           51
78
```

In some situations, you might need to apply Boolean conditional logic to "filter out" some rows of data, based on a conditional condition that's applied to a column value.

Listing 3.19 displays the contents of the CSV file people.csv and Listing 3.20 displays the contents of people_pandas.py that illustrates how to define a Pandas DataFrame that reads the CSV file and manipulates the data.

LISTING 3.19: people.csv

```
fname,lname,age,gender,country
john,smith,30,m,usa
jane,smith,31,f,france
jack,jones,32,m,france
dave,stone,33,m,italy
sara,stein,34,f,germany
eddy,bower,35,m,spain
```

LISTING 3.20: people_pandas.py

```python
import pandas as pd

df = pd.read_csv('people.csv')
df.info()
print('fname:')
print(df['fname'])
print('_____')
print('age over 33:')
print(df['age'] > 33)
print('_____')
print('age over 33:')
myfilter = df['age'] >  33
print(df[myfilter])
```

Listing 3.20 populate the Pandas DataFrame df with the contents of the CSV file people.csv. The next portion of Listing 3.20 displays the structure of df, followed by the first names of all the people. The next portion of Listing 3.20 displays a tabular list of six rows containing either True or False depending on whether a person is over 33 or at most 33, respectively. The final portion of Listing 3.20 displays a tabular list of two rows containing all the details of the people who are over 33. The output from Listing 3.20 is here:

```
myfilter = df['age'] >  33
<class 'pandas.core.frame.DataFrame'>
RangeIndex: 6 entries, 0 to 5
Data columns (total 5 columns):
fname       6 non_null object
lname       6 non_null object
age         6 non_null int64
gender      6 non_null object
country     6 non_null object
dtypes: int64(1), object(4)
memory usage: 320.0+ bytes
fname:
0     john
1     jane
2     jack
3     dave
4     sara
5     eddy
Name: fname, dtype: object
```

```
age over 33:
0      False
1      False
2      False
3      False
4       True
5       True
Name: age, dtype: bool
```
```
age over 33:
  fname  lname  age gender country
4  sara  stein   34      f  france
5  eddy  bower   35      m  france
```

PANDAS DATAFRAMES AND EXCEL SPREADSHEETS

Listing 3.21 displays the contents of `write_people_xlsx.py` that illustrates how to read data from a CSV file and then create an Excel spreadsheet with that data.

LISTING 3.21: write_people_xlsx.py

```
import pandas as pd

df1 = pd.read_csv("people.csv")
df1.to_excel("people.xlsx")

#optionally specify the sheet name:
#df1.to_excel("people.xlsx", sheet_name='Sheet_name_1')
```

Listing 3.21 initializes the Pandas DataFrame `df1` with the contents of the CSV file `people.csv`, and then invokes the `to_excel()` method in order to save the contents of the DataFrame to the Excel spreadsheet `people.xlsx`.

Listing 3.22 displays the contents of `read_people_xlsx.py` that illustrates how to read data from the Excel spreadsheet `people.xlsx` and create a `Pandas DataFrame` with that data.

LISTING 3.22: read_people_xlsx.py

```
import pandas as pd

df = pd.read_excel("people.xlsx")
print("Contents of Excel spreadsheet:")
print(df)
```

Listing 3.22 is straightforward: the `Pandas DataFrame df` is initialized with the contents of the spreadsheet `people.xlsx` (whose contents are the same as `people.csv`) via the `Pandas` function `read_excel()`. The output from Listing 3.22 is here:

```
df1:
   Unnamed: 0 fname  lname  age gender  country
0           0  john  smith   30      m      usa
```

```
1          1   jane   smith   31     f    france
2          2   jack   jones   32     m    france
3          3   dave   stone   33     m     italy
4          4   sara   stein   34     f  germany
5          5   eddy   bower   35     m     spain
```

SELECT, ADD, AND DELETE COLUMNS IN DataFrames

This section contains short code blocks that illustrate how to perform operations on a DataFrame that resemble the operations on a Python dictionary. For example, getting, setting, and deleting columns works with the same syntax as the analogous Python dict operations, as shown here:

```
df = pd.DataFrame.from_dict(dict([('A', [1,2,3]), ('B', [4,5,6])]),
              orient='index', columns=['one', 'two', 'three'])

print(df)
```

The output from the preceding code snippet is here:

```
   one   two   three
A    1     2       3
B    4     5       6
```

Now look at the following operation that appends a new column to the contents of the DataFrame df:

```
df['four'] = df['one'] * df['two']
print(df)
```

The output from the preceding code block is here:

```
   one   two   three   four
A    1     2       3      2
B    4     5       6     20
```

The following operation squares the contents of a column in the DataFrame df:

```
df['three'] = df['two'] * df['two']
print(df)
```

The output from the preceding code block is here:

```
   one   two   three   four
A    1     2       4      2
B    4     5      25     20
```

The following operation inserts a column of random numbers in index position 1 (which is the second column) in the DataFrame df:

```
import numpy as np
rand = np.random.randn(2)
```

```
df.insert(1, 'random', rand)
print(df)
```

The output from the preceding code block is here:

```
   one     random  two  three  four
A    1  -1.703111    2      4     2
B    4   1.139189    5     25    20
```

The following operation appends a new column called flag that contains True or False, based on whether or not the numeric value in the "one" column is greater than 2:

```
import numpy as np
rand = np.random.randn(2)
df.insert(1, 'random', rand)
print(df)
```

The output from the preceding code block is here:

```
   one     random  two  three  four   flag
A    1  -1.703111    2      4     2  False
B    4   1.139189    5     25    20   True
```

Columns can be deleted, as shown in following code snippet that deletes the "two" column:

```
del df['two']
print(df)
```

The output from the preceding code block is here:

```
one     random  three  four   flag
A    1  -0.460401      4     2  False
B    4   1.211468     25    20   True
```

Columns can be deleted via the pop() method, as shown in following code snippet that deletes the "three" column:

```
three = df.pop('three')
print(df)
```

```
   one     random  four   flag
A    1  -0.544829     2  False
B    4   0.581476    20   True
```

When inserting a scalar value, it will naturally be propagated to fill the column:

```
df['foo'] = 'bar'
print(df)
```

The output from the preceding code snippet is here:

```
   one     random  four   flag  foo
A    1  -0.187331     2  False  bar
B    4  -0.169672    20   True  bar
```

HANDLING OUTLIERS IN PANDAS

If you are unfamiliar with outliers and anomalies, please search for an online article that discusses these two concepts because this section uses `Pandas` to find outliers in a dataset. The key idea involves finding the "z score" of the values in the dataset, which involves calculating the mean `sigma` and standard deviation `std`, and then mapping each value `x` in the dataset to the value `(x-sigma)/std`.

Next, you specify a value of `z` (such as 3) and find the rows whose z score is greater than 3. These are the rows that contain values that are considered outliers. *Note that a suitable value for the z score is your decision (not some other external factor).*

Listing 3.23 displays the contents of `outliers_zscores.py` that illustrates how to find rows of a dataset whose `z-score` greater than (or less than) a specified value.

LISTING 3.23: outliers_zscores.py

```
import numpy as np
import pandas as pd
from scipy import stats
from sklearn import datasets

df = datasets.load_iris()
columns = df.feature_names
iris_df = pd.DataFrame(df.data)
iris_df.columns = columns

print("=> iris_df.shape:",iris_df.shape)
print(iris_df.head())
print()

z = np.abs(stats.zscore(iris_df))
print("z scores for iris:")
print("z.shape:",z.shape)

upper = 2.5
lower = 0.01
print("=> upper outliers:")
print(z[np.where(z > upper)])
print()

outliers = iris_df[z < lower]
print("=> lower outliers:")
print(outliers)
print()
```

Listing 3.23 initializes the variable `df` with the contents of the built-in `Iris` dataset. Next, the variable columns is initialized with the column names, and the DataFrame `iris_df` is initialized from the contents of `df.data` that contains the actual data for the `Iris` dataset. In addition, `iris_df.columns` is initialized with the contents of the variable `columns`.

The next portion of Listing 3.23 displays the shape of the DataFrame `iris_df`, followed by the `z-score` of the `iris_df` DataFrame, which is computed by subtracting the mean and then dividing by the standard deviation (performed for each row).

The last two portions of Listing 3.23 display the outliers (if any) whose `z-score` is outside the interval [0.01, 2.5]. Launch the code in Listing 3.23 and you will see the following output:

```
=> iris_df.shape: (150, 4)
   sepal length (cm)  sepal width (cm)  petal length (cm)  petal width (cm)
0              5.1               3.5                1.4               0.2
1              4.9               3.0                1.4               0.2
2              4.7               3.2                1.3               0.2
3              4.6               3.1                1.5               0.2
4              5.0               3.6                1.4               0.2

z scores for iris:
z.shape: (150, 4)

=> upper outliers:
[3.09077525 2.63038172]

=> lower outliers:
    sepal length (cm)  sepal width (cm)  petal length (cm)  petal width (cm)
73              6.1               2.8                4.7               1.2
82              5.8               2.7                3.9               1.2
90              5.5               2.6                4.4               1.2
92              5.8               2.6                4.0               1.2
95              5.7               3.0                4.2               1.2
```

PANDAS DATAFRAMES AND SCATTERPLOTS

Listing 3.24 displays the contents of `pandas_scatter_df.py` that illustrates how to generate a scatterplot from a `Pandas DataFrame`.

LISTING 3.24: *pandas_scatter_df.py*

```python
import numpy as np
import pandas as pd
import matplotlib.pyplot as plt
from pandas import read_csv
from pandas.plotting import scatter_matrix

myarray = np.array([[10,30,20], [50,40,60],[1000,2000,3000]])

rownames = ['apples', 'oranges', 'beer']
colnames = ['January', 'February', 'March']

mydf = pd.DataFrame(myarray, index=rownames, columns=colnames)

print(mydf)
print(mydf.describe())
```

```
scatter_matrix(mydf)
plt.show()
```

Listing 3.24 starts with various `import` statements, followed by the definition of the `NumPy` array `myarray`. Next, the variables `myarray` and `colnames` are initialized with values for the rows and columns, respectively. The next portion of Listing 3.24 initializes the `Pandas DataFrame` `mydf` so that the rows and columns are labeled in the output, as shown here:

```
January   February   March
apples        10         30      20
oranges       50         40      60
beer        1000       2000    3000
            January    February        March
count      3.000000    3.000000     3.000000
mean     353.333333  690.000000  1026.666667
std      560.386771 1134.504297  1709.073823
min       10.000000   30.000000    20.000000
25%       30.000000   35.000000    40.000000
50%       50.000000   40.000000    60.000000
75%      525.000000 1020.000000  1530.000000
max     1000.000000 2000.000000  3000.0000000
```

PANDAS DATAFRAMES AND SIMPLE STATISTICS

Listing 3.25 displays the contents of `housing_stats.py` that illustrates how to gather basic statistics from data in a `Pandas DataFrame`.

LISTING 3.25: housing_stats.py

```
import pandas as pd

df = pd.read_csv("housing.csv")

minimum_bdrms = df["bedrooms"].min()
median_bdrms  = df["bedrooms"].median()
maximum_bdrms = df["bedrooms"].max()

print("minimum # of bedrooms:",minimum_bdrms)
print("median  # of bedrooms:",median_bdrms)
print("maximum # of bedrooms:",maximum_bdrms)
print("")

print("median values:",df.median().values)
print("")

prices = df["price"]
print("first 5 prices:")
print(prices.head())
print("")

median_price = df["price"].median()
print("median price:",median_price)
print("")
```

```
corr_matrix = df.corr()
print("correlation matrix:")
print(corr_matrix["price"].sort_values(ascending=False))
```

Listing 3.25 initializes the Pandas DataFrame df with the contents of the CSV file hous-ing.csv. The next three variables are initialized with the minimum, median, and maximum number of bedrooms, respectively, and then these values are displayed.

The next portion of Listing 3.25 initializes the variable prices with the contents of the prices column of the Pandas DataFrame df. Next, the first five rows are printed via the prices.head() statement, followed by the median value of the prices.

The final portion of Listing 3.25 initializes the variable corr_matrix with the contents of the correlation matrix for the Pandas DataFrame df, and then displays its contents. The output from Listing 3.25 is here:

```
Apples
10
```

FINDING DUPLICATE ROWS IN PANDAS

Listing 3.26 displays the contents of duplicates.csv and Listing 3.27 displays the contents of duplicates.py that illustrates how to find duplicate rows in a Pandas DataFrame.

LISTING 3.26: duplicates.csv

```
fname,lname,level,dept,state
Jane,Smith,Senior,Sales,California
Dave,Smith,Senior,Devel,California
Jane,Jones,Year1,Mrktg,Illinois
Jane,Jones,Year1,Mrktg,Illinois
Jane,Stone,Senior,Mrktg,Arizona
Dave,Stone,Year2,Devel,Arizona
Mark,Aster,Year3,BizDev,Florida
Jane,Jones,Year1,Mrktg,Illinois
```

LISTING 3.27: duplicates.py

```
import pandas as pd

df = pd.read_csv("duplicates.csv")
print("Contents of data frame:")
print(df)
print()

print("Duplicate rows:")
#df2 = df.duplicated(subset=None)
df2 = df.duplicated(subset=None, keep='first')
print(df2)
print()
```

```
print("Duplicate first names:")
df3 = df[df.duplicated(['fname'])]
print(df3)
print()

print("Duplicate first name and level:")
df3 = df[df.duplicated(['fname','level'])]
print(df3)
print()
```

Listing 3.27 initializes the DataFrame df with the contents of the CSV file duplicates. csv, and then displays the contents of the DataFrame. The next portion of Listing 3.27 displays the duplicate rows by invoking the duplicated() method, whereas the next portion of Listing 3.27 displays only the first name fname of the duplicate rows. The final portion of Listing 3.27 displays the first name fname as well as the level of the duplicate rows. Launch the code in Listing 3.27 and you will see the following output:

```
Contents of data frame:
   fname  lname   level    dept       state
0   Jane  Smith  Senior   Sales  California
1   Dave  Smith  Senior   Devel  California
2   Jane  Jones   Year1   Mrktg    Illinois
3   Jane  Jones   Year1   Mrktg    Illinois
4   Jane  Stone  Senior   Mrktg     Arizona
5   Dave  Stone   Year2   Devel     Arizona
6   Mark  Aster   Year3  BizDev     Florida
7   Jane  Jones   Year1   Mrktg    Illinois

Duplicate rows:
0    False
1    False
2    False
3     True
4    False
5    False
6    False
7     True
dtype: bool

Duplicate first names:
   fname  lname   level   dept     state
2   Jane  Jones   Year1  Mrktg  Illinois
3   Jane  Jones   Year1  Mrktg  Illinois
4   Jane  Stone  Senior  Mrktg   Arizona
5   Dave  Stone   Year2  Devel   Arizona
7   Jane  Jones   Year1  Mrktg  Illinois

Duplicate first name and level:
   fname  lname   level   dept     state
3   Jane  Jones   Year1  Mrktg  Illinois
4   Jane  Stone  Senior  Mrktg   Arizona
7   Jane  Jones   Year1  Mrktg  Illinois
```

Listing 3.28 displays the contents of `drop_duplicates.py` that illustrates how to drop duplicate rows in a `Pandas DataFrame`.

LISTING 3.28: drop_duplicates.py

```
import pandas as pd

df = pd.read_csv("duplicates.csv")
print("Contents of data frame:")
print(df)
print()

fname_filtered = df.drop_duplicates(['fname'])
print("Drop duplicate first names:")
print(fname_filtered)
print()

fname_lname_filtered = df.drop_duplicates(['fname','lname'])
print("Drop duplicate first and last names:")
print(fname_lname_filtered)
print()
```

Listing 3.28 initializes the `DataFrame df` with the contents of the `CSV` file `duplicates.csv`, and then displays the contents of the DataFrame. The next portion of Listing 3.28 deletes the rows that have duplicate `fname` values, followed by a code block that drops rows with duplicate `fname` and `lname` values. Launch the code in Listing 3.28 and you will see the following output:

```
Contents of data frame:
   fname  lname   level    dept      state
0  Jane   Smith   Senior   Sales   California
1  Dave   Smith   Senior   Devel   California
2  Jane   Jones   Year1    Mrktg     Illinois
3  Jane   Jones   Year1    Mrktg     Illinois
4  Jane   Stone   Senior   Mrktg      Arizona
5  Dave   Stone   Year2    Devel      Arizona
6  Mark   Aster   Year3    BizDev     Florida
7  Jane   Jones   Year1    Mrktg     Illinois


Drop duplicate first names:
   fname  lname   level    dept      state
0  Jane   Smith   Senior   Sales   California
1  Dave   Smith   Senior   Devel   California
6  Mark   Aster   Year3    BizDev     Florida

Drop duplicate first and last names:
   fname  lname   level    dept      state
0  Jane   Smith   Senior   Sales   California
1  Dave   Smith   Senior   Devel   California
```

```
2  Jane  Jones  Year1  Mrktg   Illinois
4  Jane  Stone  Senior Mrktg   Arizona
5  Dave  Stone  Year2  Devel   Arizona
6  Mark  Aster  Year3  BizDev  Florida
```

FINDING MISSING VALUES IN PANDAS

Listing 3.29 displays the contents of `employees2.csv` and Listing 3.30 displays the contents of `missing_values.py` that illustrates how to display rows of a DataFrame that have missing values in a Pandas DataFrame.

LISTING 3.29: employees2.csv

```
name,year,month
Jane-Smith,2015,Aug
Jane-Smith,2015,Aug
Dave-Smith,2020,
Dave-Stone,Apr
Jane-Jones,2018,Dec
Jane-Stone,2017,Feb
Jane-Stone,2017,Feb
Mark-Aster,Oct
Jane-Jones,NaN,Jun
```

LISTING 3.30: missing_values.py

```
import pandas as pd
import matplotlib.pyplot as plt
import numpy as np

df = pd.read_csv("employees2.csv")

print("=> contents of CSV file:")
print(df)
print()

#NA:  Not Available (Pandas)
#NaN: Not a Number (Pandas)
#NB:  NumPy uses np.nan() to check for NaN values

df = pd.read_csv("employees2.csv")

print("=> contents of CSV file:")
print(df)
print()

print("=> any NULL values per column?")
print(df.isnull().any())
print()

print("=> count of NAN/MISSING values in each column:")
print(df.isnull().sum())
print()
```

```
print("=> count of NAN/MISSING values in each column:")
print(pd.isna(df).sum())
print()

print("=> count of NAN/MISSING values in each column (sorted):")
print(df.isnull().sum().sort_values(ascending=False))
print()

nan_null = df.isnull().sum().sum()
miss_values = df.isnull().any().sum()

print("=> count of NaN/MISSING values:",nan_null)
print("=> count of MISSING values:",miss_values)
print("=> count of NaN values:",nan_null-miss_values)
```

Listing 3.30 initializes the DataFrame df with the contents of the CSV file employees2.csv, and then displays the contents of the DataFrame. The next portion of Listing 3.30 displays the number of null values that appear in any row or column. The next portion of Listing 3.30 displays the fields and the names of the fields that have null values.

The next portion of Listing 3.30 displays the number of duplicate rows, followed by the row numbers that are duplicates. Launch the code in Listing 3.30 and you will see the following output:

```
=> contents of CSV file:
          name     year month
0   Jane-Smith   2015.0    Aug
1   Jane-Smith   2015.0    Aug
2   Dave-Smith   2020.0    NaN
3   Dave-Stone      NaN    Apr
4   Jane-Jones   2018.0    Dec
5   Jane-Stone   2017.0    Feb
6   Jane-Stone   2017.0    Feb
7   Mark-Aster      NaN    Oct
8   Jane-Jones      NaN    Jun


=> any NULL values per column?
name      False
year       True
month      True
dtype: bool


=> count of NAN/MISSING values in each column:
name      0
year      3
month     1
dtype: int64


=> count of NAN/MISSING values in each column:
name      0
year      3
month     1
dtype: int64
```

```
=> count of NAN/MISSING values in each column (sorted):
year     3
month    1
name     0
dtype: int64

=> count of NaN/MISSING values: 4
=> count of MISSING values: 2
=> count of NaN values: 2
```

SORTING DATAFRAMES IN PANDAS

Listing 3.31 displays the contents of `sort_df.py` that illustrates how to sort the rows in a Pandas DataFrame.

LISTING 3.31: sort_df.py

```python
import pandas as pd

df = pd.read_csv("duplicates.csv")
print("Contents of data frame:")
print(df)
print()

df.sort_values(by=['fname'], inplace=True)
print("Sorted (ascending) by first name:")
print(df)
print()

df.sort_values(by=['fname'], inplace=True,ascending=False)
print("Sorted (descending) by first name:")
print(df)
print()

df.sort_values(by=['fname','lname'], inplace=True)
print("Sorted (ascending) by first name and last name:")
print(df)
print()
```

Listing 3.31 initializes the DataFrame df with the contents of the CSV file duplicates. csv, and then displays the contents of the DataFrame. The next portion of Listing 3.31 displays the rows in *ascending* order based on the first name, and the next code block displays the rows in *descending* order based on the first name.

The final code block in Listing 3.31 displays the rows in ascending order based on the first name as well as the last name. Launch the code in Listing 3.31 and you will see the following output:

```
Contents of data frame:
   fname   lname   level    dept      state
0   Jane   Smith   Senior   Sales   California
1   Dave   Smith   Senior   Devel   California
```

```
2    Jane   Jones   Year1   Mrktg     Illinois
3    Jane   Jones   Year1   Mrktg     Illinois
4    Jane   Stone   Senior  Mrktg      Arizona
5    Dave   Stone   Year2   Devel      Arizona
6    Mark   Aster   Year3   BizDev     Florida
7    Jane   Jones   Year1   Mrktg     Illinois

Sorted (ascending) by first name:
     fname  lname   level    dept        state
1    Dave   Smith   Senior   Devel   California
5    Dave   Stone   Year2    Devel      Arizona
0    Jane   Smith   Senior   Sales   California
2    Jane   Jones   Year1    Mrktg     Illinois
3    Jane   Jones   Year1    Mrktg     Illinois
4    Jane   Stone   Senior   Mrktg      Arizona
7    Jane   Jones   Year1    Mrktg     Illinois
6    Mark   Aster   Year3    BizDev     Florida

Sorted (descending) by first name:
     fname  lname   level    dept        state
6    Mark   Aster   Year3    BizDev     Florida
0    Jane   Smith   Senior   Sales   California
2    Jane   Jones   Year1    Mrktg     Illinois
3    Jane   Jones   Year1    Mrktg     Illinois
4    Jane   Stone   Senior   Mrktg      Arizona
7    Jane   Jones   Year1    Mrktg     Illinois
1    Dave   Smith   Senior   Devel   California
5    Dave   Stone   Year2    Devel      Arizona

Sorted (ascending) by first name and last name:
     fname  lname   level    dept        state
1    Dave   Smith   Senior   Devel   California
5    Dave   Stone   Year2    Devel      Arizona
2    Jane   Jones   Year1    Mrktg     Illinois
3    Jane   Jones   Year1    Mrktg     Illinois
7    Jane   Jones   Year1    Mrktg     Illinois
0    Jane   Smith   Senior   Sales   California
4    Jane   Stone   Senior   Mrktg      Arizona
6    Mark   Aster   Year3    BizDev     Florida
```

WORKING WITH GROUPBY() IN PANDAS

Listing 3.32 displays the contents of `groupby1.py` that illustrates how to invoke the Pandas `groupby()` method in order to compute subtotals of feature values.

LISTING 3.32: groupby1.py

```
import pandas as pd

# colors and weights of balls:
data = {'color':['red','blue','blue','red','blue'],
        'weight':[40,50,20,30,90]}
df1 = pd.DataFrame(data)
```

```
print("df1:")
print(df1)
print()
print(df1.groupby('color').mean())
print()

red_filter = df1['color']=='red'
print(df1[red_filter])
print()
blue_filter = df1['color']=='blue'
print(df1[blue_filter])
print()

red_avg = df1[red_filter]['weight'].mean()
blue_avg = df1[blue_filter]['weight'].mean()
print("red_avg,blue_avg:")
print(red_avg,blue_avg)
print()

df2 = pd.DataFrame({'color':['blue','red'],'weight':[red_avg,blue_avg]})
print("df2:")
print(df2)
print()
```

Listing 3.32 defines the variable data containing color and weight values, and then initializes the DataFrame df with the contents of the variable data. The next two code blocks define red_filter and blue_filter that match the rows whose colors are red and blue, respectively, and then prints the matching rows.

The next portion of Listing 3.32 defines the two filters red_avg and blue_avg that calculate the average weight of the red value and the blue values, respectively. The last code block in Listing 3.32 defines the DataFrame df2 with a color column and a weight column, where the latter contains the average weight of the red values and the blue values. Launch the code in Listing 3.32 and you will see the following output:

```
initial data frame:
df1:
   color  weight
0    red      40
1   blue      50
2   blue      20
3    red      30
4   blue      90


color  weight
blue   53.333333
red    35.000000

   color  weight
0    red      40
3    red      30
```

```
   color  weight
1  blue       50
2  blue       20
4  blue       90


red_avg,blue_avg:
35.0 53.333333333333336

df2:
   color      weight
0  blue   35.000000
1   red   53.333333
```

AGGREGATE OPERATIONS WITH THE TITANIC.CSV DATASET

Listing 3.33 displays the contents of `aggregate2.py` that illustrates how to perform aggregate operations with columns in the CSV file `titanic.csv`.

LISTING 3.33: aggregate2.py

```python
import pandas as pd

#Loading titanic.csv in Seaborn:
#df = sns.load_dataset('titanic')
df = pd.read_csv("titanic.csv")

# convert floating point values to integers:
df['survived'] = df['survived'].astype(int)

# specify column and aggregate functions:
aggregates1 = {'embark_town': ['count', 'nunique', 'size']}

# group by 'deck' value and apply aggregate functions:
result = df.groupby(['deck']).agg(aggregates1)
print("=> Grouped by deck:")
print(result)
print()

# some details regarding count() and nunique():
# count() excludes NaN values whereas size() includes them
# nunique() excludes NaN values in the unique counts

# group by 'age' value and apply aggregate functions:
result2 = df.groupby(['age']).agg(aggregates1)
print("=> Grouped by age (before):")
print(result2)
print()

# some "age" values are missing (so drop them):
df = df.dropna()
```

```
# convert floating point values to integers:
df['age'] = df['age'].astype(int)

# group by 'age' value and apply aggregate functions:
result3 = df.groupby(['age']).agg(aggregates1)
print("=> Grouped by age (after):")
print(result3)
print()
```

Listing 3.33 initializes the DataFrame df with the contents of the CSV file titanic.csv. The next code snippet converts floating point values to integer, followed by defining the variable aggregates1 that specifies the functions count(), nunique(), and size() that will be invoked on the embark_town field.

The next code snippet initializes the variable result after invoking the groupby() method on the deck field, followed by invoking the agg() method.

The next code block performs the same computation to initialize the variable result2, except that the groupby() function is invoked on the age field instead of the embark_town field. Notice the comment section regarding the count() and nunique() functions: let's drop the rows with missing values via df.dropna() and investigate how that affects the calculations.

After dropping the rows with missing values, the final code block initializes the variable result3 in exactly the same way that result2 was initialized. Launch the code in Listing 3.33 and the output is shown here:

```
=> Grouped by deck:
        embark_town
              count nunique size
deck
A                15       2   15
B                45       2   47
C                59       3   59
D                33       2   33
E                32       3   32
F                13       3   13
G                 4       1    4

=> Grouped by age (before):
          age
        count nunique size
age
0.42        1       1    1
0.67        1       1    1
0.75        2       1    2
0.83        2       1    2
0.92        1       1    1
 ...      ...     ...  ...
70.00       2       1    2
70.50       1       1    1
71.00       2       1    2
74.00       1       1    1
80.00       1       1    1

[88 rows x 3 columns]
```

```
=> Grouped by age (after):
      age
    count nunique size
age
0        1        1       1
1        1        1       1
2        3        1       3
3        1        1       1
4        3        1       3
6        1        1       1
11       1        1       1
14       1        1       1
15       1        1       1
// details omitted for brevity
60       2        1       2
61       2        1       2
62       1        1       1
63       1        1       1
64       1        1       1
65       2        1       2
70       1        1       1
71       1        1       1
80       1        1       1
```

WORKING WITH apply() AND applymap() IN PANDAS

Earlier in this chapter you saw an example of the Pandas apply() method for modifying the categorical values of a feature in the CSV file shirts.csv. This section contains more examples of the apply() method, along with examples of the mapappy() method.

Listing 3.34 displays the contents of apply1.py that illustrates how to invoke the Pandas apply() method in order to compute the sum of a set of values.

LISTING 3.34: apply1.py

```python
import pandas as pd

df = pd.DataFrame({'X1': [1,2,3], 'X2': [10,20,30]})

def cube(x):
  return x * x * x

df1 = df.apply(cube)
# same result:
# df1 = df.apply(lambda x: x * x * x)

print("initial data frame:")
print(df)
print("cubed values:")
print(df1)
```

Listing 3.34 initializes the DataFrame df with columns X1 and X2, where the values for X2 are 10 times the corresponding values in X1. Next, the Python function cube() returns the cube of its argument. Listing 3.34 then defines the variable df1 by invoking the apply() function, which specifies the user-defined Python function cube(), and then prints the values of df as well as df1. Launch the code in Listing 3.34 and you will see the following output:

```
initial data frame:
    X1   X2
0    1   10
1    2   20
2    3   30
cubed values:
    X1      X2
0    1    1000
1    8    8000
2   27   27000
```

Listing 3.35 displays the contents of apply2.py that illustrates how to invoke the Pandas apply() method in order to compute the sum of a set of values.

LISTING 3.35: apply2.py

```python
import pandas as pd
import numpy as np

df = pd.DataFrame({'X1': [10,20,30], 'X2': [50,60,70]})

df1 = df.apply(np.sum, axis=0)
df2 = df.apply(np.sum, axis=1)

print("initial data frame:")
print(df)
print("add values (axis=0):")
print(df1)
print("add values (axis=1):")
print(df2)
```

Listing 3.35 is a variation of Listing 3.34: the variables df1 and df2 contain the column-wise sum and the row-wise sum, respectively, of the DataFrame df. Launch the code in Listing 3.35 and you will see the following output:

```
    X1   X2
0   10   50
1   20   60
2   30   70
add values (axis=0):
X1       60
X2      180
dtype: int64
add values (axis=1):
0        60
1        80
2       100
dtype: int64
```

Listing 3.36 displays the contents of `mapapply1.py` that illustrates how to invoke the `Pandas` `mapapply()` method in order to compute the sum of a set of values.

LISTING 3.36: mapapply1.py

```
import pandas as pd
import math

df = pd.DataFrame({'X1': [1,2,3], 'X2': [10,20,30]})
df1 = df.applymap(math.sqrt)

print("initial data frame:")
print(df)
print("square root values:")
print(df1)
```

Listing 3.36 is yet another variant of Listing 3.34: in this case, the variable `df1` is defined by invoking the `applymap()` function on the variable `df`, which in turn references (but does not execute) the `math.sqrt()` function. Next, a `print()` statement displays the contents of `df`, followed by a `print()` statement that displays the contents of `df1`: it is at this point that the built-in `math.sqrt()` function is invoked in order to calculate the square root of the values in `df`. Launch the code in Listing 3.36 and you will see the following output:

```
initial data frame:
   X1  X2
0   1  10
1   2  20
2   3  30

square root values:
         X1         X2
0  1.000000  3.162278
1  1.414214  4.472136
2  1.732051  5.477226
```

Listing 3.37 displays the contents of `mapapply2.py` that illustrates how to invoke the `Pandas` `mapapply()` method in order to convert strings to lowercase and uppercase.

LISTING 3.37: mapapply2.py

```
import pandas as pd

df = pd.DataFrame({'fname': ['Jane'], 'lname': ['Smith']},
                  {'fname': ['Dave'], 'lname': ['Jones']})

df1 = df.applymap(str.lower)
df2 = df.applymap(str.upper)

print("initial data frame:")
print(df)
```

```
print()
print("lowercase:")
print(df1)
print()
print("uppercase:")
print(df2)
print()
```

Listing 3.37 initializes the variable `df` with two first and last name pairs, and then defines the variables `df1` and `df2` by invoking the `applymap()` method to the variable `df`. The variable `df1` converts its input values to lowercase, whereas the variable `df2` converts its input values to uppercase. Launch the code in Listing 3.37 and you will see the following output:

```
initial data frame:
        fname   lname
fname   Jane    Smith
lname   Jane    Smith

lowercase:
        fname   lname
fname   jane    smith
lname   jane    smith

uppercase:
        fname   lname
fname   JANE    SMITH
lname   JANE    SMITH
```

USEFUL ONE-LINE COMMANDS IN PANDAS

This section contains an eclectic mix of one-line commands in Pandas (some of which you have already seen in this chapter) that are useful to know:

Save a DataFrame to a CSV file (comma separated and without indices):

```
df.to_csv("data.csv", sep=",", index=False)
```

List the column names of a DataFrame:

```
df.columns
```

Drop missing data from a DataFrame:

```
df.dropna(axis=0, how='any')
```

Replace missing data in a DataFrame:

```
df.replace(to_replace=None, value=None)
```

Check for NANs in a DataFrame:

```
pd.isnull(object)
```

Drop a feature in a DataFrame:

```
df.drop('feature_variable_name', axis=1)
```

Convert object type to float in a DataFrame:

```
pd.to_numeric(df["feature_name"], errors='coerce')
```

Convert data in a DataFrame to NumPy array:

```
df.as_matrix()
```

Display the first n rows of a DataFrame:

```
df.head(n)
```

Get data by feature name in a DataFrame:

```
df.loc[feature_name]
```

Apply a function to a DataFrame, such as multiplying all values in the "height" column of the DataFrame by 3:

```
df["height"].apply(lambda height: 3 * height)
```

OR:

```
def multiply(x):
    return x * 3
df["height"].apply(multiply)
```

Rename the fourth column of the DataFrame as "height":

```
df.rename(columns = {df.columns[3]:'height'}, inplace=True)
```

Get the unique entries of the column "first" in a DataFrame:

```
df["first"].unique()
```

Create a DataFrame with columns first and last from an existing DataFrame:

```
new_df = df[["first", "last"]]
```

Sort the data in a DataFrame:

```
df.sort_values(ascending = False)
```

Filter the data column named "size" to display only values equal to 7:

```
df[df["size"] == 7]
```

Select the first row of the "height" column in a DataFrame:

```
df.loc([0], ['height'])
```

WHAT IS TEXTHERO?

`Texthero` is a `Python`-based open source toolkit that functions as a layer of abstraction over `Pandas`, and its home page is here:

https://github.com/jbesomi/texthero

`Texthero` leverages very useful `Python` libraries for `NLP`, such as `Gensim`, `NLTK`, `SpaCy`, and `Sklearn`. Moreover, `Texthero` supports the following functionality:

- NER and topic modeling (for NLP) I
- TF-IDF, term frequency, and word-embeddings (for NLP)
- DBSCAN, Hierarchical, k-Means, and Meanshift algorithms
- various types of text visualization

Open a command shell and install texthero with the following command:

```
pip3 install texthero
```

`Texthero` supports various other algorithms, including dimensionality reduction algorithms for machine learning. Navigate to the following link for documentation and other information about `Texthero`:

https://texthero.org/docs/getting-started

DATA VISUALIZATION IN PANDAS

Although `Matplotlib` and `Seaborn` are often the "go to" Python libraries for data visualization, you can also use `Pandas` for such tasks.

Listing 3.38 displays the contents `pandas_viz1.py` that illustrates how to render various types of charts and graphs using `Pandas` and `Matplotlib`.

LISTING 3.38: pandas_viz1.py

```
import pandas as pd
import numpy as np
import matplotlib.pyplot as plt

df = pd.DataFrame(np.random.rand(16,3), columns=['X1','X2','X3'])
print("First 5 rows:")
print(df.head())
print()

print("Diff of first 5 rows:")
print(df.diff().head())
print()

# bar chart:
#ax = df.plot.bar()
```

```
# horizontal stacked bar chart:
#ax = df.plot.barh(stacked=True)

# vertical stacked bar chart:
ax = df.plot.bar(stacked=True)

# stacked area graph:
#ax = df.plot.area()

# non-stacked area graph:
#ax = df.plot.area(stacked=False)

#plt.show(ax)
```

Listing 3.38 initializes the `DataFrame` `df` with a 16x3 matrix of random numbers, followed by the contents of `df`. The bulk of Listing 3.38 contains code snippets for generating a bar chart, a horizontal stacked bar chart, a vertical stacked bar chart, a stacked area graph, and a nonstacked area graph. You can uncomment the individual code snippet that displays the graph of your choice with the contents of `df`. Launch the code in Listing 3.38 and you will see the following output:

```
First 5 rows:
          X1         X2         X3
0   0.051089   0.357183   0.344414
1   0.800890   0.468372   0.800668
2   0.492981   0.505133   0.228399
3   0.461996   0.977895   0.471315
4   0.033209   0.411852   0.347165

Diff of first 5 rows:
          X1         X2         X3
0        NaN        NaN        NaN
1   0.749801   0.111189   0.456255
2  -0.307909   0.036760  -0.572269
3  -0.030984   0.472762   0.242916
4  -0.428787  -0.566043  -0.124150
```

SUMMARY

This chapter introduced you to `Pandas` for creating labeled `DataFrames` and displaying metadata of `Pandas` `DataFrames`. Then you learned how to create `Pandas` `DataFrames` from various sources of data, such as random numbers and hard-coded data values.

You also learned how to read Excel spreadsheets and perform numeric calculations on that data, such as the minimum, mean, and maximum values in numeric columns. Then you saw how to create `Pandas` `DataFrames` from data stored in `CSV` files. In addition, you learned how to generate a scatterplot from data in a `Pandas` `DataFrame`.

Then you got a brief introduction to `JSON`, along with an example of converting a `Python` dictionary to `JSON`-based data (and vice versa). Finally, you learned about `Texthero`, which is an open source `Python`-based toolkit that is a layer of abstraction over `Pandas`.

## CHAPTER 4

PANDAS AND SQL

This chapter shows you how to use Pandas in order to create a variety of charts and graphs, as well as examples of Python3 and Pandas code with databases. You will see a simple example of using MongoDB, which is a popular NoSQL database. In addition, you will see some of the features of SQLite and SQLAlchemy, and how to access both of them through Python code, followed by Python code that accesses MySQL.

The first section contains code samples of data visualization in Pandas, such as bar charts, area charts, and line graphs. The second section shows you how to use Fugue in conjunction with Pandas in order to access data from a database. The third section returns to MySQL, where you will see how to read MySQL data into a Pandas DataFrame and then save the dataframe as an Excel spreadsheet.

The fourth section provides a short description of SQLite, which is a database that is available on mobile devices, such as Android and iOS. As you can probably surmise from its name, SQLite supports a subset of SQL. You can invoke SQL commands in SQLite in various ways (such as SQLiteStudio) that are discussed in this section.

The final section provides an overview of SQLite, which is a command line tool for managing databases that is available on mobile devices. The section also introduces related tools, such as SQLiteStudio (an IDE for sqlite), DB Browser, and SQLiteDict.

PANDAS AND DATA VISUALIZATION

The following subsections contain Python-based code samples that use Pandas in order to render the following types of charts and graphs:

- bar chart
- horizontal stacked bar chart
- vertical stacked bar chart

- nonstacked area chart
- stacked area chart

Pandas and Bar Charts

Listing 4.1 displays the contents of `pandas_barchart.py` that shows you how to render a bar chart in `Pandas`.

LISTING 4.1: pandas_barchart.py

```
import pandas as pd
import numpy as np
import matplotlib.pyplot as plt

df = pd.DataFrame(np.random.rand(16,3), columns=['X1','X2','X3'])
print("First 5 rows:")
print(df.head())
print()

print("Diff of first 5 rows:")
print(df.diff().head())
print()

# bar chart:
ax = df.plot.bar()
plt.show()
```

Listing 4.1 starts with `import` statements and then initializes the `Pandas DataFrame df1` with a set of data values. Launch the code in Listing 4.1 and you will see the following output:

```
First 5 rows:
          X1        X2        X3
0   0.752462  0.742749  0.950918
1   0.957054  0.836334  0.547507
2   0.022269  0.994618  0.861796
3   0.038466  0.911388  0.545711
4   0.483224  0.468873  0.412120

Diff of first 5 rows:
          X1        X2        X3
0        NaN       NaN       NaN
1   0.204591  0.093585 -0.403411
2  -0.934785  0.158284  0.314289
3   0.016197 -0.083230 -0.316085
4   0.444758 -0.442515 -0.133591
```

Figure 4.1 displays the bar chart that is generated by the code in Listing 4.1.

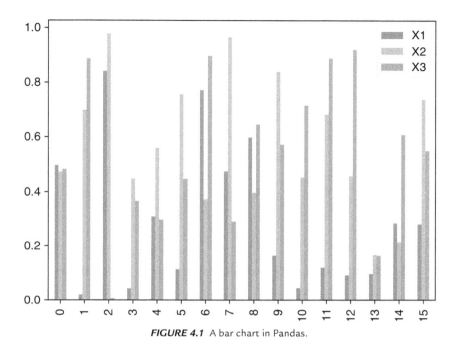

FIGURE 4.1 A bar chart in Pandas.

Pandas and Horizontally Stacked Bar Charts

Listing 4.2 displays the contents of `pandas_hstacked_bar1.py` that shows you how to render a horizontally stacked bar chart in `Pandas`.

LISTING 4.2: pandas_hstacked_bar1.py

```
import pandas as pd
import numpy as np
import matplotlib.pyplot as plt

df = pd.DataFrame(np.random.rand(16,3), columns=['X1','X2','X3'])
print("First 5 rows:")
print(df.head())
print()

print("Diff of first 5 rows:")
print(df.diff().head())
print()

# horizontal stacked bar chart:
ax = df.plot.barh(stacked=True)
plt.show()
```

Listing 4.2 starts with `import` statements and then initializes the `Pandas DataFrame df1` with a set of data values. Launch the code in Listing 4.2 and you will see the following output:

```
First 5 rows:
        X1          X2          X3
0   0.272391    0.737949    0.617566
1   0.532135    0.234155    0.720543
2   0.500043    0.740288    0.930658
3   0.565021    0.846596    0.379988
4   0.340198    0.063606    0.841024

Diff of first 5 rows:
         X1          X2          X3
0       NaN         NaN         NaN
1   0.259743   -0.503794    0.102977
2  -0.032091    0.506133    0.210115
3   0.064977    0.106308   -0.550671
4  -0.224823   -0.782989    0.461036
```

Figure 4.2 displays the horizontally stacked bar chart that is generated by the code in Listing 4.2.

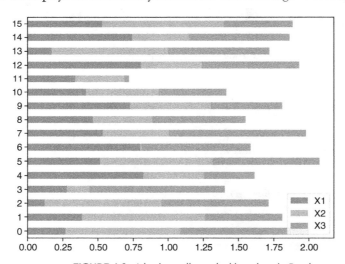

FIGURE 4.2. A horizontally stacked bar chart in Pandas.

Pandas and Vertically Stacked Bar Charts

Listing 4.3 displays the contents of `pandas_vstacked_bar1.py` that shows you how to render a vertically stacked bar chart in `Pandas`.

LISTING 4.3: *pandas_vstacked_bar1.py*

```
import pandas as pd
import numpy as np
import matplotlib.pyplot as plt

df = pd.DataFrame(np.random.rand(16,3), columns=['X1','X2','X3'])
print("First 5 rows:")
```

```
print(df.head())
print()

print("Diff of first 5 rows:")
print(df.diff().head())
print()

# vertical stacked bar chart:
ax = df.plot.bar(stacked=True)
plt.show()
```

Listing 4.3 starts with `import` statements and then initializes the `Pandas DataFrame df1` with a set of data values. Launch the code in Listing 4.3 and you will see the following output:

```
First 5 rows:
          X1         X2         X3
0   0.529936   0.100616   0.683788
1   0.924753   0.320835   0.823198
2   0.925181   0.043236   0.349372
3   0.496390   0.739566   0.759168
4   0.168874   0.241563   0.320381

Diff of first 5 rows:
          X1         X2         X3
0        NaN        NaN        NaN
1   0.394817   0.220219   0.139410
2   0.000428  -0.277599  -0.473826
3  -0.428791   0.696330   0.409796
4  -0.327516  -0.498003  -0.438787
```

Figure 4.3 displays the vertically stacked bar chart that is generated by the code in Listing 4.3.

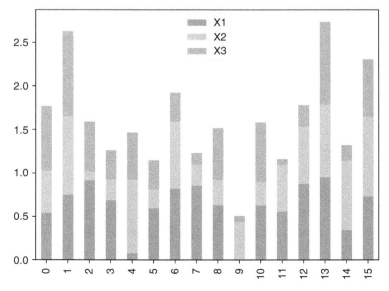

FIGURE 4.3. A vertically stacked bar chart in Pandas.

Pandas and Nonstacked Area Charts

Listing 4.4 displays the contents of pandas_area_nonstacked.py that shows you how to render a nonstacked area chart in Pandas.

LISTING 4.4: pandas_area_nonstacked.py

```
import pandas as pd
import numpy as np
import matplotlib.pyplot as plt

df = pd.DataFrame(np.random.rand(16,3), columns=['X1','X2','X3'])
print("First 5 rows:")
print(df.head())
print()

print("Diff of first 5 rows:")
print(df.diff().head())
print()

# non-stacked area graph:
ax = df.plot.area(stacked=False)
plt.show()
```

Listing 4.4 starts with import statements and then initializes the Pandas DataFrame df1 with a set of data values. Launch the code in Listing 4.4 and you will see the following output:

```
First 5 rows:
        X1        X2        X3
0   0.347024  0.887191  0.431096
1   0.201923  0.097674  0.521704
2   0.763501  0.516445  0.266348
3   0.055767  0.870355  0.679274
4   0.180045  0.621363  0.152446

Diff of first 5 rows:
        X1        X2        X3
0      NaN       NaN       NaN
1 -0.145101 -0.789517  0.090608
2  0.561577  0.418771 -0.255356
3 -0.707734  0.353910  0.412926
4  0.124278 -0.248992 -0.526828
```

Figure 4.4 displays the nonstacked area chart that is generated by the code in Listing 4.4.

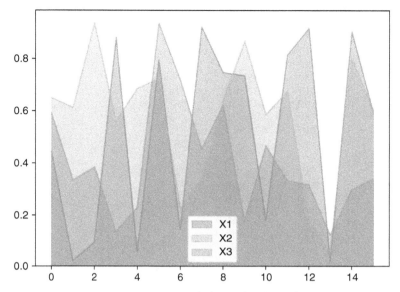

FIGURE 4.4 A Nonstacked area chart in Pandas.

Pandas and Stacked Area Charts

Listing 4.5 displays the contents of `pandas_area_stacked.py` that shows you how to render a stack area chart in `Pandas`.

LISTING 4.5: pandas_area_stacked.py

```
import pandas as pd
import numpy as np
import matplotlib.pyplot as plt

df = pd.DataFrame(np.random.rand(16,3), columns=['X1','X2','X3'])
print("First 5 rows:")
print(df.head())
print()

print("Diff of first 5 rows:")
print(df.diff().head())
print()

# stacked area graph:
ax = df.plot.area()
plt.show()
```

Listing 4.5 starts with `import` statements and then initializes the `Pandas DataFrame df1` with a set of data values. Launch the code in Listing 4.5 and you will see the following output:

```
First 5 rows:
         X1        X2        X3
0  0.801187  0.635952  0.585165
1  0.776911  0.393118  0.887285
2  0.248293  0.785893  0.409110
3  0.557084  0.402462  0.180559
4  0.201810  0.456198  0.576540

Diff of first 5 rows:
         X1        X2        X3
0       NaN       NaN       NaN
1 -0.024276 -0.242834  0.302120
2 -0.528618  0.392775 -0.478175
3  0.308790 -0.383431 -0.228551
4 -0.355274  0.053737  0.395981
```

Figure 4.5 displays the stacked area chart that is generated by the code in Listing 4.5.

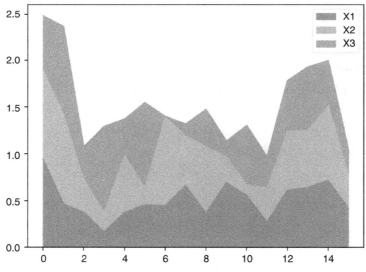

FIGURE 4.5. A stacked area chart in Pandas.

This concludes the portion of the chapter regarding `Pandas` and basic charts and graphs.

WHAT IS FUGUE?

`Fugue` a `Python`-based library that enables you to invoke `SQL`-like queries against `Pandas` DataFrames via `FugueSQL`. Install `Fugue` with the following command (specify a different version if you need to do so):

```
pip3.7 install fugue
```

Listing 4.6 displays the contents of `fugue1.py` that illustrates how to populate a `Pandas` DataFrame and then invoke various `SQL` commands to retrieve a subset of the data from the `Pandas` DataFrame.

LISTING 4.6: fugue1.py

```
import pandas as pd
from fugue_sql import fsql

df1 = pd.DataFrame({'fnames': ['john', 'dave', 'sara', 'eddy'],
                    'lnames': ['smith','stone','stein','bower'],
                    'ages':   [30,33,34,35],
                    'gender': ['m','m','f','m']})

print("=> DataFrame:")
print(df1)
print()

# Example #1: select users who are older than 33:
query_1 = """
SELECT fnames, lnames, ages, gender FROM df1
WHERE ages > 33
PRINT
"""

# display the extracted data:
fsql(query_1).run()
```

Listing 4.6 starts with `import` statements and then initializes the `Pandas` DataFrame `df1` with a set of data values. The next portion of Listing 4.6 constructs a query that retrieves the data values of all users who are older than 33. Launch the code in Listing 4.6 and you will see the following output:

```
=> DataFrame:
  fnames lnames  ages gender
0  john   smith   30     m
1  dave   stone   33     m
2  sara   stein   34     f
3  eddy   bower   35     m

ANTLR runtime and generated code versions disagree: 4.8!=4.9
ANTLR runtime and generated code versions disagree: 4.8!=4.9
ANTLR runtime and generated code versions disagree: 4.8!=4.9
ANTLR runtime and generated code versions disagree: 4.8!=4.9
PandasDataFrame
fnames:str|lnames:str|ages:long|gender:str
----------+----------+---------+----------
sara      |stein     |34       |f
eddy      |bower     |35       |m
Total count: 2
```

MYSQL, SQLALCHEMY, AND PANDAS

There are several ways to interact with a MySQL database, one of which is via SQLAlchemy. The Python code samples in subsequent sections rely on SQLAlchemy (which is briefly described in the next section) and Pandas.

What Is SQLAlchemy?

SQLAlchemy is an ORM (Object Relational Mapping), which serves as a "bridge" between Python code and a database. Install SQLAlchemy with this command:

```
pip3 install sqlalchemy
```

SQLAlchemy handles the task of converting Python function invocations into the appropriate SQL statements, as well as providing support for custom SQL statements. In addition, SQLAlchemy supports multiple databases, including MySQL, Oracle, PostgreSQL, and SQLite.

Read MySQL Data via SQLAlchemy

The previous section showed you how to install SQLAlchemy, and install Pandas (if you haven't done so already) with this command:

```
pip3 install pandas
```

The Pandas functionality in the code samples involves the intuitively named read_sql() method and the related read_sql_query() method, both of which read the contents of a MySQL table.

Listing 4.7 displays the contents of read_sql_data.py that reads the contents of the people table.

LISTING 4.7: read_sql_table.py

```
from sqlalchemy import create_engine
import pymysql
import pandas as pd

engine = create_engine('mysql+pymysql://root:yourpassword@127.0.0.1',po
ol_recycle=3600)
dbConn = engine.connect()
frame   = pd.read_sql("select * from mytools.people", dbConn);

pd.set_option('display.expand_frame_repr', False)
print(frame)
dbConn.close()
```

Listing 4.7 starts with several import statements that are required in order to access a MySQL database. The next portion of code initializes the variable engine as a reference to MySQL, followed by dbConn that is a database connection. Next, the variable frame is initialized with the rows in the people table. Launch the following command in a command shell:

```
python3 read_sql_table.py
```

Pandas and SQL • **129**

You will see the following output generated by the preceding command:

```
   fname  lname  age gender  country
0  john   smith  30     m       usa
1  jane   smith  31     f     france
2  jack   jones  32     m     france
3  dave   stone  33     m      italy
4  sara   stein  34     f    germany
5  eddy   bower  35     m      spain
```

Listing 4.8 displays the contents of `sql_query.py` that reads the contents of the `people` table.

LISTING 4.8: sql_query.py

```
from sqlalchemy import create_engine
import pymysql
import pandas as pd
engine = create_engine('mysql+pymysql://root:yourpassword@127.0.0.1',po
ol_recycle=3600)

query_1 = '''
select * from mytools.people
'''

print("create dataframe from table:")
df_2 = pd.read_sql_query(query_1, engine)

print("dataframe:")
print(df_2)
```

Listing 4.8 starts with several `import` statements followed by initializing the variable `engine` as a reference to a MySQL instance. Next, the variable `query_1` is defined as a string variable that specifies a SQL statement that selects all the rows of the `people` table, followed by the variable `df_2` (a dataframe) that returns the result of executing the SQL statement specified in the variable `query_1`. The final code snippet displays the contents of the `people` table. Launch the following command in a command shell:

```
python3 sql_query.py
```

You will see the following output generated by the preceding command:

```
   fname  lname  age gender  country
0  john   smith  30     m       usa
1  jane   smith  31     f     france
2  jack   jones  32     m     france
3  dave   stone  33     m      italy
4  sara   stein  34     f    germany
5  eddy   bower  35     m      spain
```

Launch the following Python script in a command shell:

```
python3 sql_query.py
```

You will see the following output generated by the preceding command:

```
   fname  lname age gender  country
0  john   smith  30      m      usa
1  jane   smith  31      f   france
2  jack   jones  32      m   france
3  dave   stone  33      m    italy
4  sara   stein  34      f  germany
5  eddy   bower  35      m    spain
```

EXPORT SQL DATA FROM PANDAS TO EXCEL

Listing 4.9 displays the contents of `sql_query_excel.py` that reads the contents of the `people` table into a `Pandas` DataFrame and then exports the latter to an `Excel` file.

LISTING 4.9: sql_query_excel.py

```python
from sqlalchemy import create_engine
import pymysql
import pandas as pd

engine = create_engine('mysql+pymysql://root:yourpassword@127.0.0.1/',po
ol_recycle=3600)

query_1 = '''
select * from mytools.people
'''

print("create dataframe from table:")
df_2 = pd.read_sql_query(query_1, engine)

print("Contents of Pandas dataframe:")
print(df_2)

import openpyxl
print("saving dataframe to people.xlsx")
df_2.to_excel('people.xlsx', index=False)
```

Listing 4.9 contains several `import` statements followed by the variable `engine` that is initialized to an "endpoint" from which a `MySQL` database can be accessed. The next code snippet initializes the variable `query_1` as a string that contains a simple `SQL SELECT` statement.

Next, the variable `df_2` is a `Pandas` DataFrame that initialized to the result of invoking the `SQL` statement defined in the variable `query_1`, after which the contents of `df_2` are displayed. The final portion of code in Listing 4.9 saves the contents of `df_2` to an `Excel` document called `people.xlsx`. Launch the following command in a command shell:

```
python3 sql_query_excel.py
```

The preceding command will generate the following output:

```
Creating dataframe from table people
Contents of Pandas dataframe:
   fname  lname age gender  country
0  john   smith  30      m      usa
1  jane   smith  31      f   france
```

```
2    jack    jones    32        m      france
3    dave    stone    33        m       italy
4    sara    stein    34        f     germany
..    ...     ...     ..       ...        ...
73   jane    smith    31        f      france
74   jack    jones    32        m      france
75   dave    stone    33        m       italy
76   sara    stein    34        f     germany
77   eddy    bower    35        m       spain

[78 rows x 5 columns]
saving dataframe to people.xlsx
```

NOTE *You might need to launch the earlier* Python *script using* Python 3.7 *instead of* Python 3.8 *or* Python 3.9.

The next section contains Pandas-related functionality that does not involve any database connectivity. Since the previous portion of this chapter contains Pandas-related functionality, it's a convenient a convenient location for this material. However, if you prefer, you can skip this section with no loss of continuity and proceed to the following section that discusses SQLite.

MYSQL AND CONNECTOR/PYTHON

MySQL provides a connector/Python API as another mechanism for connecting to a MySQL database. This section contains some simple Python code samples that rely on connector/Python to connect to a database and retrieve rows from a database table.

Before delving into the code samples, keep in mind that MySQL 8 uses mysql_native_password instead of caching_sha2_password. As a result, you need to specify a value for auth_plugin (which is not specified in various online code samples). Here is the error message:

```
mysql.connector.errors.NotSupportedError: Authentication
plugin 'caching_sha2_password' is not supported
```

The solution is highlighted in the Python code sample in the next section.

Establishing a Database Connection

Listing 4.10 displays the contents of mysql_conn1.py that illustrates how to establish a connector/Python database connection.

LISTING 4.10: mysql_conn1.py

```
import mysql.connector

cnx = mysql.connector.connect(user='root',
                              password='yourpassword',
                              host='localhost',
                              database='employees',
                              auth_plugin='mysql_native_password')
```

```
cnx.close()
```

Listing 4.10 contains an `import` statement in order to set the appropriate path for `Python` 3.9. If the code executes correctly on your system without these two lines of code, then you can safely delete them.

The next code snippet is an `import` statement, followed by initializing the variable `cnx` as a database connection. Note the snippet shown in bold, which is required for `MySQL` 8 in order to connect to a `MySQL` database, as described in the introductory portion of this section. Launch the code in Listing 4.10, and if you don't see any error messages, then the code worked correctly.

Reading Data From a Database Table

Listing 4.11 displays the contents of `mysql_pandas.py` that illustrates how to establish a database connection and retrieve the rows in a database table.

LISTING 4.11: mysql_pandas.py

```
import mysql.connector

mydb = mysql.connector.connect(user='root',
                            password='yourpassword',
                            host='localhost',
                            database='employees',
                            auth_plugin='mysql_native_password')

mycursor = mydb.cursor()

# select all rows from the employees table:
mycursor.execute('SELECT * FROM employees')

import pandas as pd

# populate a Pandas data frame with the data:
table_rows = mycursor.fetchall()
df = pd.DataFrame(table_rows)

print("data frame:")
print(df)

mydb.close()
```

Listing 4.11 starts with the same `import` statement as Listing 4.10 and for the same purpose. The next code snippet is an import statement, followed by initializing the variable `cnx` as a database connection. Note the snippet shown in bold, which is required for `MySQL` 8 in order to connect to a `MySQL` database. Launch the code in Listing 4.11 and if everything worked correctly you will see the following output:

```
=> Contents of data frame:
      0     1                    2
0  1000  2000          Developer
```

```
1  2000  3000          Project Lead
2  3000  4000           Dev Manager
3  4000  4000   Senior Dev Manager
```

Creating a Database Table

Listing 4.12 displays the contents of create_fun_table.py that illustrates how to establish a database connection and create a database table.

LISTING 4.12: create_fun_table.py

```
my_table = (
    "CREATE TABLE 'for_fun' ("
    "  'dept_no' char(4) NOT NULL,"
    "  'dept_name' varchar(40) NOT NULL,"
    "  PRIMARY KEY ('dept_no'), UNIQUE KEY 'dept_name' ('dept_name')"
    ") ENGINE=InnoDB")

DB_NAME = 'for_fun_db'

import mysql.connector
cnx = mysql.connector.connect(user='root',
                              password='yourpassword',
                              host='localhost',
                              database='mytools')
cursor = cnx.cursor()

try:
  print("Creating table {}: ".format(my_table), end='')
  cursor.execute(my_table)
except mysql.connector.Error as err:
  if err.errno == errorcode.ER_TABLE_EXISTS_ERROR:
    print("already exists.")
  else:
    print(err.msg)
else:
  print("Table created:",my_table)

cursor.close()

cnx.close()
```

Listing 4.12 starts by initializing the variable my_table as a string that contains a SQL statement for creating a MySQL table. The next portion of Listing 4.12 initializes the variable cnx as a connection to the mytools database, and then initializes the variable cursor as a database cursor.

The next portion of Listing 4.12 contains a try/catch block in order to create the table for_fun that is specified in the string variable my_table. The except block catches the connection-related error and displays an appropriate message if the error occurred because the specified table already exists, or for some other reason.

Launch the code in Listing 4.12 and if everything worked correctly you will see the following output:

```
Creating table CREATE TABLE 'for_fun' ('dept_no' char(4) NOT NULL,
'dept_name' varchar(40) NOT NULL,  PRIMARY KEY ('dept_no'), UNIQUE KEY
'dept_name' ('dept_name')) ENGINE=InnoDB: Table created: CREATE TABLE
'for_fun' ('dept_no' char(4) NOT NULL,  'dept_name' varchar(40) NOT
NULL,  PRIMARY KEY ('dept_no'), UNIQUE KEY 'dept_name' ('dept_name'))
ENGINE=InnoDB
```

Now open a command shell and from the MySQL prompt enter the following command:

```
MySQL [mytools]> desc for_fun;
+-----------+-------------+------+-----+---------+-------+
| Field     | Type        | Null | Key | Default | Extra |
+-----------+-------------+------+-----+---------+-------+
| dept_no   | char(4)     | NO   | PRI | NULL    |       |
| dept_name | varchar(40) | NO   | UNI | NULL    |       |
+-----------+-------------+------+-----+---------+-------+
2 rows in set (0.060 sec)
```

WRITING PANDAS DATA TO A MYSQL TABLE

Listing 4.13 displays the contents of pandas_write_sql.py that shows you how to write data from a Pandas DataFrame into a MySQL table.

LISTING 4.13: pandas_write_sql.py

```
import pandas as pd

data = pd.DataFrame({
    'book_id':[12345, 12346, 12347],
    'title':['Python Programming', 'Learn MySQL', 'Data Science
Cookbook'],
    'price':[29, 23, 27]
})

import mysql.connector
mydb = mysql.connector.connect (
        host="localhost",
        user="root",
        password="yourpassword",
        database = "mytools",
        auth_plugin='mysql_native_password'
        )

from sqlalchemy import create_engine

engine = create_engine('mysql+pymysql://root:yourpasswo
rd@127.0.0.1:3306/mytools',pool_recycle=3600)
dbConn = engine.connect()
```

```
# The to_sql writes data into the book_details table:
data.to_sql('book_details', engine, if_exists='append', index=False)

df = pd.read_sql("SELECT * FROM book_details", dbConn);
pd.set_option('display.expand_frame_repr', False)
print("Rows from book_details table:")
print(df)
dbConn.close()
```

Listing 4.13 starts by initializing the variable data as a Pandas DataFrame with data values, followed by the variable mydb that is initialized as an instance for a database connection.

The next portion of Listing 4.13 instantiates the variables engine and also the variable dbConn that will be invoked while writing data to the database. Next, the variable data invokes its to_sql() method that also specifies the table book_details, the engine variable, and also uses append mode to the database if the table already exists.

The final portion of Listing 4.13 populates the variable df with all the data in the book_details table and then displays its contents before closing the database connection. Now launch the code in Listing 4.13 and if everything worked correctly you will see the following output:

```
Rows from book_details table:
   book_id              title  price
0    12345   Python Programming     29
1    12346         Learn MySQL     23
2    12347  Data Science Cookbook    27
```

Navigate to the MySQL prompt and enter the following statements:

```
mysql> use mytools;
Database changed
mysql> desc book_details;
+---------+--------+------+-----+---------+-------+
| Field   | Type   | Null | Key | Default | Extra |
+---------+--------+------+-----+---------+-------+
| book_id | bigint | YES  |     | NULL    |       |
| title   | text   | YES  |     | NULL    |       |
| price   | bigint | YES  |     | NULL    |       |
+---------+--------+------+-----+---------+-------+
3 rows in set (0.00 sec)
mysql> select * from book_details;
+---------+----------------------+-------+
| book_id | title                | price |
+---------+----------------------+-------+
|   12345 | Python Programming   |    29 |
|   12346 | Learn MySQL          |    23 |
|   12347 | Data Science Cookbook |   27 |
+---------+----------------------+-------+
3 rows in set (0.00 sec)
```

Now launch the code in Listing 4.13 again and then execute the preceding SQL statement again:

```
mysql> select * from book_details;
+----------+----------------------+-------+
| book_id  | title                | price |
+----------+----------------------+-------+
|    12345 | Python Programming   |    29 |
|    12346 | Learn MySQL          |    23 |
|    12347 | Data Science Cookbook |   27 |
|    12345 | Python Programming   |    29 |
|    12346 | Learn MySQL          |    23 |
|    12347 | Data Science Cookbook |   27 |
+----------+----------------------+-------+
6 rows in set (0.00 sec)
```

As you can see, there are now 6 crows in the book_details table. The reason for the insertion of the same three rows of data is the append value in the following SQL statement:

```
data.to_sql('book_details', engine, if_exists='append', index=False)
```

This concludes the portion of the chapter pertaining to Pandas and MySQL The next section introduces you to SQLite, which is an RDBMS that is available on multiple platforms.

READ XML DATA IN PANDAS

Listing 4.14 displays the contents of books.xml and Listing 4.15 displays the contents of pandas_read_xml.py that shows you how to read the contents of an XML document in Pandas.

LISTING 4.14: books.xml

```
<?xml version="1.0" encoding="UTF-8"?>
<books>
  <book>
   <name>SQL Fundamentals</name>
  </book>
  <book>
   <name>SVG Fundamentals</name>
  </book>
  <book>
   <name>Python and Machine Learning</name>
  </book>
</books>
```

LISTING 4.15: pandas_read_xml.py

```
# this code might require Python3.7
import pandas as pd

filename="books.xml"

df = pd.read_xml(filename)
print("XML data:")
print(df)
```

Listing 4.15 starts by initializing the variable with the name of an existing XML document and then invokes the Pandas `read_xml()` method in order to populate the variable df with data from the XML document, after which the contents of df are printed. Now launch the code in Listing 4.15 and if everything worked correctly you will see the following output:

```
Rows from book_details table:

XML data:
              name
0  SQL Fundamentals
1  SVG Fundamentals
2  Python and Machine Learning
```

READ JSON DATA IN PANDAS

Listing 4.16 displays the contents of `pandas_read_json.py` that shows you how to read a JSON string in Pandas.

LISTING 4.16: pandas_read_json.py

```python
from io import StringIO
import pandas as pd

books =  '{"name": "SQL Fundamentals"}\n{"name": "SQL Fundamentals"}\
n{"name": "Python and Machine Learning"}\n'

json = StringIO(books)
result = pd.read_json(json, lines=True)

print("json:",result)
```

Listing 4.16 starts with two `import` statements and then initializes the variable `books` with a string of name/value pairs. Next, the variable `json` is initialized as a JSON string based on the contents of `books`. Then the variable `result` is initialized by invoking the Pandas `read_json()` method with the variable `json`, after which its contents are printed. Now launch the code in Listing 4.16 and if everything worked correctly you will see the following output:

```
XML data:
              name
0  SQL Fundamentals
1  SVG Fundamentals
2  Python and Machine Learning
```

Listing 4.17 displays the contents of `books.json` and Listing 4.18 displays the contents of `pandas_read_json.py` that shows you how to read the contents of a JSON file in Pandas.

LISTING 4.17: books.json

```
[
{"name": "SQL Fundamentals"},
{"name": "SQL Fundamentals"},
{"name": "Python and Machine Learning"}
]
```

LISTING 4.18: pandas_read_json2.py

```
import pandas as pd

filename="books.json"

df = pd.read_json(filename)
print("JSON data:")
print(df.to_string())
```

Listing 4.18 is similar to Listing 4.16, but this time without the use of the `StringIO`, and the contents of the DataFrame `df` are printed by invoking the `to_string()` method. Now launch the code in Listing 4.18 and if everything worked correctly you will see the following output:

```
JSON data:
                name
0   SQL Fundamentals
1   SVG Fundamentals
2   Python and Machine Learning
```

WORKING WITH JSON-BASED DATA

A `JSON` object consists of data represented as colon-separated name/value pairs and data objects are separated by commas. An object is specified inside curly braces { }, and an array of objects is indicated by square brackets [ ]. Note that character-valued data elements are inside a pair of double quotes "" (but no quotes for numeric data).

Here is a simple example of a `JSON` object:

```
{ "fname":"Jane", "lname":"Smith", "age":33, "city":"SF" }
```

Here is a simple example of an array of `JSON` objects (note the outer enclosing square brackets):

```
[
{ "fname":"Jane", "lname":"Smith", "age":33, "city":"SF" },
{ "fname":"John", "lname":"Jones", "age":34, "city":"LA" },
{ "fname":"Dave", "lname":"Stone", "age":35, "city":"NY" },
]
```

Python Dictionary and JSON

The `Python json` library enables you to work with `JSON`-based data in `Python`.

Listing 4.19 displays the contents of `dict2json.py` that illustrates how to convert a `Python` dictionary to a `JSON` string.

LISTING 4.19: dict2json.py

```
import json

dict1 = {}
dict1["fname"] = "Jane"
dict1["lname"] = "Smith"
dict1["age"]   = 33
dict1["city"]  = "SF"

print("Python dictionary to JSON data:")
print("dict1:",dict1)
json1 = json.dumps(dict1, ensure_ascii=False)
print("json1:",json1)
print("")

# convert JSON string to Python dictionary:
json2 = '{"fname":"Dave", "lname":"Stone", "age":35, "city":"NY"}'
dict2 = json.loads(json2)
print("JSON data to Python dictionary:")
print("json2:",json2)
print("dict2:",dict2)
```

Listing 4.19 invokes the `json.dumps()` function to perform the conversion from a `Python` dictionary to a `JSON` string. Launch the code in Listing 4.19 and you will see the following output:

```
Python dictionary to JSON data:
dict1: {'fname': 'Jane', 'lname': 'Smith', 'age': 33, 'city': 'SF'}
json1: {"fname": "Jane", "lname": "Smith", "age": 33, "city": "SF"}

JSON data to Python dictionary:
json2: {"fname":"Dave", "lname":"Stone", "age":35, "city":"NY"}
dict2: {'fname': 'Dave', 'lname': 'Stone', 'age': 35, 'city': 'NY'}
```

Python, Pandas, and JSON

Listing 4.20 displays the contents of `pd_python_json.py` that illustrates how to convert a `Python` dictionary to a `Pandas DataFrame` and then convert the DataFrame to a `JSON` string.

LISTING 4.20: pd_python_json.py

```
import json
import pandas as pd

dict1 = {}
dict1["fname"] = "Jane"
dict1["lname"] = "Smith"
dict1["age"]   = 33
dict1["city"]  = "SF"

df1 = pd.DataFrame.from_dict(dict1, orient='index')
print("Pandas df1:")
print(df1)
```

```
print()

json1 = json.dumps(dict1, ensure_ascii=False)
print("Serialized to JSON1:")
print(json1)
print()

print("Data frame to JSON2:")
json2 = df1.to_json(orient='split')
print(json2)
```

Listing 4.20 initializes a `Python` dictionary `dict1` with multiple attributes for a user (first name, last name, and so forth). Next, the DataFrame `df1` is created from the `Python` dictionary `dict1`, and its contents are displayed.

The next portion of Listing 4.20 initializes the variable `json1` by serializing the contents of `dict1`, and its contents are displayed. The last code block in Listing 4.20 initializes the variable `json2` to the result of converting the DataFrame `df1` to a JSON string. Launch the code in Listing 4.20 and you will see the following output:

```
dict1: {'fname': 'Jane', 'lname': 'Smith', 'age': 33, 'city': 'SF'}
Pandas df1:
                0
fname        Jane
lname       Smith
age            33
city           SF


Serialized to JSON1:
{"fname": "Jane", "lname": "Smith", "age": 33, "city": "SF"}


Data frame to JSON2:
{"columns":[0],"index":["fname","lname","age","city"],"data":[["Jane"],[
"Smith"],[33],["SF"]]}
json1: {"fname": "Jane", "lname": "Smith", "age": 33, "city": "SF"}
```

PANDAS AND REGULAR EXPRESSIONS (OPTIONAL)

This section is marked "optional" because the code snippets require an understanding of regular expressions. If you are not ready to learn about regular expressions, you can skip this section with no loss of continuity.

Listing 4.21 displays the contents `pandas_regexs.py` that illustrates how to extract data from a `Pandas DataFrame` using regular expressions.

LISTING 4.21: pandas_regexs.py

```
import pandas as pd

schedule = ["Monday: Prepare lunch at 12:30pm for VIPs",
```

```
                    "Tuesday: Yoga class from 10:00am to 11:00am",
                    "Wednesday: PTA meeting at library at 3pm",
                    "Thursday: Happy hour at 5:45 at Julie's house.",
                    "Friday: Prepare pizza dough for lunch at 12:30pm.",
                    "Saturday: Early shopping for the week at 8:30am.",
                    "Sunday: Neighborhood bbq block party at 2:00pm."]

# create a Pandas DataFrame:
df = pd.DataFrame(schedule, columns = ['dow_of_week'])

# convert to lowercase:
df = df.applymap(lambda s:s.lower() if type(s) == str else s)
print("df:")
print(df)
print()

# character count for each string in df['dow_of_week']:
print("string lengths:")
print(df['dow_of_week'].str.len())
print()

# the number of tokens for each string in df['dow_of_week']
print("number of tokens in each string in df['dow_of_week']:")
print(df['dow_of_week'].str.split().str.len())
print()

# the number of occurrences of digits:
print("number of digits:")
print(df['dow_of_week'].str.count(r'\d'))
print()

# display all occurrences of digits:
print("show all digits:")
print(df['dow_of_week'].str.findall(r'\d'))
print()

# display hour and minute values:
print("display (hour, minute) pairs:")
print(df['dow_of_week'].str.findall(r'(\d?\d):(\d\d)'))
print()

# create new columns from hour:minute value:
print("hour and minute columns:")
print(df['dow_of_week'].str.extract(r'(\d?\d):(\d\d)'))
print()
```

Listing 4.21 initializes the variable `schedule` with a set of strings, each of which specifies a daily to-do item for an entire week. The format for each to-do item is of the form `day:task`, where is a day of the week and task is a string that specifies what needs to be done on that particular day.

Next, the DataFrame `df1` is initialized with the contents of `schedule`, followed by an example of defining a lambda expression that converts string-based values to lower case, as shown here:

```
df = df.applymap(lambda s:s.lower() if type(s) == str else s)
```

The preceding code snippet is useful because you do not need to specify individual columns of a DataFrame: the code ignores any nonstring values (such as integers and floating point values).

The next pair of code blocks involve various operations using the methods `applymap()`, `split()`, and `len()` that you have seen in previous examples. The next code block displays the number of digits in each to-do item by means of the regular expression in the following code snippet:

```
print(df['dow_of_week'].str.count(r'\d'))
```

The next code block displays the actual digits (instead of the number of digits) in each to-do item by means of the regular expression in the following code snippet:

```
print(df['dow_of_week'].str.findall(r'\d'))
```

The final code block displays the strings of the form hour:minutes by means of the regular expression in the following code snippet:

```
print(df['dow_of_week'].str.findall(r'(\d?\d):(\d\d)'))
```

As mentioned in the beginning of this section, you can learn more about regular expressions by reading one of the appendices of this book. Launch the code in Listing 4.21 and you will see the following output:

```
=> df:
                                            dow_of_week
0            monday: prepare lunch at 12:30pm for vips
1          tuesday: yoga class from 10:00am to 11:00am
2              wednesday: pta meeting at library at 3pm
3        thursday: happy hour at 5:45 at julie's house.
4    friday: prepare pizza dough for lunch at 12:30pm.
5     saturday: early shopping for the week at 8:30am.
6       sunday: neighborhood bbq block party at 2:00pm.

=> string lengths:
0    41
1    43
2    40
3    46
4    49
5    48
6    47
Name: dow_of_week, dtype: int64

=> number of tokens in each string in df['dow_of_week']:
0    7
1    7
2    7
3    8
4    8
5    8
6    7
Name: dow_of_week, dtype: int64
```

```
=> number of digits:
0    4
1    8
2    1
3    3
4    4
5    3
6    3
Name: dow_of_week, dtype: int64

=> show all digits:
0                [1, 2, 3, 0]
1    [1, 0, 0, 0, 1, 1, 0, 0]
2                         [3]
3                   [5, 4, 5]
4                [1, 2, 3, 0]
5                   [8, 3, 0]
6                   [2, 0, 0]
Name: dow_of_week, dtype: object

=> display (hour, minute) pairs:
0               [(12, 30)]
1    [(10, 00), (11, 00)]
2                       []
3                [(5, 45)]
4               [(12, 30)]
5                [(8, 30)]
6                [(2, 00)]
Name: dow_of_week, dtype: object

=> hour and minute columns:

      0    1
0    12   30
1    10   00
2   NaN  NaN
3     5   45
4    12   30
5     8   30
6     2   00
```

WHAT IS SQLITE?

SQLite is a light weight, portable, and open source RDBMS that is available on Windows, Linux, and MacOS, as well as Android and iOS. The official website is here:

https://www.sqlite.org

Here is where you can find a tutorial for some of the most commonly used SQLite commands:

https://www.sqlitetutorial.net/sqlite-commands/

In addition, `SQLite` is `ACID`-compliant and also implements most `SQL` standards. Let's look at some features of `SQLite` and the installation process, both of which are discussed in two subsections.

SQLite Features

`SQLite` provides several useful features, some of which are listed below:

- doesn't require a separate server process or system to operate
- no system administration
- no external dependencies
- can operate in a serverless environment.
- available in multiple platforms (Unix, Linux, Mac, Windows)
- ACID transactions
- full support for all features in SQL92

SQLite Installation

Navigate to the following Web site and download the distribution for your operating system:

https://www.sqlite.org/download.html

The second step is to unzip the downloaded file in a convenient location, which we'll assume is the directory `$HOME/sqlite3_home`.

Note that if you have a MacBook then the directory that contains the `sqlite3` executable is automatically in the `PATH` variable. Just to be sure, type the following command to see if the `sqlite3` is accessible:

```
which sqlite3
```

If the preceding command returns a blank line, then you need to include the path to the `bin` directory where `sqlite3` is located. For example, if the preceding directory is `$HOME/sqlite3_home/bin`, then update the `PATH` environment variable as follows:

```
export PATH=/$HOME/sqlite_home/bin:$PATH
```

Create a Database and a Table

The following sequence of commands show you how to launch `sqlite` and create a database called `test.db`:

```
$ sqlite3 test.db
SQLite version 3.28.0 2019-04-15 14:49:49
Enter ".help" for usage hints.
sqlite>
sqlite> .help
.auth ON|OFF          Show authorizer callbacks
.backup ?DB? FILE     Backup DB (default "main") to FILE
.bail on|off          Stop after hitting an error.  Default OFF
.binary on|off        Turn binary output on or off.  Default OFF
.cd DIRECTORY         Change the working directory to DIRECTORY
.changes on|off       Show number of rows changed by SQL
```

```
// details omitted for brevity
.trace ?OPTIONS?        Output each SQL statement as it is run
.vfsinfo ?AUX?          Information about the top-level VFS
.vfslist                List all available VFSes
.vfsname ?AUX?          Print the name of the VFS stack
.width NUM1 NUM2 ...    Set column widths for "column" mode
sqlite> .databases
databases
main: /tmp/test.db
sqlite> .quit
List the files in the current directory and you will see the following:
-rw-r--r--   1 oswaldcampesato  staff        0 Aug  5 10:36 test.db
```

Now create a table called `books` in `sqlite3` by executing the following sequence of commands:

```
$ sqlite3 test.db
SQLite version 3.28.0 2019-04-15 14:49:49
Enter ".help" for usage hints.
sqlite>
sqlite> CREATE TABLE books(author text, title text, year integer, price
real);
sqlite> .tables
books
sqlite> select * from books;
sqlite> # insert data later
sqlite>
sqlite> .quit
```

Insert, Select, and Delete Table Data

The following sequence of commands show you how perform data-related operations with the books table in the database called "test.db":

```
$ sqlite3 test.db
SQLite version 3.28.0 2019-04-15 14:49:49
Enter ".help" for usage hints.
sqlite> INSERT INTO books(author, title, year, price)
VALUES ("John Doe", "Unix Tips", "2020", "34.95");
sqlite> select * from books;
John Doe|Unix Tips|2020|34.95
sqlite> delete from books;
sqlite> select * from books;
sqlite>
sqlite> .tables
books
sqlite> drop table books;
sqlite>
sqlite> .quit
```

Launch SQL Files

Listing 4.22 displays the contents of create_table.sql and Listing 4.23 displays the contents of insert_data.sql.

LISTING 4.22: create_table.sql

```
CREATE TABLE books2(author text, title text, year integer, price real);
```

LISTING 4.23: insert_data.sql

```
INSERT INTO books2(author, title, year, price)
VALUES ("Oswald Campesato", "C Programming", "2018", "35.95");
```

Launch the preceding SQL files as follows:

```
sqlite3 test.db < create_table.sql
sqlite3 test.db < insert_data.sql
```

Let's return to the sqlite3 prompt and check the structure of the table books2 and its contents:

```
$ sqlite3 test.db
SQLite version 3.28.0 2019-04-15 14:49:49
Enter ".help" for usage hints.
sqlite>
sqlite> .schema books2
CREATE TABLE books2(author text, title text, year integer, price real);
sqlite> select * from books2;
Oswald Campesato|C Programming|2018|35.95
```

Drop Tables and Databases

```
$ sqlite3 test.db
SQLite version 3.28.0 2019-04-15 14:49:49
Enter ".help" for usage hints.
sqlite>
sqlite> drop table books2;
sqlite> .tables
sqlite>
$ sqlite3 test.db

SQLite version 3.28.0 2019-04-15 14:49:49
Enter ".help" for usage hints.
sqlite>
sqlite> .tables
sqlite>
sqlite> .quit
```

Now remove the database test.db by invoking the bash rm command, as shown here:

```
rm test.db
sqlite> .quit
```

Load CSV Data Into a sqlite Table

Listing 4.24 displays the contents of rainfall.csv that contains 65 rows of data and Listing 4.25 displays the contents of load_rainfall.sql.

LISTING 4.24: rainfall.csv

```
CREATE
2023-01-02,0
2023-01-03,1
2023-01-04,0
2023-01-05,2
2023-01-06,3
// details omitted for brevity
2023-03-27,60
2023-03-28,29
2023-03-29,26
2023-03-30,44
2023-03-31,8
```

LISTING 4.25: load_rainfall.sql

```
DROP TABLE IF EXISTS rainfall;
CREATE TABLE rainfall ("day" TEXT, "centimeters" REAL);

.mode csv
.import rainfall.csv rainfall
```

Listing 4.25 drops the table `rainfall` if it already exists, and then creates the `rainfall` table with a text column and a real-valued column called `day` and `centimeters`, respectively. Now launch the code in Listing 4.25, and then navigate to the `sqlite3` prompt to check the number of rows in the `rainfall` table:

```
sqlite3 mytools.db
SQLite version 3.28.0 2019-04-15 14:49:49
Enter ".help" for usage hints.
sqlite> select count(*) from rainfall;
65
sqlite> .quit
```

In the next section, you will learn how to write `Python` code for managing data in `sqlite3` and also learn how to extract data from the `rainfall` table in order to generate a histogram using `Pandas`.

PYTHON AND SQLITE

This section contains an assortment of `Python` files that illustrate how to perform various operations in `sqlite3`, which are the counterpart to the examples that you learned how to perform from the `sqlite3` prompt. Note that the `Python` code samples use the `mytools.db` database instead of the `test.db` database.

Connect to a sqlite3 Database

Listing 4.26 displays the contents of `connect_db.py` that shows you how to connect to a `sqlite3` database in `Python`.

LISTING 4.26: connect_db.py

```
import sqlite3

con = sqlite3.connect("mytools.db")
cursor = con.cursor()
con.commit()
con.close()
```

Listing 4.26 is a "do nothing" Python code sample that simply connects to the mytools.db database.

Create a Table in a sqlite3 Database

Listing 4.27 displays the contents of connect_db.py that shows you how to connect to a sqlite3 database in Python.

LISTING 4.27: create_table.py

```
import sqlite3

con = sqlite3.connect("mytools.db")
cursor = con.cursor()

cursor.execute(
  CREATE TABLE books(author text, title text, year integer, price real);
)

con.commit()
con.close()
```

Listing 4.27 creates a cursor and then executes the SQL create statement in order to create the table books in the mytools.db database.

Insert Data in a sqlite3 Table

Listing 4.28 displays the contents of insert_data.py that shows you how to insert data in a sqlite3 table in Python.

LISTING 4.28: insert_data.py

```
import sqlite3

con = sqlite3.connect("mytools.db")
cursor = con.cursor()

sql = """ INSERT INTO books(author, title, year, price)
          VALUES ("Tom Smith", "Intro to TypeScript", "2022", "39.95")
"""

cursor.execute(sql)
```

```
con.commit()
con.close()
```

Listing 4.28 creates a cursor and then executes the SQL insert statement in order to insert data in the table books in the mytools.db database.

Select Data From a sqlite3 Table

Listing 4.29 displays the contents of select_data.py that shows you how to insert data in a sqlite3 table in Python.

LISTING 4.29: select_data.py

```
import sqlite3

con = sqlite3.connect("mytools.db")
cursor = con.cursor()

sql = """ SELECT * FROM books; """

cursor.execute(sql)

row_count = 0
all_rows = cursor.fetchall()

print("Contents of table books:")
for row in all_rows:
  row_count += 1
  print("row:",row)

con.commit()
con.close()

print("row count:",row_count)
print()
```

Listing 4.29 creates a cursor and then executes the SQL select statement in order to select data from the table books in the mytools.db database. The next portion of Listing 4.29 initializes the variable all_rows as a reference to the data in the books table, followed by a loop that iterates through the elements in all_rows and prints their contents. Notice that the final code snippet displays the numbers of rows in the books table.

Populate a Pandas Dataframe From a sqlite3 Table

Listing 4.30 displays the contents of read_sqlite3_into_pandas.py that shows you how to populate a Pandas DataFrame with data from a sqlite3 table in Python.

LISTING 4.30: read_sqlite3_into_pandas.py

```
import sqlite3
import pandas as pd
```

```
con = sqlite3.connect("mytools.db")
df = pd.read_sql_query("SELECT * FROM books;", con)
con.close()

print("=> Contents of book table:")
print(df)
```

Listing 4.30 creates a cursor and then executes the SQL select statement in order to select data from the table books in the mytools.db database. The next portion of Listing 4.30 initializes the df with the contents of the books table by invoking the Pandas method read_sql_query(). The next code snippet in Listing 4.30 displays the contents of the Pandas DataFrame df. Launch the code in Listing 4.30 and you will see the following output:

```
=> Contents of book table:
        author                title  year   price
0    John Doe            Unix Tips  2020   34.95
1    Oswald C        C Programming  2018   35.95
2   Tom Smith  Intro to TypeScript  2022   39.95
```

Although you can perform SQL operations from the command line, just like you can with MySQL, it's probably easier to work with SQLite in an IDE. In fact, a very robust IDE is SQLiteStudio, which is discussed in the next section.

Histogram With Data From a sqlite3 Table (1)

Listing 4.31 displays the contents of rainfall_hist1.py that shows you how to define a simple SQL query in order to create a histogram based on the data from the rainfall table.

LISTING 4.31: rainfall_hist1.py

```
import sqlite3
import pandas as pd

sql = """
  SELECT
  cast(centimeters/10.00 as int)*10 as cent_floor,
  count(*) as count
FROM rainfall
GROUP by 1
ORDER by 1;
"""

con = sqlite3.connect("mytools.db")
df = pd.read_sql_query(sql, con)
con.close()

print("=> Histogram of Rainfall:")
print(df)
```

Listing 4.31 starts with two import statements and then initializes the string variable sql with a SQL statement involving the table rainfall. Next, the variable con is initialized as a database connection to the database mytools.db.

The next portion of Listing 4.31 invokes the `read_sql_query()` method to read the contents of the `rainfall` table and populate the `DataFrame` `df` with that data. Finally, the connection is closed and the contents of `df` are printed. Now launch the code in Listing 4.31 and you will see the following output:

```
=> Histogram of Rainfall:
   cent_floor   count
0           0     27
1          10     14
2          20      9
3          30      9
4          40      3
5          50      2
6          60      1
```

If you want to replace the value 10.00 with a variable, you can use the following code snippet:

```
factor = 10.00
sql = "SELECT cast(centimeters/"+str(factor)+" as int)*"+str(factor)+"
as cent_floor, count(*) as count FROM rainfall GROUP by 1 ORDER by 1;"
```

However, the preceding style can quickly become cumbersome for longer and more complex SQL statements.

Histogram With Data From a sqlite3 Table (2)

Listing 4.32 displays the contents of `rainfall_hist2.py` that shows you how to define a simple SQL query in order to create a histogram based on the data from the `rainfall` table.

LISTING 4.32: rainfall_hist2.py

```
import sqlite3
import pandas as pd

sql = """
select
  bucket_floor,
  'FROM ' || bucket_floor || ' TO ' || bucket_ceiling as bucket_name,
  count(*) as count
from (
  select
    cast(centimeters/10.00 as int)*10 as bucket_floor,
    cast(centimeters/10.00 as int)*10 + 10 as bucket_ceiling
  from rainfall
) x
group by 1, 2
order by 1;
"""
con = sqlite3.connect("mytools.db")
df = pd.read_sql_query(sql, con)
con.close()
```

```
print("=> Histogram of Rainfall:")
print(df)
```

Listing 4.32 is similar to the previous example, along with some fine tuning in order to print a more detailed version of the data. Now launch the code in Listing 4.32 and you will see the following output:

```
=> Histogram of Rainfall:
     bucket_floor     bucket_name     count
0               0    FROM  0 TO 10       27
1              10    FROM 10 TO 20       14
2              20    FROM 20 TO 30        9
3              30    FROM 30 TO 40        9
4              40    FROM 40 TO 50        3
5              50    FROM 50 TO 60        2
6              60    FROM 60 TO 70        1
```

WORKING WITH sqlite3 TOOLS

The previous two sections showed you how to work directly with `sqlite3`, either through the `sqlite3` prompt or from the command line. The following subsections briefly discuss the following useful tools for working with `sqlite3`:

- SQLiteStudio
- DB Browser
- SQLiteDict

SQLiteStudio Installation

`SQLiteStudio` is an open source IDE for `SQLite` that enables you to perform many database operations, such as creating, updating, and dropping tables and views. Navigate to the following Web site, download the distribution for your operating system, and perform the specified installation steps:

https://sqlitestudio.pl/

https://mac.softpedia.com/get/Developer-Tools/SQLiteStudio.shtml

Figure 4.6 displays the structure of the `employees` table whose definition is the same as the `employees` table in the `mytools` database in `MySQL`.

Figure 4.7 displays a screenshot of three rows in the `employees` table, where you can insert a fourth row of data in the top row that is pre-populated with `NULL` values.

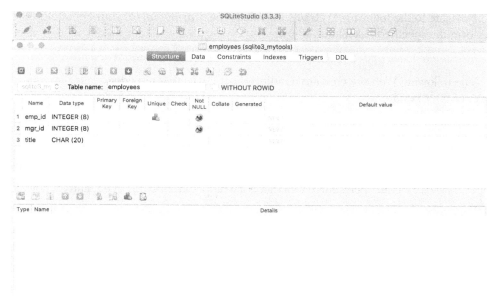

FIGURE 4.6. The employees table.

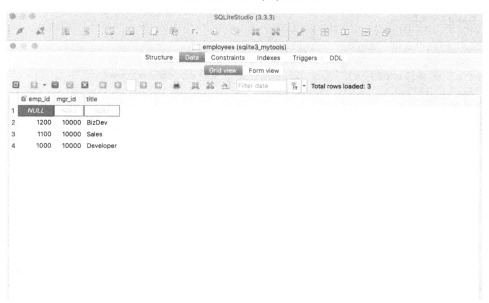

FIGURE 4.7 Three rows in the employees table.

DB Browser for SQLite Installation

DB Browser is an open source and visual-oriented tool for SQLite that that enables you to perform various database-related operations, such as creating and updating files. Moreover, this tool enables you to manage data through an interface that resembles a spreadsheet.

Navigate to the following Web site, download the distribution for your operating system, and perform the specified installation steps:

https://www.macupdate.com/app/mac/38584/db-browser-for-sqlite/download/secure

The following Web site contains a multitude of URLs that provide details regarding the features of DB Browser:

https://sqlitebrowser.org

SQLiteDict (Optional)

SQLiteDict is an open source tool that is a wrapper around sqlite3, and it's downloadable here:

https://pypi.org/project/sqlitedict/

SQLiteDict enables you to persist dictionaries to a file on the file system, as illustrated by the code in Listing 4.33.

LISTING 4.33: sqlitesavedict1.py

```
# pip3 install sqlitedict

from sqlitedict import SqliteDict

mydict = SqliteDict('./my_db.sqlite', autocommit=True)
mydict['pasta'] = 'pasta'
mydict['pizza'] = 'pizza'

for key, value in mydict.iteritems():
  print("key:",key," value:",value)

# dictionary functions work:
print("length:",len(mydict))
mydict.close()

# a client instance:
myclient = MongoClient("localhost",27017)
```

Listing 4.33 contains an import statement followed by the variable mydict that is initialized as a dictionary that includes the two strings pasta and pizza. The next code snippet contains a look that displays the key/value pairs of mydict, followed by the length of the mydict dictionary. The next close snippet closes the dictionary and then launches a MongoDB client at the default port. Now launch the code in Listing 4.33 and you will see the following output:

```
key: pasta   value: pasta
key: pizza   value: pizza
number of items: 2
```

Listing 4.34 illustrates how to read the contents of the file that was saved in Listing 4.33.

LISTING 4.34: sqlitereaddict1.py

```
# pip3 install sqlitedict

# read the contents of my_db.sqlite
# and note no autocommit=True
with SqliteDict('./my_db.sqlite') as mydict:
  print("old:", mydict['pasta'])
  mydict['pasta'] = u"more pasta"
  print("new:", mydict['pasta'])
  mydict['pizza'] = range(10)
  mydict.commit()
  # this is not persisted to disk:
  mydict['dish'] = u"deep dish"

# open the same file again:
with SqliteDict('./my_db.sqlite') as mydict:
  print("pasta:",mydict['pasta'])
  # this line will cause an error:
  #print("dish  value:",mydict['dish'])
```

Listing 4.34 contains a block of code that reads the existing value of past from `mydict`, then updates its value, and then saves its new value. The final code block in Listing 4.34 reads the stored contents and displays the key/value pairs. Now launch the code in Listing 4.34 and you will see the following output:

```
old: pasta
new: more pasta
pasta: more pasta
```

Check the online documentation for information regarding other functionality that is available through `sqlitedict`.

WORKING WITH BEAUTIFUL SOUP

Beautiful Soup is a `Python` library that enables you to parse data from `HTML` Web pages and `XML` documents. If you are familiar with `XPath`, then you already understand what you can do with Beautiful Soup (which supports a subset of `XPath` functionality).

Beautiful Soup can traverse the tree-like structure of `HTML` Web pages and `XML` documents (which include `SVG` documents) in order to extract the desired data or text.

Moreover, Beautiful Soup works with documents on the file system of your laptop as well as data that has been "scraped" from a live `HTML` Web page. Just to give you an idea, Beautiful Soup can easily extract the data from each row in the following Web page:

```
<html>
<body>
  <table>
   <tr><td>50</td><td>80</td></tr>
   <tr><td>150</td><td>180</td></tr>
  </table>
</body>
</html>
```

Parsing an HTML Web Page

Listing 4.35 displays of `sample.html` and Listing 4.36 displays the contents of `bsoup1.py` that extracts data from `sample.html` and then uses `Pandas` to render a bar chart.

LISTING 4.35: sample.html

```
<html>
<body>
  <table>
   <tr>
      <td>50</td>
      <td>80</td>
      <td>72</td>
      <td>68</td>
   </tr>
   <tr>
      <td>150</td>
      <td>180</td>
      <td>172</td>
      <td>168</td>
   </tr>
  </table>
</body>
</html>
```

LISTING 4.36: bsoup1.py

```
import pandas as pd

# pip3 install BeautifulSoup4
from bs4 import BeautifulSoup

# read file and parse HTML:
filename="sample.html"
with open(filename) as f:
  content = f.read()
  soup = BeautifulSoup(content, 'html.parser')

print("=> table data:")
#table = soup.table
table = soup.find("table")
print(table)
print()

print("=> table rows:")
rows = soup.find_all('tr')
for row in rows:
  print ("=> found row:",row)
print()

"""
# scraping a live HTML Web page:
# pip3 install requests
```

```
import requests
URL = "https://www.yahoo.com"
page = requests.get(URL)
soup = BeautifulSoup(page.content, 'html.parser')
"""
```

Listing 4.36 starts with `import` statements and then initializes the variable `content` with the contents of the `HTML` Web page `sample.html`. After the contents of the variable `content` are printed, the next code block populates the variable `table` with the set of tables that are in `sample.html` via the variable `content`, and a simple look displays the set of tables.

The next portion of Listing 4.36 finds all the `<tr>` elements and populates the variable `rows` with that data. A simple loop iterates through the contents of the variable `rows` and prints each data row. Now launch the code in Listing 4.36 and you will see the following output:

```
=> table data:
<table>
<tr>
<td>50</td>
<td>80</td>
<td>72</td>
<td>68</td>
</tr>
<tr>
<td>150</td>
<td>180</td>
<td>172</td>
<td>168</td>
</tr>
</table>

=> table rows:
=> found row: <tr>
<td>50</td>
<td>80</td>
<td>72</td>
<td>68</td>
</tr>
=> found row: <tr>
<td>150</td>
<td>180</td>
<td>172</td>
<td>168</td>
</tr>
```

BEAUTIFUL SOUP AND PANDAS

The code sample in this section uses Beautiful Soup to extract data values from an HTML table in the Web page sample.html that you saw in the previous section. That data is used to populate a `Pandas DataFrame`, after which a bar chart is displayed using a `Pandas` API and `Matplotlib` API, both of which are displayed in bold at the end of Listing 4.38. Although `Matplotlib` is not discussed until Chapter 5, the code snippet is very intuitive and does not require any substantive knowledge of `Matplotlib`.

Listing 4.37 displays the contents of `bsoup2.py` that shows you how to render a bar chart in Pandas.

LISTING 4.37: bsoup2.py

```
from bs4 import BeautifulSoup
import numpy as np
import pandas as pd

# read file and parse HTML:
filename="sample.html"
with open(filename) as f:
  content = f.read()
  soup = BeautifulSoup(content, 'html.parser')

rows = soup.find_all('tr')
all_data = []
for row in rows:
  row_items = row.find_all('td')
  print("row_items:",row_items)
  # create an array of <td> for each row:
  values = [td.get_text() for td in row_items]
  print("values:",values)
  # convert to integers:
  values = np.asarray(values)
  values = values.astype(int)
  print("values:",values)
  # append to matrix:
  all_data.append(values)
  print()
print("all_data:",all_data)

df = pd.DataFrame(all_data)
print("df:")
print(df)

# bar chart:
ax = df.plot.bar()
plt.show()
```

Listing 4.37 starts with import statements and then. Now launch the code in Listing 4.37 and you will see the following output:

```
row_items: [<td>50</td>, <td>80</td>, <td>72</td>, <td>68</td>]
values: ['50', '80', '72', '68']
values: [50 80 72 68]

row_items: [<td>150</td>, <td>180</td>, <td>172</td>, <td>168</td>]
values: ['150', '180', '172', '168']
values: [150 180 172 168]

all_data: [array([50, 80, 72, 68]), array([150, 180, 172, 168])]
```

```
df:
       0     1     2     3
0    50    80    72    68
1   150   180   172   168
```

Figure 4.8 displays the bar chart that is populated with data from the HTML Web page sample.html.

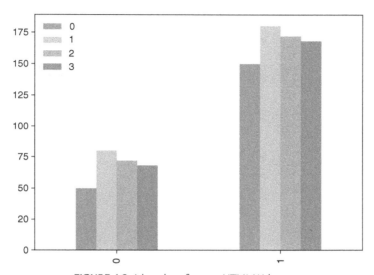

FIGURE 4.8 A bar chart from an HTML Web page.

BEAUTIFUL SOUP AND LIVE HTML WEB PAGES

The code sample in this section uses Beautiful Soup to parse the contents of a live HTML Web page. The key difference in this section is the inclusion of a code snippet for scraping the contents of an online HTML Web page.

Listing 4.38 displays the contents of bsoup3.py that shows you how to render a bar chart in Pandas.

LISTING 4.38: bsoup3.py

```
from bs4 import BeautifulSoup

import re
import requests

URL = "https://www.yahoo.com"
page = requests.get(URL)
soup = BeautifulSoup(page.content, 'html.parser')

print("-----------------------")
print("page before:")
```

```
print(page.text)
print("-----------------------")
print()

divs = soup.find('div')
print("-----------------------")
print("<div> elements:")
print(divs)
print("-----------------------")
print()

tables = soup.find('tables')
print("-----------------------")
print("table elements:")
print(tables)
print("-----------------------")
print()

#links = soup.find('html/head/links')
links = soup.find('links')
print("-----------------------")
print("link elements:")
print(links)
print("-----------------------")
print()
```

Listing 4.38 starts with `import` statements and then initializes the variable `content` with the contents of the HTML Web page located at the specified URL. After the text in the variable `page` are printed, the next code block populates the variable `divs` with the set of `<div>` elementals in that are in Web page. In a similar fashion, the next two code blocks display the tables and the link elements in the Web page. Now launch the code in Listing 4.38 and you will see the following output:

```
row_items:
-----------------------
page before:
<!DOCTYPE html>
<html id="atomic" lang="en-US" class="atomic   l-out Pos-r https fp fp-
default dt-default mini-uh-on uh-topbar-on ltr desktop Desktop bkt201">
<head>
    <meta http-equiv="X-UA-Compatible" content="IE=edge">

    <title>Yahoo | Mail, Weather, Search, Politics, News, Finance,
Sports & Videos</title><meta http-equiv="x-dns-prefetch-control"
content="on"><link rel="dns-prefetch" href="//s.yimg.com"><link
rel="preconnect" href="//s.yimg.com"><link rel="dns-prefetch" href="//
search.yahoo.com"><link rel="preconnect" href="//search.yahoo.com"><link
rel="dns-prefetch" href="//11.at.atwola.com"><link rel="preconnect"
href="//11.at.atwola.com"><link rel="dns-prefetch" href="//geo.yahoo.
com"><link rel="preconnect" href="//geo.yahoo.com"><link rel="dns-
prefetch" href="//video-api.yql.yahoo.com"><link rel="preconnect"
href="//video-api.yql.yahoo.com">
// detail omitted for brevity
</div>
```

```
----------------------

----------------------
table elements:
None
----------------------

----------------------
link elements:
None
----------------------
```

This concludes the brief section regarding Beautiful Soup. The following Web page contains documentation and code snippets that show you how to use various features of Beautiful Soup:

https://beautiful-soup-4.readthedocs.io/en/latest/

SUMMARY

This chapter showed you how to use `Python3` and `Pandas` code with databases. You learned how to use basic functionality of `MongoDB`, which is a popular `NoSQL` database. In addition, you saw some of the features of `SQLite` and `SQLAlchemy`, and how to access both of them through Python code, followed by Python code that accesses `MySQL`.

In addition, you got an overview of `SQLite`, which is a command line tool for managing databases that is available on mobile devices. Finally, you learned about related tools, such as `SQLiteStudio` (an **IDE** for `sqlite`), `DB Browser`, and `SQLiteDict`.

## CHAPTER 5

MATPLOTLIB FOR DATA VISUALIZATION

This chapter introduces data visualization, along with a collection of `Python`-based code samples that use `Matplotlib` to render charts and graphs. In addition, this chapter contains visualization code samples that combine `Pandas` and `Matplotlib`.

The first part of this chapter briefly discusses data visualization, with a short list of some data visualization tools, and a list of various types of visualization (bar graphs, pie charts, and so forth).

The first part of this chapter contains a very short introduction to `Matplotlib`, followed by short code samples that display the available styles in colors in `Matplotlib`.

The second part of this chapter contains an assortment of `Python` code samples that render horizontal lines, slanted lines, and parallel lines. This section also contains a set of code samples that show you how to render a grid of points in several ways.

The third part of this chapter shows you how to load images, display a checkerboard pattern, and plotting trigonometric function in `Matplotlib`. The fourth section contains examples of rendering charts and graphs in `Matplotlib`, which includes histograms, bar charts, pie charts, and heat maps.

The fourth section contains code samples for rendering 3D charts, financial data, and data from a sqlite3 database. The fifth section is optional because it requires some knowledge of working with time series datasets.

WHAT IS DATA VISUALIZATION?

Data visualization refers to presenting data in a graphical manner, such as bar charts, line graphs, heat maps, and many other specialized representations. As you probably know, big data comprises massive amounts of data, which leverages data visualization tools to assist in making better decisions.

A key role for good data visualization is to tell a meaningful story, which in turn focuses on useful information that resides in datasets that can contain many data points (i.e., billions of rows of data). Another aspect of data visualization is its effectiveness: how well does it convey the trends that might exist in the dataset?

There are many open source data visualization tools available, some of which are listed here (many others are available):

- Matplotlib
- Seaborn
- Bokeh
- YellowBrick
- Tableau
- D3.js (JavaScript and SVG)

Incidentally, in case you have not already done so, it would be helpful to install the following `Python` libraries (using `pip3`) on your computer so that you can launch the code samples in this chapter:

```
pip3 install matplotlib
pip3 install seaborn
pip3 install bokeh
```

Types of Data Visualization

Bar graphs, line graphs, and pie charts are common ways to present data, and yet many other types exist, some of which are listed below:

- `2D/3D Area Chart`
- `Bar Chart`
- `Gantt Chart`
- `Heat Map`
- `Histogram`
- `Polar Area`
- `Scatter Plot (2D or 3D)`
- `Timeline`

The `Python` code samples in the next several sections illustrate how to perform visualization via rudimentary APIs from `matplotlib`.

WHAT IS MATPLOTLIB?

`Matplotlib` is a plotting library that supports `NumPy`, `SciPy`, and toolkits such as `wxPython` (among others). `Matplotlib` supports only version 3 of `Python`: support for version 2 of `Python` was available only through 2020. `Matplotlib` is a multiplatform library that is built on `NumPy` arrays.

The plotting-related code samples in this chapter use `pyplot`, which is a `Matplotlib` module that provides a `MATLAB`-like interface. Here is an example of using `pyplot` to plot a smooth curve based on negative powers of Euler's constant e:

```
import matplotlib.pyplot as plt
import numpy as np
xvals = np.linspace(0, 10, 100)
```

```
yvals = np.exp(-xvals)
plt.plot(xvals, yvals)
plt.show()
```

Keep in mind that the code samples that plot line segments assume that you are familiar with the equation of a (non-vertical) line in the plane: `y = m*x + b`, where `m` is the slope and `b` is the y-intercept.

Furthermore, some code samples use `NumPy` APIs such as `np.linspace()`, `np.array()`, `np.random.rand()`, and `np.ones()` that are discussed in Chapter 3, so you can refresh your memory regarding these APIs.

MATPLOTLIB STYLES

Listing 5.1 displays the contents of `mpl_styles.py` that illustrates how to plot a pie chart in `Matplotlib`.

LISTING 5.1: mpl_styles.py

```
import matplotlib.pyplot as plt

print("plt.style.available:")
styles = plt.style.available

for style in styles:
  print("style:",style)
```

Listing 5.1 contains an `import` statement, followed by the variable `styles` that is initialized with the set of available styles in Matplotlib. The final portion of Listing 5.1 contains a loop that iterates through the values in the styles variable. Now launch the code in Listing 5.1 and you will see the following output:

```
plt.style.available:
style: Solarize_Light2
style: _classic_test_patch
style: bmh
style: classic
style: dark_background
style: fast
style: fivethirtyeight
style: ggplot
style: grayscale
style: seaborn
style: seaborn-bright
style: seaborn-colorblind
style: seaborn-dark
style: seaborn-dark-palette
style: seaborn-darkgrid
style: seaborn-deep
style: seaborn-muted
style: seaborn-notebook
style: seaborn-paper
style: seaborn-pastel
```

```
style: seaborn-poster
style: seaborn-talk
style: seaborn-ticks
style: sea born-white
style: seaborn-whitegrid
style: tableau-colorblind10
```

DISPLAY ATTRIBUTE VALUES

Listing 5.2 displays the contents of `mat_attrib_values.py` that displays the attribute values of an object in `Matplotlib` (subplots are discussed later in this chapter).

LISTING 5.2: mat_attrib_values.py

```python
import matplotlib.pyplot as plt

fig, ax = plt.subplots()

print("=> attribute values:")
print(plt.getp(fig))
```

Listing 5.2 contains an `import` statement, followed by the variables `fig` and `ax` that are initialized by invoking the `subplots()` method of the `plt` class. The next block of code prints the attribute values in `fig` wby invoking the `plt.getp()` method. Launch the code in Listing 5.2 and you will see the following output:

```
=> attribute values:
    agg_filter = None
    alpha = None
    animated = False
    axes = [<AxesSubplot:>]
    children = [<matplotlib.patches.Rectangle object at 0x11c34f0...
    clip_box = None
    clip_on = True
    clip_path = None
    constrained_layout = False
    constrained_layout_pads = (0.04167, 0.04167, 0.02, 0.02)
    contains = None
    default_bbox_extra_artists = [<AxesSubplot:>, <matplotlib.spines.
Spine object a...
    dpi = 100.0
    edgecolor = (1.0, 1.0, 1.0, 1.0)
    facecolor = (1.0, 1.0, 1.0, 1.0)
    figheight = 4.8
    figure = None
    figwidth = 6.4
    frameon = True
    gid = None
    in_layout = True
    label =
    path_effects = []
    picker = None
    rasterized = None
    size_inches = [6.4 4.8]
```

```
sketch_params = None
snap = None
tight_layout = False
transform = IdentityTransform()
transformed_clip_path_and_affine = (None, None)
url = None
visible = True
window_extent = TransformedBbox(Bbox(x0=0.0, y0=0.0, x1=6.4, ...
zorder = 0
```

COLOR VALUES IN Matplotlib

Listing 5.3 displays the contents of mat_colors.py that displays the colors that are available in Matplotlib.

LISTING 5.3: heatmap1.py

```
import matplotlib
import matplotlib.pyplot as plt

colors = plt.colormaps()

col_count=5
idx=0
for color in colors:
  if(color.endswith("_r") == False):
    print(color," ",end="")
    idx += 1
    if(idx % col_count == 0):
      print()
print()
print("=> color count:",idx)
```

Listing 5.3 contains two import statements, after which the variable colors is initialized with the list of available colors. The next portion of Listing 5.3 contains a loop that iterates through the colors variable, and prints the value of each color, provided that it does not have the suffix "_r" in its name. A newline is printed each time that five colors have been printed. Now launch the code in Listing 5.3 and you will see the following output:

```
Accent   Blues   BrBG   BuGn   BuPu
CMRmap   Dark2   GnBu   Greens   Greys
OrRd   Oranges   PRGn   Paired   Pastel1
Pastel2   PiYG   PuBu   PuBuGn   PuOr
PuRd   Purples   RdBu   RdGy   RdPu
RdYlBu   RdYlGn   Reds   Set1   Set2
Set3   Spectral   Wistia   YlGn   YlGnBu
YlOrBr   YlOrRd   afmhot   autumn   binary
bone   brg   bwr   cividis   cool
coolwarm   copper   cubehelix   flag   gist_earth
gist_gray   gist_heat   gist_ncar   gist_rainbow   gist_stern
gist_yarg   gnuplot   gnuplot2   gray   hot
hsv   inferno   jet   magma   nipy_spectral
```

```
ocean   pink   plasma   prism   rainbow
seismic   spring   summer   tab10   tab20
tab20b   tab20c   terrain   turbo   twilight
twilight_shifted   viridis   winter
=> color count: 83
```

Now let's proceed to the next section that contains a fast-paced set of basic code samples that display various types of line segments.

CUBED NUMBERS IN Matplotlib

Listing 5.4 displays the contents of cubed_numbers.py that illustrates how to plot a set of points using Matplotlib.

LISTING 5.4: cubed_numbers.py

```python
import matplotlib.pyplot as plt

plt.plot([1, 2, 3, 4], [1, 8, 27, 64])
plt.axis([0, 5, 0, 70])
plt.xlabel("Integers (1-4)")
plt.ylabel("Cubed Integers")
plt.show()
```

Listing 5.4 plots a set of integer-valued points whose x-coordinate is between 1 and 4 inclusive and whose y-coordinate is the cube of the corresponding x-coordinate. The code sample also labels the horizontal axis and the vertical axis. Figure 5.1 displays these points in Listing 5.4.

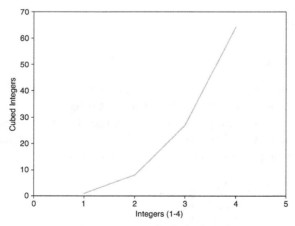

FIGURE 5.1 A graph of cubed numbers.

HORIZONTAL LINES IN Matplotlib

Listing 5.5 displays the contents of hlines1.py that illustrates how to plot horizontal lines using Matplotlib. Recall that the equation of a non-vertical line in the 2D plane is $y = m*x + b$, where m is the slope of the line and b is the y-intercept of the line.

LISTING 5.5: hlines1.py

```
import numpy as np
import matplotlib.pyplot as plt

# top line
x1 = np.linspace(-5,5,num=200)
y1 = 4 + 0*x1

# middle line
x2 = np.linspace(-5,5,num=200)
y2 = 0 + 0*x2

# bottom line
x3 = np.linspace(-5,5,num=200)
y3 = -3 + 0*x3

plt.axis([-5, 5, -5, 5])
plt.plot(x1,y1)
plt.plot(x2,y2)
plt.plot(x3,y3)
plt.show()
```

Listing 5.5 uses the `np.linspace()` API in order to generate a list of 200 equally spaced numbers for the horizontal axis, all of which are between −5 and 5. The three lines defined via the variables y1, y2, and y3, are defined in terms of the variables x1, x2, and x3, respectively.

Figure 5.2 displays three horizontal line segments whose equations are contained in Listing 5.5.

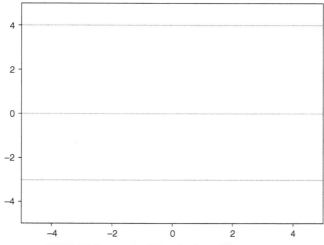

FIGURE 5.2 A graph of three horizontal line segments.

SLANTED LINES IN Matplotlib

Listing 5.6 displays the contents of `diagonallines.py` that illustrates how to plot slanted lines.

LISTING 5.6: *diagonallines.py*

```python
import matplotlib.pyplot as plt
import numpy as np

x1 = np.linspace(-5,5,num=200)
y1 = x1

x2 = np.linspace(-5,5,num=200)
y2 = -x2

plt.axis([-5, 5, -5, 5])
plt.plot(x1,y1)
plt.plot(x2,y2)
plt.show()
```

Listing 5.6 defines two lines using the technique that you saw in Listing 5.5, except that these two lines define y1 = x1 and y2 = -x2, which produces slanted lines instead of horizontal lines.

Figure 5.3 displays two slanted line segments whose equations are defined in Listing 5.6.

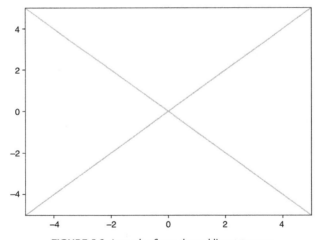

FIGURE 5.3 A graph of two slanted line segments.

PARALLEL SLANTED LINES IN Matplotlib

If two lines in the Euclidean plane have the same slope, then they are parallel. Listing 5.7 displays the contents of parallellines1.py that illustrates how to plot parallel slanted lines.

LISTING 5.7: *parallellines1.py*

```python
import matplotlib.pyplot as plt
import numpy as np
```

```
# lower line
x1 = np.linspace(-5,5,num=200)
y1 = 2*x1

# upper line
x2 = np.linspace(-5,5,num=200)
y2 = 2*x2 + 3

# horizontal axis
x3 = np.linspace(-5,5,num=200)
y3 = 0*x3 + 0

# vertical axis
plt.axvline(x=0.0)

plt.axis([-5, 5, -10, 10])
plt.plot(x1,y1)
plt.plot(x2,y2)
plt.plot(x3,y3)
plt.show()
```

Listing 5.7 defines three lines using the technique that you saw in Listing 5.6, where two lines are slanted and parallel and the third line is horizontal. Launch the code in Listing 5.7 and you will see the result displayed in Figure 5.4.

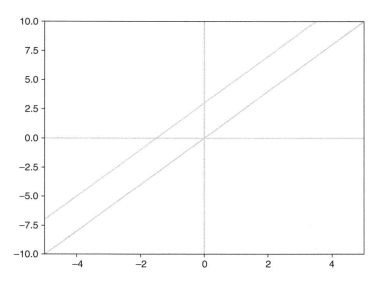

FIGURE 5.4 A graph of two slanted parallel line segments.

A GRID OF POINTS IN Matplotlib

Listing 5.8 displays the contents of plotgrid.py that illustrates how to plot a simple grid.

LISTING 5.8: multi_lines.py

```
import matplotlib.pyplot as plt

x_coord = [50, 300, 175, 50]
y_coord = [50, 50,  150, 50]
plt.plot(x_coord,y_coord)
plt.scatter(x_coord,y_coord)

for x,y in zip(x_coord,y_coord):
  plt.text(x,y,'Coord ({x},{y})'.format(x=x,y=y))

x_coord = [ 175, 300,  50, 175]
y_coord = [  50, 150, 150, 50]
plt.plot(x_coord,y_coord)
plt.scatter(x_coord,y_coord)

for x,y in zip(x_coord,y_coord):
  plt.text(x,y,'Coord ({x},{y})'.format(x=x,y=y))
plt.show()
```

Listing 5.8 defines the `NumPy` variable `points` that defines a 2D list of points with three rows and four columns. The `Pyplot` API `plot()` uses the `points` variable to display a grid-like pattern. Figure 5.5 displays a grid of points as defined in Listing 5.8.

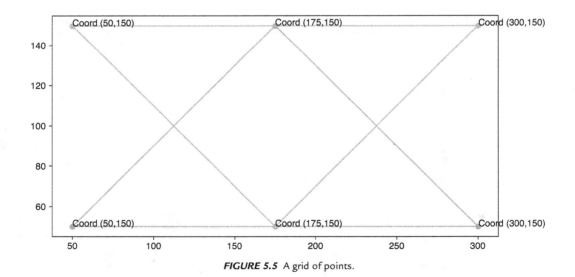

FIGURE 5.5 A grid of points.

A DOTTED GRID IN Matplotlib

Listing 5.9 displays the contents of `plotdottedgrid1.py` that illustrates how to plot a "dotted" grid pattern.

LISTING 5.9: plotdottedgrid1.py

```
import numpy as np
import pylab
from itertools import product
import matplotlib.pyplot as plt

fig = pylab.figure()
ax = fig.add_subplot(1,1,1)

ax.grid(which='major', axis='both', linestyle='--')

[line.set_zorder(3) for line in ax.lines]
fig.show() # to update

plt.gca().xaxis.grid(True)
plt.show()
```

Listing 5.9 is similar to the code in Listing 5.8 in that both of them plot a grid-like pattern; however, the former renders a "dotted" grid pattern whereas the latter renders a "dotted" grid pattern by specifying the value `'--'` for the `linestyle` parameter.

The next portion of Listing 5.9 invokes the `set_zorder()` method that controls which items are displayed on top of other items, such as dots on top of lines, or vice versa. The final portion of Listing 5.9 invokes the `gca().xaxis.grid(True)` chained methods to display the vertical grid lines.

You can also use the `plt.style` directive to specify a style for figures. The following code snippet specifies the classic style of Matplotlib:

```
plt.style.use('classic')
```

Figure 5.6 displays a "dashed" grid pattern based on the code in Listing 5.9.

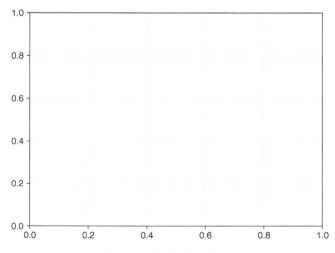

FIGURE 5.6 A "dashed" grid pattern.

TWO LINES AND A LEGEND IN Matplotlib

Listing 5.10 displays the contents of `plotgrid2.py` that illustrates how to display a colored grid.

LISTING 5.10: two_lines_legend.py

```
import matplotlib.pyplot as plt

# FIRST PLOT:
vals_x = [91,93,95,96,97,98,99,99,104,115]
vals_y = [1500,2000,3000,2500,1200,1500,2900,3200,5200,6500]
plt.plot(vals_x, vals_y) # alternate style
#plt.plot(vals_x, vals_y, label='First List')

# SECOND PLOT:
vals_x2 = [91,93,95,96,97,98,99,99,104,115]
vals_y2 = [1005,1006,1007,1008,1009,2031,3100,2033,3034,4035]
plt.plot(vals_x2, vals_y2)
#plt.plot(vals_x2, vals_y2, label='Second List') # alternate style

# generate line plot:
plt.plot(vals_x, vals_y)
plt.title("Random Pairs of Numbers")
plt.xlabel("Random X Values")
plt.ylabel("Random Y Values")
plt.legend(['First List','Second List'])
#plt.legend() # alternate style
plt.show()
```

Listing 5.10 defines the `NumPy` variable `data` that defines a 2D set of points with ten rows and ten columns. The Pyplot API `plot()` uses the `data` variable to display a colored grid-like pattern.

Figure 5.7 displays a colored grid whose equations are contained in Listing 5.10.

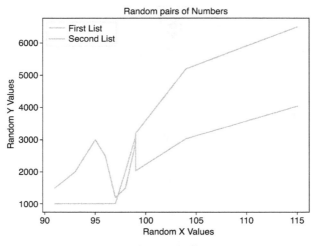

FIGURE 5.7 A colored grid of line segments.

LOADING IMAGES IN Matplotlib

Listing 5.11 displays the contents of `load_images2.py` that illustrates how to display an image.

LISTING 5.11: load_images2.py

```
from sklearn.datasets import load_digits
from matplotlib import pyplot as plt

digits = load_digits()
#set interpolation='none'

fig = plt.figure(figsize=(3, 3))
plt.imshow(digits['images'][66], cmap="gray", interpolation='none')
plt.show()
```

Listing 5.11 starts with two `import` statements and then the `digits` variable is initialized with the contents of the `digits` dataset. The next portion of Listing 5.11 displays the contents of one of the images in the `digits` dataset. Now launch the code in Listing 5.11 and you will see the image in Figure 5.8.

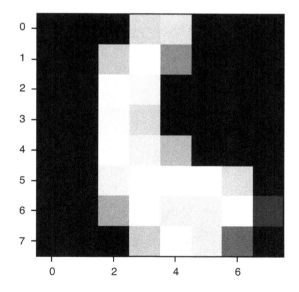

FIGURE 5.8 Loading an image in Matplotlib.

A CHECKERBOARD IN Matplotlib

Listing 5.12 displays the contents of `checkerboard1.py` that illustrates how to display a checkerboard.

LISTING 5.12: checkerboard1.py

```
import matplotlib.pyplot as plt
from matplotlib import colors
import numpy as np

data = np.random.rand(10, 10) * 20

# create discrete colormap
cmap = colors.ListedColormap(['red', 'blue'])
bounds = [0,10,20]
norm = colors.BoundaryNorm(bounds, cmap.N)

fig, ax = plt.subplots()
ax.imshow(data, cmap=cmap, norm=norm)

# draw gridlines
ax.grid(which='major', axis='both', linestyle='-', color='k',
linewidth=2)
ax.set_xticks(np.arange(-.5, 10, 1));
ax.set_yticks(np.arange(-.5, 10, 1));

plt.show()
```

Listing 5.12 defines the NumPy variable data that defines a 2D set of points with ten rows and ten columns. The Pyplot API plot() uses the data variable to display a colored grid-like pattern. Figure 5.9 displays a colored grid whose equations are contained in Listing 5.12.

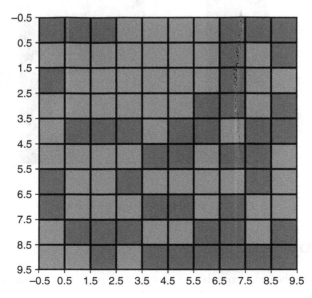

FIGURE 5.9 A checkerboard.

RANDOMIZED DATA POINTS IN `Matplotlib`

Listing 5.13 displays the contents of `lin_reg_plot.py` that illustrates how to plot a graph of random points.

LISTING 5.13: lin_plot_reg.py

```
import numpy as np
import matplotlib.pyplot as plt

trX = np.linspace(-1, 1, 101) # Linear space of 101 and [-1,1]

#Create the y function based on the x axis
trY = 2*trX + np.random.randn(*trX.shape)*0.4+0.2

#create figure and scatter plot of the random points
plt.figure()
plt.scatter(trX,trY)

# Draw one line with the line function
plt.plot (trX, .2 + 2 * trX)
plt.show()
```

Listing 5.13 defines the `NumPy` variable `trX` that contains 101 equally spaced numbers that are between −1 and 1 (inclusive). The variable `trY` is defined in two parts: the first part is `2*trX` and the second part is a random value that is partially based on the length of the one-dimensional array `trX`. The variable `trY` is the sum of these two "parts," which creates a "fuzzy" line segment.

The next portion of Listing 5.13 creates a scatterplot based on the values in `trX` and `trY`, followed by the Pyplot API `plot()` that renders a line segment. Figure 5.10 displays a random set of points based on the code in Listing 5.13.

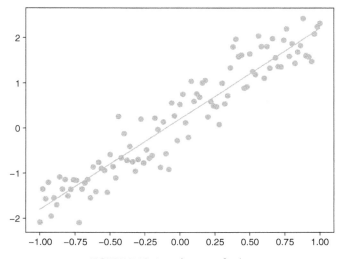

FIGURE 5.10 A random set of points.

A SET OF LINE SEGMENTS IN Matplotlib

Listing 5.14 displays the contents of `line_segments.py` that illustrates how to plot a set of connected line segments in Matplotlib.

LISTING 5.14: line_segments.py

```
import numpy as np
import matplotlib.pyplot as plt

x = [7,11,13,15,17,19,23,29,31,37]

plt.plot(x) # OR: plt.plot(x, 'ro-') or bo
plt.ylabel('Height')
plt.xlabel('Weight')
plt.show()
```

Listing 5.14 defines the array x that contains a hard-coded set of values. The Pyplot API `plot()` uses the variable x to display a set of connected line segments. Figure 5.11 displays the result of launching the code in Listing 5.14.

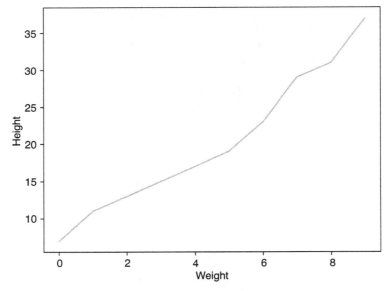

FIGURE 5.11 A set of connected line segments.

PLOTTING MULTIPLE LINES IN Matplotlib

Listing 5.15 displays the contents of `plt_array2.py` that illustrates the ease with which you can plot multiple lines in Matplotlib.

LISTING 5.15: plt_array2.py

```
import matplotlib.pyplot as plt

x = [7,11,13,15,17,19,23,29,31,37]
data = [[8, 4, 1], [5, 3, 3], [6, 0, 2], [1, 7, 9]]
plt.plot(data, 'd-')
plt.show()
```

Listing 5.15 defines the array data that contains a hard-coded set of values. The Pyplot API plot() uses the variable data to display a line segment. Figure 5.12 displays multiple lines based on the code in Listing 5.15.

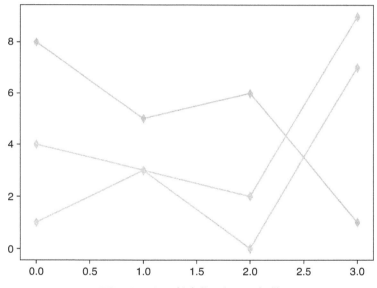

FIGURE 5.12 Multiple lines in Matplotlib.

TRIGONOMETRIC FUNCTIONS IN Matplotlib

In case you're wondering, you can display the graph of trigonometric functions as easily as you can render "regular" graphs using Matplotlib. Listing 5.16 displays the contents of sincos. py that illustrates how to plot a sine function and a cosine function in Matplotlib.

LISTING 5.16: sincos.py

```
import numpy as np
import math

x = np.linspace(0, 2*math.pi, 101)
s = np.sin(x)
c = np.cos(x)
```

```
import matplotlib.pyplot as plt
plt.plot (s)
plt.plot (c)
plt.show()
```

Listing 5.16 defines the `NumPy` variables x, s, and c using the `NumPy` APIs `linspace()`, `sin()`, and `cos()`, respectively. Next, the Pyplot API `plot()` uses these variables to display a sine function and a cosine function.

Figure 5.13 displays a graph of two trigonometric functions based on the code in Listing 5.16.

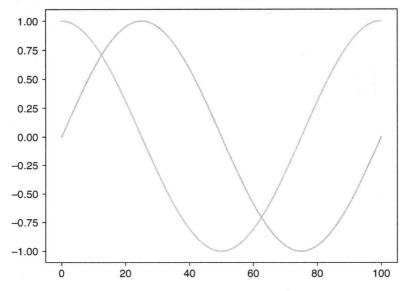

FIGURE 5.13 Sine and cosine trigonometric functions.

Now let's look at a simple dataset consisting of discrete data points, which is the topic of the next section.

A HISTOGRAM IN Matplotlib

Listing 5.17 displays the contents of `histogram1.py` that illustrates how to plot a histogram using `Matplotlib`.

LISTING 5.17: histogram1.py

```
import matplotlib.pyplot as plt

x = [1, 2, 3, 4, 5, 6, 7, 4]

plt.hist(x, bins = [1, 2, 3, 4, 5, 6, 7])
plt.title("Histogram")
plt.legend(["bar"])
plt.show()
```

Listing 5.17 is straightforward: the variable x is initialized as a set of numbers, followed by a block of code that renders a histogram based on the data in the variable x. Launch the code in Listing 5.17 and you will see the histogram that is shown in Figure 5.14.

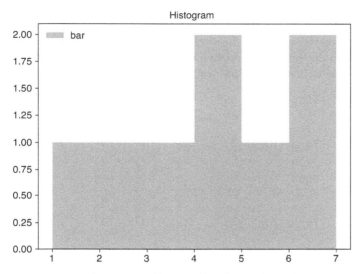

FIGURE 5.14 A histogram based on random values.

HISTOGRAM WITH DATA FROM A sqlite3 TABLE

Listing 5.18 displays the contents of `rainfall_hist2.py` that shows you how to define a simple SQL query in order to create a histogram based on the data from the rainfall table.

LISTING 5.18: rainfall_hist3.py

```
import sqlite3
import pandas as pd
import matplotlib.pyplot as plt

sql = """
  SELECT
  cast(centimeters/5.00 as int)*5 as cent_floor,
  count(*) as count
FROM rainfall
GROUP by 1
ORDER by 1;
"""

con = sqlite3.connect("mytools.db")
df = pd.read_sql_query(sql, con)
con.close()

print("=> Histogram of Rainfall:")
print(df)
```

```
#df.hist(column='count', bins=7, grid=False, rwidth=1.0, color='red')
df.hist(column='count', bins=14, grid=False, rwidth=.8, color='red')
plt.show()
```

Listing 5.18 starts with several `import` statements and then initializes the variable `sql` with a `SQL` statement that selects data from the `rainfall` table. The next portion of Listing 5.18 initializes the variable con for accessing the `mytools.db` database, and then populates the `Pandas DataFrame df` with the result of executing the `SQL` statement contained in the variable `sql`. Now launch the code in Listing 5.18 and you will see the following output:

```
=> Histogram of Rainfall:
     bucket_floor      bucket_name   count
0                0     FROM 0 TO 10      27
1               10    FROM 10 TO 20      14
2               20    FROM 20 TO 30       9
3               30    FROM 30 TO 40       9
4               40    FROM 40 TO 50       3
5               50    FROM 50 TO 60       2
6               60    FROM 60 TO 70       1
```

You will see the histogram that is shown in Figure 5.15.

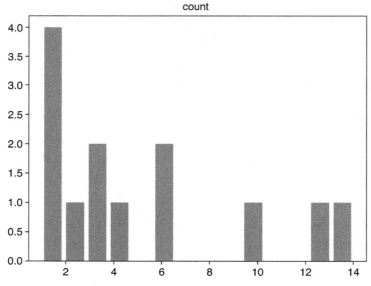

FIGURE 5.15 A histogram based on rainfall data.

PLOT BAR CHARTS Matplotlib

Listing 5.19 displays the contents of `barchart1.py` that illustrates how to plot a bar chart in `Matplotlib`.

LISTING 5.19: barchart1.py

```
import matplotlib.pyplot as plt

x = [3, 1, 3, 12, 2, 4, 4]
y = [3, 2, 1, 4, 5, 6, 7]

plt.bar(x, y)

plt.title("Bar Chart")
plt.legend(["bar"])
plt.show()
```

Listing 5.19 contains an import statement followed by the variables x and y that are initialized as a list of numbers. Next, the bar chart is generated by invoking the bar() method of the plt class. The final block of code sets the title and legend for the bar chart and then displays the bar chart. Launch the code in Listing 5.19 and you will see the pie chart displayed in Figure 5.16.

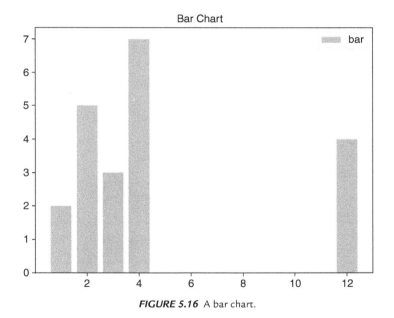

FIGURE 5.16 A bar chart.

Listing 5.20 displays the contents of barchart2.py that illustrates how to plot a bar chart in Matplotlib.

LISTING 5.20: barchart2.py

```
import matplotlib.pyplot as plt

plt.bar([0.25,1.25,2.25,3.25,4.25],
        [50,40,70,80,20],
        label="GDP1",width=.5)
```

```
plt.bar([.75,1.75,2.75,3.75,4.75],
        [80,20,20,50,60],
        label="GDP2", color='r',width=.5)

plt.legend()
plt.xlabel('Months')
plt.ylabel('GDP (Billion Euross)')
plt.title('Bar Chart Comparison')
```

Listing 5.20 contains an `import` statement followed by the definition of two bar charts that are displayed in a side-by-side manner. Notice that the definition of each bar chart involves specifying the x and y (even though they are not explicitly included), followed by a value for the `label` and `width` arguments. The final block of code sets the legend and labels for the horizontal and vertical axes. Now launch the code in Listing 5.20 and you will see the pie chart displayed in Figure 5.17.

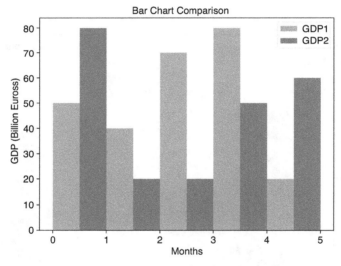

FIGURE 5.17 Two bar charts.

PLOT A PIE CHART Matplotlib

Listing 5.21 displays the contents of `piechart1.py` that illustrates how to plot a pie chart in Matplotlib.

LISTING 5.21: piechart1.py

```
import numpy as np

# data to display on plots
x = [1, 2, 3, 4]
```

```
# explode the first wedge:
e =(0.1, 0, 0, 0)

plt.pie(x, explode = e)
plt.title("Pie chart")
plt.show()
```

Listing 5.21 contains an `import` statement followed by the variables x and e that are initialized as a list of numbers. The values for x are used to calculate the relative size of each "slice" of the pie chart, and the values for the variable e indicate that the first pie slice is "exploded" slightly (indicated by the value 0.1 in e). Launch the code in Listing 5.21 and you will see the pie chart displayed in Figure 5.18.

Pie chart

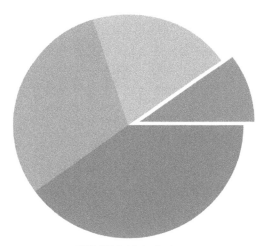

FIGURE 5.18 A pie chart.

HEAT MAPS IN Matplotlib

Listing 5.22 displays the contents of `heatmap1.py` that illustrates how to render a heat map in Matplotlib.

LISTING 5.22: heatmap1.py

```
import numpy as np

data = np.random.random((16, 16))
plt.imshow(data, cmap='tab20_r', interpolation='nearest')
plt.show()
```

Listing 5.22 contains an import statement, followed by the variable data that is initialized as a 16x16 matrix of random values. The next code snippet renders the heat map, and the final code snippet displays the heat map. Now launch the code in Listing 5.22 and you will see the image that is shown in Figure 5.19.

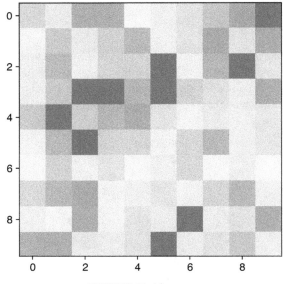

FIGURE 5.19 A heat map.

SAVE PLOT AS A PNG FILE

Listing 5.23 displays the contents of `matplot2png.py` that shows you how to save a graphics image as a PNG file.

LISTING 5.23: matplot2png.py

```
import matplotlib.pyplot as plt
import numpy as np

outfile="graph1.png"

plt.figure()
plt.plot(range(6))

fig, ax = plt.subplots()

ax.plot([2, 3, 4, 5, 5, 6, 6],
        [5, 7, 1, 3, 4, 6 ,8])

ax.plot([1, 2, 3, 4, 5],
        [2, 3, 4, 5, 6])

x = np.linspace(0, 12, 100)
plt.plot(np.sin(x))
```

```
plt.plot(np.linspace(-4,4,50))

plt.savefig(outfile, dpi=300)
```

Listing 5.23 contains `import` statements, followed by the variable `outfile` that is initialized with the name of the PNG file that will be saved to the file system. The contents of the PNG file consist of a sine wave and a set of line segments. Launch the code in Listing 5.23 and you will see the image that is shown in Figure 5.20.

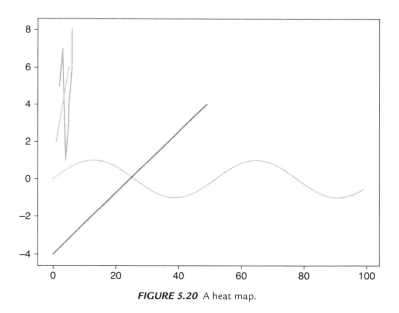

FIGURE 5.20 A heat map.

WORKING WITH SWEETVIZ

`SweetViz` is an open-source `Python` module that generates remarkably detailed visualizations in the form of HTML Web pages based on literally five lines of `Python` code.

As a simple illustration, Listing 5.24 shows the contents of `sweetviz1.py` that generates a visualization of various aspects of the `Iris` dataset that is available in Scikit-learn.

LISTING 5.24: sweetviz1.py

```
import sweetviz as sv
import seaborn as sns

df = sns.load_dataset('iris')
report = sv.analyze(df)
report.show_html()
```

Listing 5.24 starts with two `import` statements, followed an initialization of the variable `df` with the contents of the `Iris` dataset. The next code snippet initializes the variable report as the result of invoking the `analyze()` method in `SweetViz`, followed by a code snippet that generates an HTML Web page with the result of the analysis.

Now launch the code from the command line and you will see a new HTML Web page called `SWEETVIZ_REPORT.html` in the same directory. Figure 5.21 displays the contents of the Web page `SWEETVIZ_REPORT.html`.

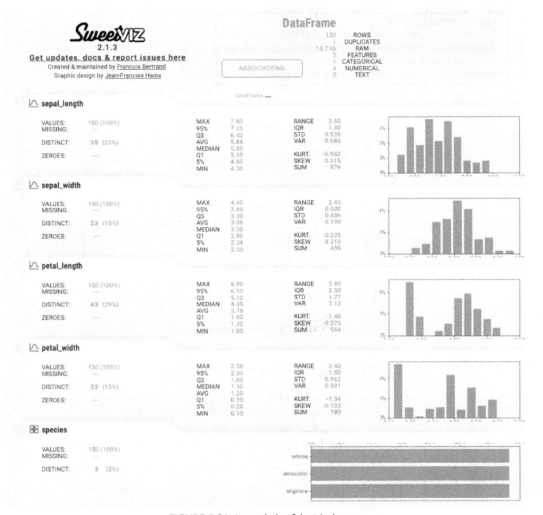

FIGURE 5.21 An analysis of the Iris dataset.

WORKING WITH SKIMPY

`Skimpy` is an open-source `Python` module that generates an analysis of a dataset directly from the command line: no `Python` code is required. Install `Skimpy` with the following command:

```
pip3 install skimpy
```

Launch the following command to analysis the `Titanic` dataset (or a dataset of your own choice) that redirects the output to a text file (the latter is optional):

```
skimpy titanic.csv >titanic_out.txt
```

Figure 5.22 displays the contents of the generated output from the preceding command.

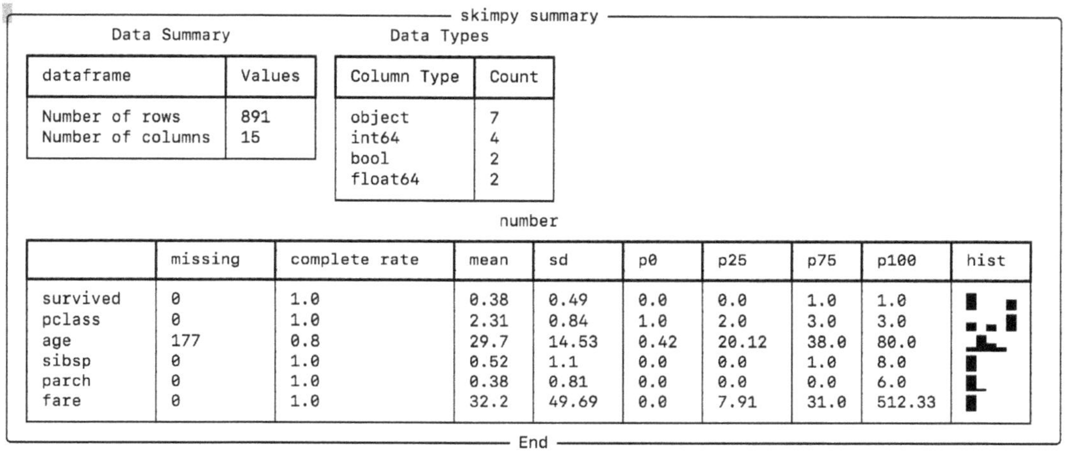

```
───────────────── skimpy summary ─────────────────
        Data Summary                   Data Types
┌──────────────────┬────────┐   ┌─────────────┬───────┐
│ dataframe        │ Values │   │ Column Type │ Count │
├──────────────────┼────────┤   ├─────────────┼───────┤
│ Number of rows   │ 891    │   │ object      │ 7     │
│ Number of columns│ 15     │   │ int64       │ 4     │
└──────────────────┴────────┘   │ bool        │ 2     │
                                 │ float64     │ 2     │
                                 └─────────────┴───────┘
                              number
```

	missing	complete rate	mean	sd	p0	p25	p75	p100	hist
survived	0	1.0	0.38	0.49	0.0	0.0	1.0	1.0	
pclass	0	1.0	2.31	0.84	1.0	2.0	3.0	3.0	
age	177	0.8	29.7	14.53	0.42	20.12	38.0	80.0	
sibsp	0	1.0	0.52	1.1	0.0	0.0	1.0	8.0	
parch	0	1.0	0.38	0.81	0.0	0.0	0.0	6.0	
fare	0	1.0	32.2	49.69	0.0	7.91	31.0	512.33	

```
──────────── End ────────────
```

FIGURE 5.22 An analysis of the Titanic dataset.

3D CHARTS IN Matplotlib

Listing 5.25 displays the contents of `matplot_3d.py` that illustrates how to render a 3D plot in `Matplotlib`.

LISTING 5.25: matplot_3d.py

```python
import matplotlib.pyplot as plt
import numpy as np

zline = np.linspace(0,40,1000)
xline = 2*np.sin(2*zline)
yline = 3*np.cos(3*zline)

ax = plt.axes(projection="3d")
ax.plot3D(xline,yline,zline,'red',linewidth=4)
plt.show()
```

Listing 5.25 contains `import` statements, followed by the variables `zline`, `xline`, and `yline` that are initialized via the `NumPy` methods `linspace()`, `sin()`, and `cos()`, respectively. The next portion of Listing 5.25 initializes the variable `ax` in order to display a 3D effort, which is rendered by the final code snippet. Launch the code in Listing 5.25 and you will see the image that is shown in Figure 5.23.

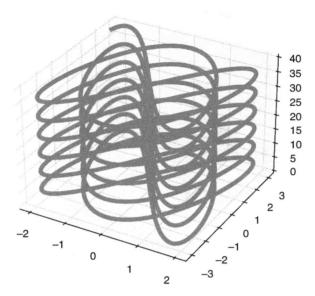

FIGURE 5.23 A 3D plot.

PLOTTING FINANCIAL DATA WITH MPLFINANCE

The section contains a `Python`-based code sample that shows you how to plot financial data for a given stock. First, make sure that you have the necessary `Python` library installed, as shown here:

```
pip3 install mplfinance
```

Listing 5.26 displays the contents of `financial_mpl.py` and illustrates how to plot financial data in `Matplotlib`.

LISTING 5.26: financial_mpl.py

```
import matplotlib.pyplot as plt
import pandas as pd

csvfile="aapl.csv"
daily = pd.read_csv(csvfile,index_col=0,parse_dates=True)
daily.index.name = 'Date'

print("daily.head():")
print(daily.head())
print()
print("daily.tail():")
print(daily.tail())
import mplfinance as mpf
mpf.plot(daily)
```

```
#Plot types: ohlc, candle, line, renko, and pnf
```

Listing 5.26 contains `import` statements, followed by the variable `csvfile` that contains AAPL data for the years 2017 and 2018. Next, the variable `daily` is initialized with the contents of `aapl.csv`, followed by a block of code that prints the first 5 lines and the final 5 lines of data in `aapl.csv`.

The final code snippet invokes the `plot()` method of the class `mpf` (which is imported from `mplfinance`) in order to render a chart. Now launch the code in Listing 5.26 and you will see the following output:

```
daily.head():
                 Open         High     ...    Adj Close     Volume
Date                                    ...
2017-01-03   115.800003   116.330002   ...   114.311760   28781900
2017-01-04   115.849998   116.510002   ...   114.183815   21118100
2017-01-05   115.919998   116.860001   ...   114.764473   22193600
2017-01-06   116.779999   118.160004   ...   116.043915   31751900
2017-01-09   117.949997   119.430000   ...   117.106812   33561900

[5 rows x 6 columns]

daily.tail():
                 Open         High     ...    Adj Close     Volume
Date                                    ...
2018-01-12   176.179993   177.360001   ...   177.089996   25418100
2018-01-16   177.899994   179.389999   ...   176.190002   29565900
2018-01-17   176.149994   179.250000   ...   179.100006   34386800
2018-01-18   179.369995   180.100006   ...   179.259995   31193400
2018-01-19   178.610001   179.580002   ...   178.460007   31269600

[5 rows x 6 columns]
```

Figure 5.24 displays a plot of financial data based on the code in Listing 5.29.

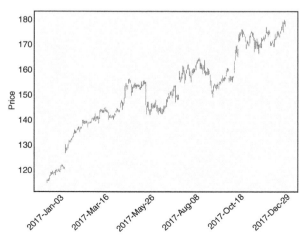

FIGURE 5.24 Plot of financial data.

CHARTS AND GRAPHS WITH DATA FROM Sqlite3

Listing 5.27 displays the contents of `rainfall_multiple.py` that shows you how to generate multiple charts and graphs from that that is extracted from a `sqlite3` database.

LISTING 5.27: rainfall_multiple.py

```python
import sqlite3
import pandas as pd
import matplotlib.pyplot as plt

sql = """
  SELECT
    cast(centimeters/5.00 as int)*5 as cent_floor,
    count(*) as count
FROM rainfall
GROUP by 1
ORDER by 1;
"""

con = sqlite3.connect("mytools.db")
df = pd.read_sql_query(sql, con)
con.close()

######################################
# generate 7 types of charts/graphs
# and save them as PNG or TIFF files
######################################
df.hist(column='count', bins=14, grid=False, rwidth=.8, color='red')
plt.savefig("rainfall_histogram.tiff")

df.plot.pie(y='count',figsize=(8,6))
plt.savefig("rainfall_pie.png")

df.plot.line(y='count',figsize=(8,6))
plt.savefig("rainfall_line.png")

df.plot.scatter(y='count',x='cent_floor',figsize=(8,6))
plt.savefig("rainfall_scatter.png")

df.plot.box(figsize=(8,6))
plt.savefig("rainfall_box.png")

df.plot.hexbin(x='count', y='cent_floor',gridsize=30, figsize=(8,6))
plt.savefig("rainfall_hexbin.png")
df["cent_floor"].plot.kde()
plt.savefig("rainfall_kde.png")

df["count"].hist()
df.plot.line(x='count', y='cent_floor', figsize=(8,6))
df.plot.scatter(x='count', y='cent_floor', figsize=(8,6))
df.plot.box(figsize=(8,6))
```

```
df.plot.hexbin(x='count', y='cent_floor',gridsize=30, figsize=(8,6))
df.plot.pie(y='cost', figsize=(8, 6))
df["cent_floor"].plot.kde()
```

Listing 5.27 contains several import statements and then initializes the variable sql with a SQL statement that selects data from the rainfall table. The next portion of Listing 5.27 initializes the variable con for accessing the mytools.db database, and then populates the Pandas data frame df with the result of executing the SQL statement contained in the variable sql.

The next portion of Listing 5.27 contains pairs of code snippets for rendering charts and graphs of the type of histogram, pie, line, scatter, box, hexbin, and kde, respectively. Launch the code in Listing 5.27 and you will see the following output:

```
=> Histogram of Rainfall:
      cent_floor   count
0           0       14
1           5       13
2          10        4
3          15       10
4          20        3
5          25        6
6          30        3
7          35        6
8          40        2
9          45        1
10         50        1
11         55        1
12         60        1
```

In addition to the preceding output, you will also see the following files in the same directory where you launched the code in Listing 5.27:

```
rainfall_histogram.tiff
rainfall_pie.png
rainfall_line.png
rainfall_scatter.png
rainfall_box.png
rainfall_hexbin.png
rainfall_kde.png
```

SUMMARY

This chapter started with a very short introduction to Matplotlib, along with code samples that displayed the available styles in colors in Matplotlib.

Then you learned how to render horizontal lines, slanted lines, parallel lines, and a grid of points. In addition, you learned how to load images, display checkerboard patterns, and plot trigonometric functions. Moreover, you saw how to render histograms, bar charts, pie charts, and heat maps.

Next, you saw how to create a 3D plot, how to render financial data, and render a chart with data from a sqlite3 database.

## CHAPTER 6

SEABORN FOR DATA VISUALIZATION

This chapter introduces several tools for data visualization, including `Seaborn`, `Bokeh`, and `YellowBrick`. This chapter also contains a gentle introduction to `Scikit-learn` (which is typically imported as `sklearn`).

The first part of the chapter introduces you to `Seaborn` for data visualization, which is a layer above `Matplotlib`. Although `Seaborn` does not have all of the features that are available in `Matplotlib`, `Seaborn` provides an easier set of APIs for rendering charts and graphs.

The second portion of this chapter contains a very short introduction to `Bokeh`, along with a code sample that illustrates how to create a more artistic graphics effect with relative ease in `Bokeh`.

The third part of the chapter introduces you to `Scikit-learn`, which is a very powerful `Python` library that supports many machine learning algorithms and also supports visualization. If you are new to machine learning, fear not: *this section does not require a background in machine learning in order to understand the Python code samples.*

WORKING WITH SEABORN

`Seaborn` is a `Python` library for data visualization that also provides a high-level interface to `Matplotlib`. `Seaborn` is easier to work with than `Matplotlib`, and actually extends `Matplotlib`, but keep in mind that `Seaborn` is not as powerful as `Matplotlib`.

`Seaborn` addresses two challenges of `Matplotlib`. The first involves the default `Matplotlib` parameters. `Seaborn` works with different parameters, which provides greater flexibility than the default rendering of `Matplotlib` plots. `Seaborn` addresses the limitations of the `Matplotlib` default values for features such as colors, tick marks on the upper and right axes, and the style (among others).

In addition, `Seaborn` makes it easier to plot entire data frames (somewhat like `Pandas`) than doing so in `Matplotlib`. Nevertheless, since `Seaborn` extends `Matplotlib`, knowledge of the latter is advantageous and will simplify your learning curve.

Features of Seaborn

`Seaborn` provides a nice set of features and useful methods to control the display of data, some of which are listed here:

- scale `Seaborn` plots
- set the plot style
- set the figure size
- rotate label text
- set xlim or ylim
- set log scale
- add titles

Some useful `Seaborn` methods are listed here:

```
plt.xlabel()
plt.ylabel()
plt.annotate()
plt.legend()
plt.ylim()
plt.savefig()
```

`Seaborn` supports various built-in datasets, just like `NumPy` and `Pandas`, including the `Iris` dataset and the `Titanic` dataset, both of which you will see in subsequent sections. As a starting point, the next section contains the code that displays all the available built-in datasets in `Seaborn`.

SEABORN DATASET NAMES

Listing 6.1 displays the contents dataset_names.py that displays the Seaborn built-in datasets, one of which we will use in a subsequent section in order to render a heat map in Seaborn.

LISTING 6.1: dataset_names.py

```
import seaborn as sns

names = sns.get_dataset_names()
for name in names:
  print("name:",name)
```

Listing 6.1 contains an `import` statement and then the variable `names` that is initialized with the set of built-in dataset names in `Seaborn`. The next portion contains a loop that iterates through the dataset names in the variable `names` and displays their values. Launch the code in Listing 6.1 and you will see the following output:

```
name: anagrams
name: anscombe
name: attention
name: brain_networks
name: car_crashes
```

```
name: diamonds
name: dots
name: exercise
name: flights
name: fmri
name: gammas
name: geyser
name: iris
name: mpg
name: penguins
name: planets
name: taxis
name: tips
name: titanic
```

The three-line code sample in the next section shows you how to display the rows in the built-in "tips" dataset.

Seaborn BUILT-IN DATASETS

Listing 6.2 displays the contents of seaborn_tips.py that illustrates how to read the tips dataset into a data frame and display the first five rows of the dataset.

LISTING 6.2: seaborn_tips.py

```
import seaborn as sns

df = sns.load_dataset("tips")
print(df.head())
```

Listing 6.2 is very simple: after importing seaborn, the variable df is initialized with the data in the built-in dataset tips, and the print() statement displays the first five rows of df. Note that the load_dataset() API searches for online or built-in datasets. The output from Listing 6.2 is here:

```
   total_bill   tip     sex smoker  day    time  size
0       16.99  1.01  Female     No  Sun  Dinner     2
1       10.34  1.66    Male     No  Sun  Dinner     3
2       21.01  3.50    Male     No  Sun  Dinner     3
3       23.68  3.31    Male     No  Sun  Dinner     2
4       24.59  3.61  Female     No  Sun  Dinner     4
```

THE IRIS DATASET IN SEABORN

Listing 6.3 displays the contents of seaborn_iris.py that illustrates how to plot the Iris dataset.

LISTING 6.2: seaborn_iris.py

```
import seaborn as sns
import matplotlib.pyplot as plt
```

```
# Load iris data
iris = sns.load_dataset("iris")

# Construct iris plot
sns.swarmplot(x="species", y="petal_length", data=iris)

# Show plot
plt.show()
```

Listing 6.3 imports `Seaborn` and `matplotlib.pyplot` and then initializes the variable `iris` with the contents of the built-in `Iris` dataset. Next, the `swamplot()` API displays a graph with the horizontal axis labeled `species`, the vertical axis labeled `petal_length`, and the displayed points are from the `Iris` dataset.

Figure 6.1 displays the images in the `Iris` dataset based on the code in Listing 6.3.

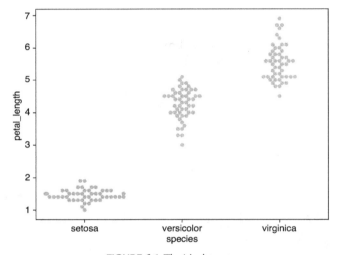

FIGURE 6.1 The Iris dataset.

THE TITANIC DATASET IN SEABORN

Listing 6.4 displays the contents of `seaborn_titanic_plot.py` that illustrates how to plot the `Titanic` dataset.

LISTING 6.4: seaborn_titanic_plot.py

```
import matplotlib.pyplot as plt
import seaborn as sns

titanic = sns.load_dataset("titanic")
g = sns.factorplot("class", "survived", "sex", data=titanic, kind="bar",
palette="muted", legend=False)

plt.show()
```

Listing 6.4 contains the same `import` statements as Listing 6.3, and then initializes the variable `titanic` with the contents of the built-in `Titanic` dataset. Next, the `factorplot()` API displays a graph with dataset attributes that are listed in the API invocation. Figure 6.2 displays a plot of the data in the `Titanic` dataset based on the code in Listing 6.4.

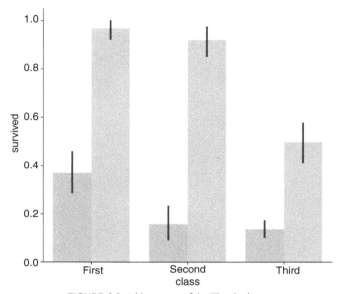

FIGURE 6.2 A histogram of the Titanic dataset.

EXTRACTING DATA FROM TITANIC DATASET IN SEABORN (1)

Listing 6.5 displays the contents of `seaborn_titanic.py` that illustrates how to extract subsets of data from the `Titanic` dataset.

LISTING 6.5: seaborn_titanic.py

```
import matplotlib.pyplot as plt
import seaborn as sns

titanic = sns.load_dataset("titanic")
print("titanic info:")
titanic.info()

print("first five rows of titanic:")
print(titanic.head())

print("first four ages:")
print(titanic.loc[0:3,'age'])

print("fifth passenger:")
print(titanic.iloc[4])
```

```
#print("first five ages:")
#print(titanic['age'].head())

#print("first five ages and gender:")
#print(titanic[['age','sex']].head())

#print("descending ages:")
#print(titanic.sort_values('age', ascending = False).head())

#print("older than 50:")
#print(titanic[titanic['age'] > 50])

#print("embarked (unique):")
#print(titanic['embarked'].unique())

#print("survivor counts:")
#print(titanic['survived'].value_counts())

#print("counts per class:")
#print(titanic['pclass'].value_counts())

#print("max/min/mean/median ages:")
#print(titanic['age'].max())
#print(titanic['age'].min())
#print(titanic['age'].mean())
#print(titanic['age'].median())
```

Listing 6.5 contains the same import statements as Listing 6.4, and then initializes the variable titanic with the contents of the built-in Titanic dataset. The next portion of Listing 6.5 displays various aspects of the Titanic dataset, such as its structure, the first five rows, the first four ages, and the details of the fifth passenger.

As you can see, there is a large block of "commented out" code that you can uncomment in order to see the associated output, such as age, gender, persons over 50, unique rows, and so forth. The output from Listing 6.5 is here:

```
#print(titanic['age'].mean())
titanic info:
<class 'pandas.core.frame.Data frame'>
RangeIndex: 891 entries, 0 to 890
Data columns (total 15 columns):
survived       891 non-null int64
pclass         891 non-null int64
sex            891 non-null object
age            714 non-null float64
sibsp          891 non-null int64
parch          891 non-null int64
fare           891 non-null float64
embarked       889 non-null object
class          891 non-null category
who            891 non-null object
adult_male     891 non-null bool
deck           203 non-null category
embark_town    889 non-null object
```

```
alive            891 non-null object
alone            891 non-null bool
dtypes: bool(2), category(2), float64(2), int64(4), object(5)
memory usage: 80.6+ KB
first five rows of titanic:
   survived   pclass     sex    age  sibsp  parch      fare embarked  class \
0         0        3    male   22.0      1      0    7.2500        S  Third
1         1        1  female   38.0      1      0   71.2833        C  First
2         1        3  female   26.0      0      0    7.9250        S  Third
3         1        1  female   35.0      1      0   53.1000        S  First
4         0        3    male   35.0      0      0    8.0500        S  Third

       who  adult_male deck  embark_town alive  alone
0      man        True  NaN  Southampton    no  False
1    woman       False    C    Cherbourg   yes  False
2    woman       False  NaN  Southampton   yes   True
3    woman       False    C  Southampton   yes  False
4      man        True  NaN  Southampton    no   True
first four ages:
0    22.0
1    38.0
2    26.0
3    35.0
Name: age, dtype: float64
fifth passenger:
survived                  0
pclass                    3
sex                    male
age                      35
sibsp                     0
parch                     0
fare                   8.05
embarked                  S
class                 Third
who                     man
adult_male             True
deck                    NaN
embark_town     Southampton
alive                    no
alone                  True
Name: 4, dtype: object
counts per class:
3    491
1    216
2    184
Name: pclass, dtype: int64
max/min/mean/median ages:
80.0
0.42
29.69911764705882
28.0
```

EXTRACTING DATA FROM TITANIC DATASET IN Seaborn (2)

Listing 6.6 displays the contents of `seaborn_titanic2.py` that illustrates how to extract subsets of data from the `Titanic` dataset.

LISTING 6.6: seaborn_titanic2.py

```
import matplotlib.pyplot as plt
import seaborn as sns

titanic = sns.load_dataset("titanic")

# Returns a scalar
# titanic.ix[4, 'age']
print("age:",titanic.at[4, 'age'])

# Returns a Series of name 'age', and the age values associated
# to the index labels 4 and 5
# titanic.ix[[4, 5], 'age']
print("series:",titanic.loc[[4, 5], 'age'])

# Returns a Series of name '4', and the age and fare values
# associated to that row.
# titanic.ix[4, ['age', 'fare']]
print("series:",titanic.loc[4, ['age', 'fare']])

# Returns a Data frame with rows 4 and 5, and columns 'age' and 'fare'
# titanic.ix[[4, 5], ['age', 'fare']]
print("data frame:",titanic.loc[[4, 5], ['age', 'fare']])

query = titanic[
    (titanic.sex == 'female')
    & (titanic['class'].isin(['First', 'Third']))
    & (titanic.age > 30)
    & (titanic.survived == 0)
]
print("query:",query)
```

Listing 6.6 contains the same `import` statements as Listing 6.5, and then initializes the variable `titanic` with the contents of the built-in `Titanic` dataset. The next code snippet displays the age of the passenger with index 4 in the dataset (which equals 35).

The following code snippet displays the ages of passengers with index values 4 and 5 in the dataset:

```
print("series:",titanic.loc[[4, 5], 'age'])
```

The next snippet displays the age and fare of the passenger with index 4 in the dataset, followed by another code snippet displays the age and fare of the passengers with index 4 and index 5 in the dataset.

The final portion of Listing 6.6 is the most interesting part: it defines a variable `query` as shown here:

```
query = titanic[
    (titanic.sex == 'female')
    & (titanic['class'].isin(['First', 'Third']))
    & (titanic.age > 30)
    & (titanic.survived == 0)
]
```

The preceding code block will retrieve the female passengers who are in either first class or third class, and who are also over 30, and who did not survive the accident. The entire output from Listing 6.6 is here:

```
age: 35.0
series: 4    35.0
5     NaN
Name: age, dtype: float64
series: age        35
fare      8.05
Name: 4, dtype: object
data frame:     age     fare
4  35.0  8.0500
5   NaN  8.4583
query:      survived  pclass    sex   age  sibsp  parch    fare embarked
class  \
18           0       3  female  31.0      1      0  18.0000       S  Third
40           0       3  female  40.0      1      0   9.4750       S  Third
132          0       3  female  47.0      1      0  14.5000       S  Third
167          0       3  female  45.0      1      4  27.9000       S  Third
177          0       1  female  50.0      0      0  28.7125       C  First
254          0       3  female  41.0      0      2  20.2125       S  Third
276          0       3  female  45.0      0      0   7.7500       S  Third
362          0       3  female  45.0      0      1  14.4542       C  Third
396          0       3  female  31.0      0      0   7.8542       S  Third
503          0       3  female  37.0      0      0   9.5875       S  Third
610          0       3  female  39.0      1      5  31.2750       S  Third
638          0       3  female  41.0      0      5  39.6875       S  Third
657          0       3  female  32.0      1      1  15.5000       Q  Third
678          0       3  female  43.0      1      6  46.9000       S  Third
736          0       3  female  48.0      1      3  34.3750       S  Third
767          0       3  female  30.5      0      0   7.7500       Q  Third
885          0       3  female  39.0      0      5  29.1250       Q  Third
```

VISUALIZING A PANDAS DATASET IN SEABORN

Listing 6.7 displays the contents of `pandas_seaborn.py` that illustrates how to display a Pandas dataset in Seaborn.

LISTING 6.7: pandas_seaborn.py

```
import pandas as pd
import random
import matplotlib.pyplot as plt
import seaborn as sns

df = pd.Data frame()

df['x'] = random.sample(range(1, 100), 25)
df['y'] = random.sample(range(1, 100), 25)

print("top five elements:")
print(df.head())
```

```
# display a density plot
#sns.kdeplot(df.y)

# display a density plot
#sns.kdeplot(df.y, df.x)

#sns.distplot(df.x)

# display a histogram
#plt.hist(df.x, alpha=.3)
#sns.rugplot(df.x)

# display a boxplot
#sns.boxplot([df.y, df.x])

# display a violin plot
#sns.violinplot([df.y, df.x])

# display a heatmap
#sns.heatmap([df.y, df.x], annot=True, fmt="d")

# display a cluster map
#sns.clustermap(df)

# display a scatterplot of the data points
sns.lmplot('x', 'y', data=df, fit_reg=False)
plt.show()
```

Listing 6.7 contains several familiar `import` statements, followed by the initialization of the Pandas variable df as a `Pandas` DataFrame. The next two code snippets initialize the columns and rows of the dataframe and the `print()` statement display the first five rows.

For your convenience, Listing 6.7 contains an assortment of "commented out" code snippets that use `Seaborn` in order to render a density plot, a histogram, a boxplot, a violin plot, a heatmap, and a cluster. Uncomment the portions that interest you in order to see the associated plot. The output from Listing 6.7 is here:

```
top five elements:
     x   y
0   52  34
1   31  47
2   23  18
3   34  70
4   71   1
```

Figure 6.3 displays a plot of the data in the `Titanic` dataset based on the code in Listing 6.7.

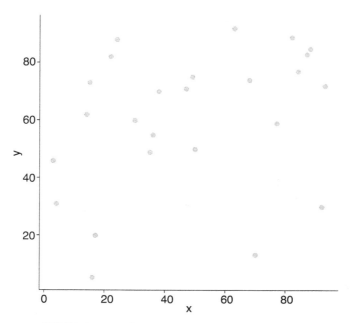

FIGURE 6.3 A Pandas DataFrame displayed via `Seaborn`.

SEABORN HEAT MAPS

Listing 6.8 displays the contents `heatmap1.py` that displays a heat map from a `Seaborn` built-in dataset.

LISTING 6.8: heatmap1.py

```
import seaborn as sns
import matplotlib.pyplot as plt

data = sns.load_dataset("flights")
data = data.pivot("month", "year", "passengers")

print("data.head():")
print(data.head())

sns.heatmap(data)
plt.show()
```

Listing 6.8 contains two `import` statements, followed by the variable data that is initialized with the contents of the `Seaborn` built-in dataset called `flights`. The next code snippet invokes the `pivot()` method that selects the attributes month, year, and passengers from the dataset. The next portion of code displays the first five rows of the dataset, followed by a code block that renders a heat map and you will see the following output:

```
data.head():
year    1949  1950  1951  1952  1953  1954  1955  1956  1957  1958  1959  1960
month
Jan      112   115   145   171   196   204   242   284   315   340   360   417
Feb      118   126   150   180   196   188   233   277   301   318   342   391
Mar      132   141   178   193   236   235   267   317   356   362   406   419
Apr      129   135   163   181   235   227   269   313   348   348   396   461
May      121   125   172   183   229   234   270   318   355   363   420   472
```

Figure 6.4 displays a heat map plot of the data in the `flights` dataset based on the code in Listing 6.8.

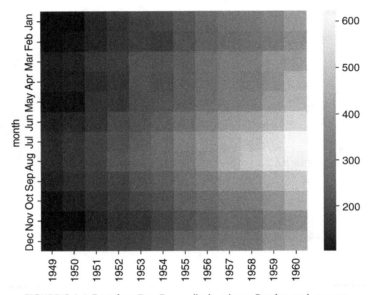

FIGURE 6.4 A Pandas DataFrame displayed as a Seaborn heat map.

SEABORN PAIR PLOTS

This section contains several Python-based code samples that show you how to use the Seaborn `pair_plot()` method to render pair plots.

Listing 6.9 displays the contents `seborn_pairplot1.py` that displays a pair plot with the Iris dataset.

LISTING 6.9: seaborn_pairplot1.py

```
import seaborn as sns
import pandas as pd
import matplotlib.pyplot as plt

# load iris data
iris = sns.load_dataset("iris")

df = pd.Data frame(iris)
```

```
# construct and display iris plot
g = sns.pairplot(df, height=2, aspect=1.0)
plt.show()
```

Listing 6.9 starts with `import` statements, followed by the variable `iris` that is initialized with the contents of the `Seaborn` built-in dataset called `iris`. The next code snippet initializes the variable df with the contents of the dataset. The final block of code generates a pair plot based on the contents of the variable df, and then displays the pair plot. Figure 6.5 displays a plot of the data in the `iris` dataset based on the code in Listing 6.9.

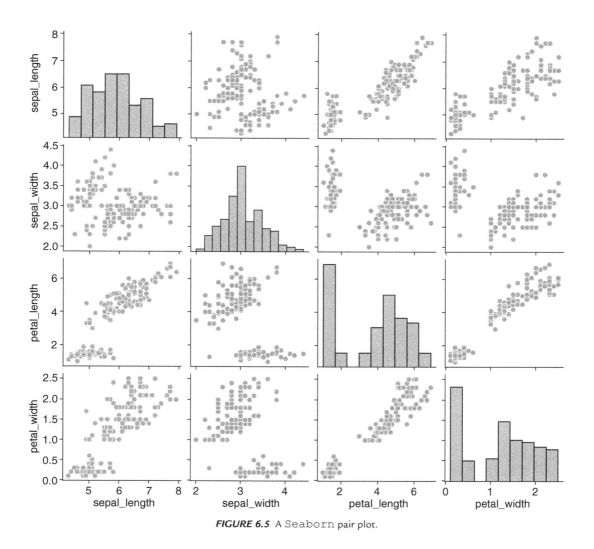

FIGURE 6.5 A `Seaborn` pair plot.

Listing 6.10 displays the contents `seborn_pairplot12.py` that renders a pair plot with the `Iris` dataset.

LISTING 6.10: seaborn_pairplot2.py

```python
import seaborn as sns
import pandas as pd
import matplotlib.pyplot as plt

# load iris data
iris = sns.load_dataset("iris")

df = pd.Data frame(iris)

# IRIS columns:
# sepal_length,sepal_width,petal_length,petal_width,species

# plot a subset of columns:
plot_columns = ['sepal_length', 'sepal_width']
sns.pairplot(df[plot_columns])
plt.show()

# specify KDE for the diagonal:
sns.pairplot(df[plot_columns], diag_kind='kde')
plt.show()
```

Listing 6.10 starts with the same code as Listing 6.9, followed by the variable `plot_columns` that contains sepal-related attributes from the iris dataset. The next code block generates a pair plot and displays its contents, followed by a code snippet that generates a pair plot with the argument `diag_kind` equal to kde.

Figure 6.6 displays a pair plot of the data in the `iris` dataset based on the code in Listing 6.10.

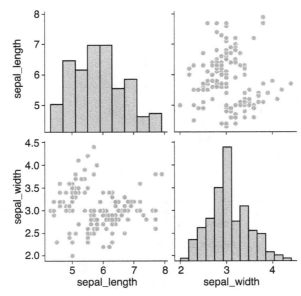

FIGURE 6.6 A Seaborn pair plot of Iris data.

Figure 6.7 displays a pair plot with the `kde` attribute value of the data in the `iris` dataset based on the code in Listing 6.10.

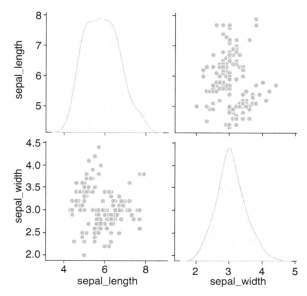

FIGURE 6.7 A Seaborn pair plot of Iris data with kde option.

WHAT IS BOKEH?

`Bokeh` is an open source project that depends on `Matplotlib` as well as `Scikit-learn`. As you will see in the subsequent code sample, `Bokeh` generates an HTML Web page that is based on `Python` code, and then launches that Web page in a browser. `Bokeh` and `D3.js` (which is a JavaScript layer of abstraction over `SVG`) both provide elegant visualization effects that support animation effects and user interaction.

`Bokeh` enables the rapid creation statistical visualization, and it works with other tools with as `Python` Flask and Django. In addition to `Python`, `Bokeh` supports Julia, Lua, and R (`JSON` files are generated instead of HTML Web pages).

Listing 6.11 displays the contents `bokeh_trig.py` that illustrates how to create a graphics effect using various Bokeh APIs.

LISTING 6.11: bokeh_trig.py

```
# pip3 install bokeh
from bokeh.plotting import figure, output_file, show
from bokeh.layouts import column
import bokeh.colors as colors
import numpy as np
import math
```

```
deltaY = 0.01
maxCount = 150
width  = 800
height = 400
band_width = maxCount/3

x = np.arange(0, math.pi*3, 0.05)
y1 = np.sin(x)
y2 = np.cos(x)

white = colors.RGB(255,255,255)

fig1 = figure(plot_width = width, plot_height = height)

for i in range(0,maxCount):
  rgb1 = colors.RGB(i*255/maxCount, 0, 0)
  rgb2 = colors.RGB(i*255/maxCount, i*255/maxCount, 0)
  fig1.line(x, y1-i*deltaY,line_width = 2, line_color = rgb1)
  fig1.line(x, y2-i*deltaY,line_width = 2, line_color = rgb2)

for i in range(0,maxCount):
  rgb1 = colors.RGB(0, 0, i*255/maxCount)
  rgb2 = colors.RGB(0, i*255/maxCount, 0)
  fig1.line(x, y1+i*deltaY,line_width = 2, line_color = rgb1)
  fig1.line(x, y2+i*deltaY,line_width = 2, line_color = rgb2)
  if (i % band_width == 0):
    fig1.line(x, y1+i*deltaY,line_width = 5, line_color = white)

show(fig1)
```

Listing 6.11 starts with a commented out `pip3` code snippet that you can launch from the command line in order to install `Bokeh` (in case you haven't done so already).

The next code block contains several `Bokeh`-related statements as well as `NumPy` and `Math`.

Notice that the variable `white` is defined as an (R,G,B) triple of integers, which represents the red, green, and blue components of a color. In particular, (255,255,255) represents the color white (check online if you are unfamiliar with RGB). The next portion of Listing 6.11 initializes some scalar variables that are used in the two `for` loops that are in the second half of Listing 6.11.

Next, the `NumPy` variable x is a range of values from 0 to `math.PI/3`, with an increment of 0.05 between successive values. Then the `NumPy` variables y1 and y2 are defined as the sine and cosine values, respectively, of the values in x. The next code snippet initializes the variable `fig1` that represents a context in which the graphics effects will be rendered. This completes the initialization of the variables that are used in the two `for` loops.

The next portion of Listing 6.11 contains the first `for` loop that creates a gradient-like effect by defining (R,G,B) triples whose values are based partially on the value of the loop variable i. For example, the variable `rgb1` ranges in a linear fashion from (0,0,0) to (255,0,0), which represent the colors black and red, respectively. The variable `rgb2` ranges in a linear fashion from (0,0,0) to (255,255,0), which represent the colors black and yellow, respectively. The next portion of the `for` loop contains two invocations of the `fig1.line()` API that renders a sine wave and a cosine wave in the context variable `fig1`.

The second `for` loop is similar to the first `for` loop: the main difference is that the variable `rgb1` varies from black to blue, and the variable `rgb2` variables from black to green. The final code snippet in Listing 6.13 invokes the `show()` method that generates an HTML Web page (with the same prefix as the `Python` file) and then launches the Web page in a browser.

Figure 6.8 displays the graphics effect based on the code in Listing 6.11. If this image is displayed as black and white, launch the code from the command line and you will see the gradient-like effects in the image.

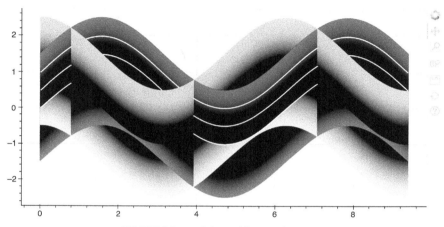

FIGURE 6.8 A Bokeh graphics sample.

The next section introduces you to `Scikit-learn`, which is a powerful `Python`-based library that supports many algorithms for machine learning. After you have read the short introduction, subsequent sections contain `Python` code samples that combine `Pandas`, `Matplotlib`, and `Scikit-learn` built-in datasets.

INTRODUCTION TO SCIKIT-LEARN

Since this book is about data visualization, you might be wondering why this chapter contains an introduction to `Scikit-learn` (also known as `Sklearn`). The reason is straightforward: the easy introduction to some `Scikit-learn` functionality is possible without a more formal learning process. In addition, this knowledge will bode well if you decide to delve into machine learning (and perhaps this section will provide additional motivation to do so).

However, a thorough understanding of `Scikit-learn` involves significantly more time and effort, especially if you plan to learn the details of the `Scikit-learn` machine learning algorithms. On the other hand, if you are not interested in learning about `Scikit-learn` at this point in time, you can skip this section and perhaps return to it when you are interested in learning this material.

`Scikit-learn` is Python's premier general-purpose machine learning library, and its home page is here:

https://scikit-learn.org/stable/

Before we discuss any code samples, please keep in mind that `Scikit-learn` is an immensely useful Python library that supports a huge number of machine learning algorithms. In particular, `Scikit-learn` supports many classification algorithms, such as logistic regression, naive Bayes, decision trees, random forests, and SVMs (support vector machines). Although entire books are available that are dedicated to `Scikit-learn`, this chapter contains only a few pages of Scikit-learn material.

If you decide that you want to acquire a deep level of knowledge about `Scikit-learn`, navigate to the Web pages that contain very detailed documentation for `Scikit-learn`. Moreover, if you have "how to" questions involving `Scikit-learn`, you can almost always find suitable answers on stack overflow (*https://stackoverflow.com/*).

`Scikit-learn` is well-suited for classification tasks as well as regression and clustering tasks in machine learning. `Scikit-learn` supports a vast collection of ML algorithms, including linear regression, logistic regression, kNN ("K nearest neighbor"), kMeans, decision trees, random forests, MLPs (multilayer perceptrons), and SVMs (support vector machines).

Moreover, `Scikit-learn` supports dimensionality reduction techniques such as PCA (principal component analysis), "hyper parameter" tuning, methods for scaling data, and is suitable for preprocessing data, cross-validation, and so forth.

Machine learning code samples often contain a combination of `Scikit-learn`, NumPy, Pandas, and Matplotlib. In addition, `Scikit-learn` provides various built-in datasets that we can display visually. One of those datasets is the `Digits` dataset, which is the topic of the next section.

The next section of this chapter provides several Python code samples that contain a combination of Pandas, Matplotlib, and the Scikit-learn built-in Digits dataset.

THE DIGITS DATASET IN `Scikit-learn`

The `Digits` dataset in `Scikit-learn` comprises 1797 small 8×8 images: each image is a hand-written digit, which is also the case for the `MNIST` dataset. Listing 6.12 displays the contents of `load_digits1.py` that illustrates how to plot the `Digits` dataset.

LISTING 6.12: load_digits1.py

```
from scikit-learn import datasets

# Load in the 'digits' data
digits = datasets.load_digits()

# Print the 'digits' data
print(digits)
```

Listing 6.12 is very straightforward: after importing the `datasets` module, the variable `digits` is initialized with the contents of the `Digits` dataset. The `print()` statement displays the contents of the `digits` variable, which is displayed here:

```
{images': array(
        [[[0.,   0.,   5., ...,       1.,   0.,   0.],
```

```
          [0.,    0.,   13.,   ...,   15.,    5.,    0.],
          [0.,    3.,   15.,   ...,   11.,    8.,    0.],
          ...,
          [0.,    4.,   11.,   ...,   12.,    7.,    0.],
          [0.,    2.,   14.,   ...,   12.,    0.,    0.],
          [0.,    0.,    6.,   ...,    0.,    0.,    0.]]),
'target': array([0, 1, 2, ..., 8, 9, 8]), 'frame': None, 'feature_
names': ['pixel_0_0', 'pixel_0_1', 'pixel_0_2', 'pixel_0_3',
'pixel_0_4', 'pixel_0_5', 'pixel_0_6', 'pixel_0_7', 'pixel_1_0',
'pixel_1_1', 'pixel_1_2', 'pixel_1_3', 'pixel_1_4', 'pixel_1_5',
'pixel_1_6', 'pixel_1_7', 'pixel_2_0', 'pixel_2_1', 'pixel_2_2',
'pixel_2_3', 'pixel_2_4', 'pixel_2_5', 'pixel_2_6', 'pixel_2_7',
'pixel_3_0', 'pixel_3_1', 'pixel_3_2', 'pixel_3_3', 'pixel_3_4',
'pixel_3_5', 'pixel_3_6', 'pixel_3_7', 'pixel_4_0', 'pixel_4_1',
'pixel_4_2', 'pixel_4_3', 'pixel_4_4', 'pixel_4_5', 'pixel_4_6',
'pixel_4_7', 'pixel_5_0', 'pixel_5_1', 'pixel_5_2', 'pixel_5_3',
'pixel_5_4', 'pixel_5_5', 'pixel_5_6', 'pixel_5_7', 'pixel_6_0',
'pixel_6_1', 'pixel_6_2', 'pixel_6_3', 'pixel_6_4', 'pixel_6_5',
'pixel_6_6', 'pixel_6_7', 'pixel_7_0', 'pixel_7_1', 'pixel_7_2',
'pixel_7_3', 'pixel_7_4', 'pixel_7_5', 'pixel_7_6', 'pixel_7_7'],
'target_names': array([0, 1, 2, 3, 4, 5, 6, 7, 8, 9]), 'images':
array([[[ 0.,    0.,    5.,   ...,    1.,    0.,    0.],
         [ 0.,    0.,   13.,   ...,   15.,    5.,    0.],
         [ 0.,    3.,   15.,   ...,   11.,    8.,    0.],
// data omitted for brevity
])}
```

Listing 6.13 displays the contents of `load_digits2.py` that illustrates how to plot one of the Digits dataset (which you can change in order to display a different digit).

LISTING 6.13: *load_digits2.py*

```
from sklearn.datasets import load_digits
from matplotlib import pyplot as plt

digits = load_digits()
#set interpolation='none'

fig = plt.figure(figsize=(3, 3))
plt.imshow(digits['images'][66], cmap="gray", interpolation='none')
plt.show()
```

Listing 6.13 imports the `load_digits` class from `Scikit-learn` in order to initialize the variable `digits` with the contents of the `Digits` dataset that is available in `Scikit-learn`. The next portion of Listing 6.13 initializes the variable `fig` and invokes the method `imshow()` of the `plt` class in order to display a number in the `Digits` dataset.

Figure 6.9 displays a plot of one of the digits in the `Digits` dataset based on the code in Listing 6.13.

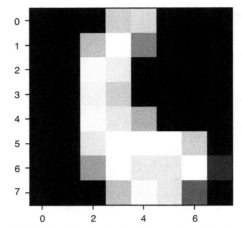

FIGURE 6.9 A digit in the Scikit-learn Digits dataset.

Listing 6.14 displays the contents of `load_digits3.py` that illustrates how to access the `Digits` dataset in `Scikit-learn`.

LISTING 6.14: load_digits3.py

```
from sklearn import datasets

digits = datasets.load_digits()
print("digits shape:",digits.images.shape)
print("data    shape:",digits.data.shape)

n_samples, n_features = digits.data.shape
print("(samples,features):", (n_samples, n_features))

import matplotlib.pyplot as plt
#plt.imshow(digits.images[-1], cmap=plt.cm.gray_r)
#plt.show()

plt.imshow(digits.images[0], cmap=plt.cm.binary,
interpolation='nearest')
plt.show()
```

Listing 6.14 starts with one `import` statement followed by the variable `digits that` contains the `Digits` dataset. The output from Listing 6.16 is here:

```
digits shape: (1797, 8, 8)
data    shape: (1797, 64)
(samples,features): (1797, 64)
```

Figure 6.10 displays an image in the `Digits` dataset based on the code in Listing 6.14.

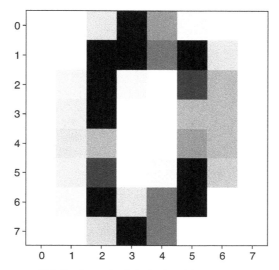

FIGURE 6.10 The digits in the Digits Dataset.

THE IRIS DATASET IN SCIKIT-LEARN

Listing 6.15 displays the contents of `scikit-learn_iris.py` that illustrates how to access the `Iris` dataset in `Scikit-learn`.

In addition to support for machine learning algorithms, `Scikit-learn` provides various built-in datasets that you can access with literally one line of code. In fact, Listing 6.15 displays the contents of `sklearn_iris1.py` that illustrates how you can easily load the `Iris` dataset into a `Pandas` DataFrame.

LISTING 6.15: sklearn_iris.py

```
import numpy as np
import pandas as pd
from scikit-learn.datasets import load_iris

iris = load_iris()

print("=> iris keys:")
for key in iris.keys():
  print(key)
print()

#print("iris dimensions:")
#print(iris.shape)
#print()

print("=> iris feature names:")
for feature in iris.feature_names:
```

```
    print(feature)
print()

X = iris.data[:, [2, 3]]
y = iris.target
print('=> Class labels:', np.unique(y))
print()

x_min, x_max = X[:, 0].min() - .5, X[:, 0].max() + .5
y_min, y_max = X[:, 1].min() - .5, X[:, 1].max() + .5

print("=> target:")
print(iris.target)
print()

print("=> all data:")
print(iris.data)
```

Listing 6.15 contains several import statements and then initializes the variable iris with the Iris dataset. Next, a for loop displays the keys in dataset, followed by another for loop that displays the feature names.

The next portion of Listing 6.15 initializes the variable X with the feature values in columns 2 and 3, and then initializes the variable y with the values of the target column.

The variable x_min is initialized as the minimum value of column 0 and then an additional 0.5 is subtracted from x_min. Similarly, the variable x_max is initialized as the maximum value of column 0 and then an additional 0.5 is added to x_max. The variables y_min and y_max are the counterparts to x_min and x_max, applied to column 1 instead of column 0.

Launch the code in Listing 6.15 and you will see the following output (truncated to save space):

```
=> iris keys:
data
target
target_names
DESCR
feature_names
filename

=> iris feature names:
sepal length (cm)
sepal width (cm)
petal length (cm)
petal width (cm)

=> Class labels: [0 1 2]

=> x_min: 0.5 x_max: 7.4
=> y_min: -0.4 y_max: 3.0
=> target:
[0 0 0 0 0 0 0 0 0 0 0 0 0 0 0 0 0 0 0 0 0 0 0 0 0 0 0 0 0 0 0 0 0 0 0 0 0
```

```
0 0 0 0 0 0 0 0 0 0 0 0 0 0 0 1 1 1 1 1 1 1 1 1 1 1 1 1 1 1 1 1 1 1 1 1 1 1 1 1 1 1
1 1 1 1 1 1 1 1 1 1 1 1 1 1 1 1 1 1 1 1 1 1 1 1 1 1 1 1 1 1 1 2 2 2 2 2 2 2 2 2 2 2
2 2 2 2 2 2 2 2 2 2 2 2 2 2 2 2 2 2 2 2 2 2 2 2 2 2 2 2 2 2 2 2 2 2 2 2 2 2 2 2 2 2
2 2]

=> all data:
[[5.1 3.5 1.4 0.2]
 [4.9 3.  1.4 0.2]
 [4.7 3.2 1.3 0.2]
 // details omitted for brevity
 [6.5 3.  5.2 2. ]
 [6.2 3.4 5.4 2.3]
 [5.9 3.  5.1 1.8]]
```

Scikit-Learn, Pandas, and the Iris Dataset

Listing 6.16 displays the contents of `pandas_iris.py` that illustrates how to load the contents of the `Iris` dataset (from Scikit-learn) into a `Pandas` DataFrame.

LISTING 6.16: pandas_iris.py

```
import numpy as np
import pandas as pd
from sklearn.datasets import load_iris

iris = load_iris()

print("=> IRIS feature names:")
for feature in iris.feature_names:
  print(feature)
print()

# Create a data frame with the feature variables
df = pd.Data frame(iris.data, columns=iris.feature_names)

print("=> number of rows:")
print(len(df))
print()

print("=> number of columns:")
print(len(df.columns))
print()

print("=> number of rows and columns:")
print(df.shape)
print()

print("=> number of elements:")
print(df.size)
print()

print("=> IRIS details:")
print(df.info())
print()
print("=> top five rows:")
print(df.head())
```

```
print()

X = iris.data[:, [2, 3]]
y = iris.target
print('=> Class labels:', np.unique(y))
```

Listing 6.16 contains several `import` statements and then initializes the variable `iris` with the Iris dataset. Next, a `for` loop displays the feature names. The next code snippet initializes the variable `df` as a `Pandas` DataFrame that contains the data from the `Iris` dataset.

The next block of code invokes some attributes and methods of a `Pandas` DataFrame to display the number of row, columns, and elements in the data frame, as well as the details of the `Iris` dataset, the first five rows, and the unique labels in the `Iris` dataset. Launch the code in Listing 6.16 and you will see the following output:

```
=> IRIS feature names:
sepal length (cm)
sepal width (cm)
petal length (cm)
petal width (cm)

=> number of rows:
150

=> number of columns:
4

=> number of rows and columns:
(150, 4)

=> number of elements:
600

=> IRIS details:
<class 'pandas.core.frame.Data frame'>
RangeIndex: 150 entries, 0 to 149
Data columns (total 4 columns):
sepal length (cm)    150 non-null float64
sepal width (cm)     150 non-null float64
petal length (cm)    150 non-null float64
petal width (cm)     150 non-null float64
dtypes: float64(4)
memory usage: 4.8 KB
None

=> top five rows:
   sepal length (cm)  sepal width (cm)  petal length (cm)  petal width (cm)
0                5.1               3.5                1.4               0.2
1                4.9               3.0                1.4               0.2
2                4.7               3.2                1.3               0.2
3                4.6               3.1                1.5               0.2
4                5.0               3.6                1.4               0.2

=> Class labels: [0 1 2]
```

ADVANCED TOPICS IN SEABORN

Listing 6.17 displays the contents `sns_kde_plot1.py` that displays a kde plot.

LISTING 6.17: sns_kde_plot1.py

```
import numpy as np
import matplotlib.pyplot as plt
import seaborn as sns

np.random.seed(1)
numerical_1 = np.random.randn(400)

np.random.seed(2)
numerical_2 = np.random.randn(400)

fig, ax = plt.subplots(figsize=(6,6))

sns.kdeplot(x=numerical_1,
            y= numerical_2,
            ax=ax,
            shade=True,
            color="blue",
            bw=1)
plt.show()
```

Listing 6.17 contains several `import` statements and then initializes the variables `numerical_1` and `numerical_2` with a set of 400 randomly generated numbers. The next code snippet initializes the figure-related variables `fig` and `ax`.

The next code snippet invokes the `kdeplot()` method of `Seaborn` and uses the values in `numerical_1` and `numerical_2` as values for the horizontal and vertical axes, respectively. The final code snippet displays the chart that is generated by the `kdeplot()` method. Now launch the code in Listing 6.17 and you will see the generated chart.

Figure 6.11 displays a plot of the data in the `Titanic` dataset based on the code in Listing 6.17.

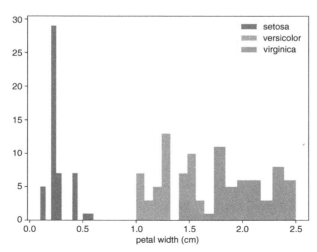

FIGURE 6.11 A Pandas DataFrame displayed via `Seaborn`.

Listing 6.18 displays the contents `sns_line_barchart1.py` that displays a line graph and a bar chart.

LISTING 6.18: sns_line_barchart1.py

```
import numpy as np

import seaborn as sns
import matplotlib.pyplot as plt

sns.set(style="white", rc={"lines.linewidth": 3})
fig, ax1 = plt.subplots(figsize=(4,4))
ax2 = ax1.twinx()
sns.barplot(x=['A','B','C','D'],
            y=[100,200,135,98],
            color='#004488',
            ax=ax1)

sns.lineplot(x=['A','B','C','D'],
             y=[4,2,5,3],
             color='r',
             marker="o",
             ax=ax2)

plt.show()
```

Listing 6.18 contains several `import` statements and then initializes the figure-related variables `fig` and `ax`, followed by the variable `ax2` that is initialized by invoking the `twinx()` method of `ax1`.

The next two code blocks generate a bar plot and a line plot, respectively, using hardcoded values for x and y. The next code snippet displays the generated bar chart and line plot. Figure 6.12 displays a bar chart and a line plot of the data in Listing 6.18.

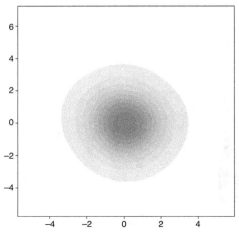

FIGURE 6.12 A bar chart and line graph.

SUMMARY

This chapter started with some basic features of `Seaborn`, which is an extension of `Matplotlib`. You saw examples of plotting lines and histograms, and also how to plot a `Pandas` DataFrame using `Seaborn`.

Next, you learned about `Bokeh`, along with an example of rendering graphics in `Bokeh`. Furthermore, you learned about `SVG` and how to render various 2D shapes, such as line segments, rectangles, circles, Bezier curves, and bar charts.

You also learned about `Scikit-learn`, including examples of working with the `Digits` and `Iris` datasets, and also how to process images. Finally, you learned how to render a bar chart and a line graph in `Scikit-learn`.

SVG AND *D3*

This appendix gives you an overview of SVG with SVG code samples that illustrate how to render various 2D shapes. SVG is an XML-based technology with support for linear gradients, radial gradients, filter effects, transforms (translate, scale, skew, and rotate), and animation effects using an XML-based syntax. Although SVG does not support 3D effects (which are available in CSS3), SVG provides some functionality that is unavailable in CSS3, such as support for arbitrary polygons, elliptic arcs, and quadratic and cubic Bézier curves.

As you will soon discover, it's possible to reference SVG documents in CSS selectors via the CSS url() function, which means you can harness the power of SVG via CSS selectors. Moreover, you can create HTML Web pages that contain a combination of D3, CSS, and pure SVG.

After you have finished reading this appendix, you will know how to use SVG elements and the required attributes for creating a variety of 2D shapes. You will also understand how to convert an SVG document into its D3 counterpart (which frequently involves the D3 .attr() method).

Please keep in mind the following points before you read this appendix. First, this appendix does not contain any tutorial-based content regarding XML, CSS3, or XSL stylesheets. However, there are plenty of online tutorials that can help you learn the basic concepts with illustrative examples. Second, a number of SVG-based code samples that are discussed in the first half of this appendix are accompanied by their corresponding D3-based counterparts, so you can choose the solution based on your preference of SVG or D3.

BASIC TWO-DIMENSIONAL SHAPES IN SVG

This section shows you how to render line segments and rectangles in SVG documents. As a simple example, SVG supports a `<line>` element for rendering line segments, and its syntax looks like this:

```
<line x1="20" y1="20" x2="100" y2="150".../>
```

An SVG `<line>` element renders line segments that connect the two points (x1,y1) and (x2,y2).

SVG supports a `<rect>` element for rendering rectangles, and its syntax looks like this:

```
<rect width="200" height="50" x="20" y="50".../>
```

The SVG `<rect>` element renders a rectangle whose width and height are specified in the `width` and `height` attributes. The upper-left vertex of the rectangle is specified by the point with coordinates `(x,y)`.

Listing A.1 displays the contents of `BasicShapes1.svg` that illustrates how to render line segments and rectangles.

LISTING A.1: BasicShapes1.svg

```
<?xml version="1.0" encoding="iso-8859-1"?>
<!DOCTYPE svg PUBLIC "-//W3C//DTD SVG 20001102//EN"
 "http://www.w3.org/TR/2000/CR-SVG-20001102/DTD/svg-20001102.dtd">

<svg xmlns="http://www.w3.org/2000/svg"
     xmlns:xlink="http://www.w3.org/1999/xlink"
     width="100%" height="100%">
 <g>
   <!-- left-side figures -->
   <line x1="20" y1="20" x2="220" y2="20"
         stroke="blue" stroke-width="4"/>

   <line x1="20" y1="40" x2="220" y2="40"
         stroke="red" stroke-width="10"/>

   <rect width="200" height="50" x="20" y="70"
         fill="red" stroke="black" stroke-width="4"/>

   <path d="M20,150 l200,0 10,50 l-200,0 z"
         fill="blue" stroke="red" stroke-width="4"/>

   <!-- right-side figures -->
   <path d="M250,20 l200,0 l-100,50 z"
         fill="blue" stroke="red" stroke-width="4"/>

   <path d="M300,100 l100,0 150,50 l-50,50 l-100,0 l-50,-50 z"
         fill="yellow" stroke="red" stroke-width="4"/>
 </g>
</svg>
```

The first SVG `<line>` element in Listing A.1 specifies the color `blue` and a `stroke-width` (i.e., line width) of 4, whereas the second SVG `<line>` element specifies the color `red` and a `stroke-width` of 10.

Notice that the first SVG `<rect>` element renders a rectangle that looks the same (except for the color) as the second SVG `<line>` element, which shows that it's possible to use different SVG elements to render a rectangle (or a line segment).

The SVG `<path>` element is probably the most flexible and powerful element because you can create arbitrarily complex shapes based on a concatenation of other SVG elements. Later in this appendix you will see an example of how to render multiple Bézier curves by means of an SVG <path> element.

An SVG <path> element contains a d attribute that specifies the points in the desired path. For example, the first SVG <path> element in Listing A.1 contains the following d attribute:

```
d="M20,150 l200,0 10,50 l-200,0 z"
```

This is how to interpret the contents of the d attribute:

- move to the absolute location point (20,150)
- draw a horizontal line segment 200 pixels to the right
- draw a line segment by moving 10 pixels to the right and 50 pixels down
- draw a horizontal line segment by moving 200 pixels to the left
- draw a line segment to the initial point (specified by z)

Similar comments apply to the other two SVG <path> elements in Listing A.1. One detail to keep in mind is that uppercase letters (C, L, M, and Q) refer to absolute positions, whereas lowercase letters (c, l, m, and q) refer to relative positions with respect to the element that is to the immediate left. Experiment with the code in Listing A.1 by using combinations of lowercase and uppercase letters to gain a better understanding of how to create different visual effects.

Figure A.1 displays the result of rendering the SVG document BasicShapes1.svg in a Chrome browser.

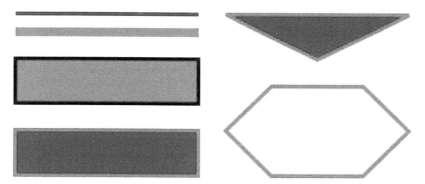

FIGURE A.1 SVG lines and rectangles.

Since you might be working primarily with D3 instead of SVG, the following three code snippets show you how to render a line segment, a rectangle, and a path in D3 using an svg variable (which will be defined in D3 code samples later in this appendix):

```
svg.append("svg:line")
    .attr("x1", 10)
    .attr("y1", 20)
    .attr("x2", 200)
    .attr("y2", 300)
    .style("stroke", "blue")
    .style("stroke-width", 3);
```

A D3 rectangle looks like:

```
svg.append("svg:rect")
       .attr("x",       10)
       .attr("y",       20)
       .attr("width",   200)
       .attr("height", 100)
       .attr("fill",    "red");
```

A D3 path looks like:

```
svg.append("svg:path")
       .attr("d", "m0,0 10,-240 a200,200 0 0,0 0,240")
       .style("fill", "yellow")
```

SVG GRADIENTS AND THE <PATH> ELEMENT

As you might have surmised, SVG supports linear gradients as well as radial gradients that you can apply to 2D shapes. For example, you can use the SVG <path> element to define elliptic arcs (using the d attribute) and then specify gradient effects. The SVG <path> element contains a d attribute for specifying the shapes in a path, as shown here:

```
<path d="specify a list of path elements" fill="..." />
```

Listing A.2 displays the contents of BasicShapesLRG1.svg that illustrate how to render 2D shapes with linear gradients and with radial gradients.

LISTING A.2: BasicShapesLRG1.svg

```
<?xml version="1.0" encoding="iso-8859-1"?>
<!DOCTYPE svg PUBLIC "-//W3C//DTD SVG 20001102//EN"
 "http://www.w3.org/TR/2000/CR-SVG-20001102/DTD/svg-20001102.dtd">

<svg xmlns="http://www.w3.org/2000/svg"
     xmlns:xlink="http://www.w3.org/1999/xlink"
     width="100%" height="100%">
  <defs>
    <linearGradient id="pattern1"
                   x1="0%" y1="100%" x2="100%" y2="0%">
      <stop offset="0%"    stop-color="yellow"/>
      <stop offset="40%"   stop-color="red"/>
      <stop offset="80%"   stop-color="blue"/>
    </linearGradient>

   <radialGradient id="pattern2">
      <stop offset="0%"    stop-color="yellow"/>
      <stop offset="40%"   stop-color="red"/>
      <stop offset="80%"   stop-color="blue"/>
   </radialGradient>
  </defs>

  <g>
  <ellipse cx="120" cy="80" rx="100" ry="50"
```

```
            fill="url(#pattern1)"/>

    <ellipse cx="120" cy="200" rx="100" ry="50"
            fill="url(#pattern2)"/>

    <ellipse cx="320" cy="80" rx="50" ry="50"
            fill="url(#pattern2)"/>

    <path d="M 505,145 v -100 a 250,100 0 0,1 -200,100"
          fill="black"/>

    <path d="M 500,140 v -100 a 250,100 0 0,1 -200,100"
          fill="url(#pattern1)"
          stroke="black" stroke-thickness="8"/>

    <path d="M 305,165 v  100 a 250,100 0 0,1  200,-100"
          fill="black"/>

    <path d="M 300,160 v  100 a 250,100 0 0,1  200,-100"
          fill="url(#pattern1)"
          stroke="black" stroke-thickness="8"/>

    <ellipse cx="450" cy="240" rx="50" ry="50"
            fill="url(#pattern1)"/>
  </g>
</svg>
```

Listing A.2 contains an SVG `<defs>` element that specifies a `<linearGradient>` element (whose `id` attribute has value `pattern1`) with three stop values using an XML-based syntax followed by a `<radialGradient>` element with three `<stop>` elements and an `id` attribute whose value is `pattern2`.

The next portion of Listing A.2 is an SVG `<g>` element, which acts as a logical container for SVG elements. In fact, it's possible to define nested `<g>` elements in an SVG document. In this example, the `<g>` element contains four `<ellipse>` elements, the first of which specifies the point $(120,80)$ as its center (cx,cy), with a major radius of 100, a minor radius of 50, and filled with the linear gradient `pattern1`, as shown here:

```
<ellipse cx="120" cy="80" rx="100" ry="50"
        fill="url(#pattern1)"/>
```

Similar comments apply to the attribute values in the other three SVG `<ellipse>` elements. In addition, the SVG `<g>` element contains four SVG `<path>` elements that render elliptic arcs. The first `<path>` element specifies a black background for the elliptic arc defined with the following d attribute:

```
d="M 505,145 v -100 a 250,100 0 0,1 -200,100"
```

Unfortunately, the SVG syntax for elliptic arcs is not fully intuitive, and it's based on the notion of major arcs and minor arcs that connect two points on an ellipse. This example is only for illustrative purposes, so we won't delve into a detailed explanation of how elliptic arcs are defined in SVG. However, the following website provides additional details: *http://www.svgbasics.com/arcs.html*. Perform an Internet search to find additional links that discuss SVG elliptic arcs (and be prepared to spend some time experimenting with your own code samples).

The second SVG <path> element in the <g> element renders the same elliptic arc with a slight offset using the linear gradient pattern1, which creates a shadow effect. The corresponding code for an ellipse in D3 is:

```
svg.append("svg:ellipse")
    .append("ellipse")
    .attr("cx",        300)
    .attr("cy",        200)
    .attr("rx",        120)
    .attr("ry",        80)
    .attr("fill",      "red")
    .attr("stroke",  "blue")
    .attr("stroke-width", 2);
```

The code for a linear gradient and a radial gradient in D3 is somewhat lengthy (depending on the number of stop colors that you define), and you can find online examples of both types of gradients in D3.

Similar comments apply to the other pair of SVG <path> elements, which render an elliptic arc with the radial gradient pattern2 (also with a shadow effect). Figure A.2 displays the result of rendering BasicShapesLRG1.svg.

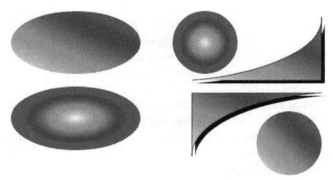

FIGURE A.2 SVG linear radial gradient arcs.

SVG <POLYGON> ELEMENT

The SVG <polygon> element contains a polygon attribute in which you can specify points that represent the vertices of a polygon. Although the SVG <polygon> element is most useful when you want to create polygons with an arbitrary number of sides, you can also use the <polygon> element to render line segments and rectangles. The syntax of the SVG <polygon> element looks like this:

```
<polygon path="specify a list of points" fill="..." />
```

Listing A.3 displays the contents of a portion of SvgCube1.svg that illustrates how to render a cube in SVG using a <polygon> element.

LISTING A.3: SvgCube1.svg

```
<?xml version="1.0" encoding="iso-8859-1"?>
<!DOCTYPE svg PUBLIC "-//W3C//DTD SVG 20001102//EN"
 "http://www.w3.org/TR/2000/CR-SVG-20001102/DTD/svg-20001102.dtd">

<svg xmlns="http://www.w3.org/2000/svg"
     xmlns:xlink="http://www.w3.org/1999/xlink"
     width="100%" height="100%">
  <!-- <defs> element omitted for brevity -->

  <!-- top face (counter clockwise) -->
  <polygon fill="url(#pattern1)"
           points="50,50 200,50 240,30 90,30"/>

  <!-- front face -->
  <rect width="150" height="150" x="50" y="50"
        fill="url(#pattern2)"/>

  <!-- right face (counter clockwise) -->
  <polygon fill="url(#pattern3)"
           points="200,50 200,200 240,180 240,30"/>
</svg>
```

Listing A.3 contains an SVG <g> element that contains the three faces of a cube, in which an SVG <polygon> element renders the top face (a parallelogram), an SVG <rect> element renders the front face, and another SVG <polygon> element renders the right face (also a parallelogram). The three faces of the cube are rendered with the linear gradient and the two radial gradients defined in the SVG <defs> element (not shown in Listing A.3). The code for a blue polygon in D3 is:

```
var points2 = "200,50 200,200 240,180 240,30";
var polygon = g1.append("polygon")
                .style("fill", "blue")
                .attr("points", points2)
                .attr("stroke", "red")
                .attr("stroke-width", 1);
```

Figure A.3 displays the result of rendering the SVG document SvgCube1.svg in a landscape-mode screenshot.

FIGURE A.3 An SVG gradient cube.

BÉZIER CURVES AND TRANSFORMS

SVG supports quadratic and cubic Bézier curves that you can render with linear gradients or radial gradients. You can also concatenate multiple Bézier curves using an SVG `<path>` element. Listing A.4 displays the contents of `BezierCurves1.svg` that illustrate how to render various Bézier curves.

NOTE *The transform-related effects are discussed later in this appendix.*

LISTING A.4: BezierCurves1.svg

```
<?xml version="1.0" encoding="iso-8859-1"?>
<!DOCTYPE svg PUBLIC "-//W3C//DTD SVG 20001102//EN"
 "http://www.w3.org/TR/2000/CR-SVG-20001102/DTD/svg-20001102.dtd">

 <svg xmlns="http://www.w3.org/2000/svg"
     xmlns:xlink="http://www.w3.org/1999/xlink"
     width="100%" height="100%">
  <!-- <defs> element omitted for brevity -->

  <g transform="scale(1.5,0.5)">
   <!-- scale a cubic Bezier curve with 'pattern1' -->
   <path d="m 0,50 C 400,200 200,-150 100,350"
         stroke="black" stroke-width="4"
         fill="url(#pattern1)"/>
  </g>

  <g transform="translate(50,50)">
    <!-- scale a red cubic Bezier curve -->
    <g transform="scale(0.5,1)">
     <path d="m 50,50 C 400,100 200,200 100,20"
           fill="red" stroke="black" stroke-width="4"/>
    </g>

    <!-- scale a yellow cubic Bezier curve -->
    <g transform="scale(1,1)">
     <path d="m 50,50 C 400,100 200,200 100,20"
           fill="yellow" stroke="black" stroke-width="4"/>
    </g>
  </g>

  <!-- translate/scale a blue cubic Bezier curve -->
  <g transform="translate(-50,50)">
    <g transform="scale(1,2)">
     <path d="M 50,50 C 400,100 200,200 100,20"
           fill="blue" stroke="black" stroke-width="4"/>
    </g>
  </g>

  <!-- translate/scale a blue cubic Bezier curve -->
  <g transform="translate(-50,50)">
   <g transform="scale(0.5, 0.5) translate(195,345)">
```

```
    <path d="m20,20 C20,50 20,450 300,200 s-150,-250 200,100"
        fill="blue" style="stroke:#880088;stroke-width:4;"/>
  </g>

  <!-- scale a cubic Bezier curve with 'pattern2' -->
  <g transform="scale(0.5, 0.5) translate(185,335)">
   <path d="m20,20 C20,50 20,450 300,200 s-150,-250 200,100"
        fill="url(#pattern2)"
        style="stroke:#880088;stroke-width:4;"/>
  </g>

  <!-- scale a reddish blue cubic Bezier curve -->
  <g transform="scale(0.5, 0.5) translate(180,330)">
   <path d="m20,20 C20,50 20,450 300,200 s-150,-250 200,100"
     fill="blue" style="stroke:#880088;stroke-width:4;"/>
  </g>

  <g transform="scale(0.5, 0.5) translate(170,320)">
   <path d="m20,20 C20,50 20,450 300,200 s-150,-250 200,100"
        fill="url(#pattern2)"
        style="stroke:black;stroke-width:4;"/>
  </g>
  </g>

  <g transform="scale(0.8,1) translate(380,120)">
   <path d="M0,0 C200,150 400,300 20,250"
        fill="url(#pattern2)"
        style="stroke:blue;stroke-width:4;"/>
  </g>

  <g transform="scale(2.0,2.5) translate(150,-80)">
   <path d="M200,150 C0,0 400,300 20,250"
        fill="url(#pattern2)"
        style="stroke:blue;stroke-width:4;"/>
  </g>
</svg>
```

Listing A.4 contains an SVG `<defs>` element that defines two linear gradients followed by ten SVG `<path>` elements, each of which renders a cubic Bézier curve. The SVG `<path>` elements are enclosed in SVG `<g>` elements whose `transform` attribute contains the SVG `scale()` function or the SVG `translate()` function (or both).

The first SVG `<g>` element invokes the SVG `scale()` function to scale the cubic Bézier curve that is specified in an SVG `<path>` element, as shown here:

```
<g transform="scale(1.5,0.5)">
    <path d="m 0,50 C 400,200 200,-150 100,350"
        stroke="black" stroke-width="4"
        fill="url(#pattern1)"/>
</g>
```

The preceding cubic Bézier curve has an initial point (0,50) with control points (400,200) and (200,-150) followed by the second control point (100,350). The Bézier curve is black, with a width of 4, and its `fill` attribute is the color defined in the `<linearGradient>` element (whose `id` attribute has value pattern1) that is defined in the SVG `<defs>` element.

The remaining SVG <path> elements are similar to the first SVG <path> element, so they will not be described.

Figure A.4 displays the result of rendering the Bézier curves that are defined in the SVG document BezierCurves1.svg in a landscape-mode screenshot.

FIGURE A.4 SVG Bézier curves.

SVG FILTERS AND SHADOW EFFECTS

You can create nice filter effects that you can apply to 2D shapes as well as text strings, and this section contains three SVG-based examples of creating such effects. Listing A.5 displays the contents of the SVG documents BlurFilterText1.svg.

LISTING A.5: BlurFilterText1.svg

```
<?xml version="1.0" encoding="iso-8859-1"?>
<!DOCTYPE svg PUBLIC "-//W3C//DTD SVG 20001102//EN"
 "http://www.w3.org/TR/2000/CR-SVG-20001102/DTD/svg-20001102.dtd">

<svg xmlns="http://www.w3.org/2000/svg"
     xmlns:xlink="http://www.w3.org/1999/xlink"
     width="100%" height="100%">
  <defs>
  <filter
     id="blurFilter1"
     filterUnits="objectBoundingBox"
     x="0" y="0"
     width="100%" height="100%">
     <feGaussianBlur stdDeviation="4"/>
  </filter>
  </defs>

<g transform="translate(50,100)">
  <text id="normalText" x="0" y="0"
        fill="red" stroke="black" stroke-width="4"
        font-size="72">
     Normal Text
  </text>

  <text id="horizontalText" x="0" y="100"
        filter="url(#blurFilter1)"
```

```
            fill="red" stroke="black" stroke-width="4"
            font-size="72">
        Blurred Text
   </text>
</g>
</svg>
```

The SVG `<defs>` element in Listing A.5 contains an SVG `<filter>` element that specifies a Gaussian blur with the following line:

```
<feGaussianBlur stdDeviation="4"/>
```

You can specify larger values for the `stdDeviation` attribute if you want to create more diffuse filter effects.

The first SVG `<text>` element that is contained in the SVG `<g>` element renders a normal text string, whereas the second SVG `<text>` element contains a `filter` attribute that references the filter (defined in the SVG `<defs>` element) to render the same text string, as shown here:

```
filter="url(#blurFilter1)"
```

Figure A.5 displays the result of rendering `BlurFilterText1.svg` that creates a filter effect in Google Chrome on a MacBook.

Normal Text

FIGURE A.5 SVG filter effect.

RENDERING TEXT ALONG AN SVG <PATH> ELEMENT

SVG enables you to render a text string along an SVG `<path>` element. Listing A.6 displays the contents of the document `TextOnQBezierPath1.svg` that illustrates how to render a text string along the path of a quadratic Bézier curve.

LISTING A.6: TextOnQBezierPath1.svg

```
<?xml version="1.0" encoding="iso-8859-1"?>
<!DOCTYPE svg PUBLIC "-//W3C//DTD SVG 20001102//EN"
 "http://www.w3.org/TR/2000/CR-SVG-20001102/DTD/svg-20001102.dtd">

<svg xmlns="http://www.w3.org/2000/svg"
     xmlns:xlink="http://www.w3.org/1999/xlink"
     width="100%" height="100%">
<defs>
  <path id="pathDefinition"
        d="m0,0 Q100,0 200,200 T300,200 z"/>
</defs>
  <g transform="translate(100,100)">
```

```
   <text id="textStyle" fill="red"
       stroke="blue" stroke-width="2"
       font-size="24">

   <textPath xlink:href="#pathDefinition">
   Sample Text that follows a path specified by a Quadratic Bezier curve
   </textPath>
   </text>
</g>
</svg>
```

The SVG `<defs>` element in Listing A.6 contains an SVG `<path>` element that defines a quadratic Bézier curve (note the `Q` in the `d` attribute). The SVG `<path>` element has an `id` attribute whose value is `pathDefinition`, which is referenced later in this code sample.

The SVG `<g>` element contains an SVG `<text>` element that specifies a text string to render, as well as an SVG `<textPath>` element that specifies the path along which the text is rendered, as shown here:

```
<textPath xlink:href="#pathDefinition">
   Sample Text that follows a path specified by a Quadratic Bezier curve
</textPath>
```

Notice that the SVG `<textPath>` element contains the attribute `xlink:href`, whose value is `pathDefinition`, which is also the `id` of the SVG `<path>` element that is defined in the SVG `<defs>` element. As a result, the text string is rendered along the path of a quadratic Bézier curve instead of rendering the text string horizontally (which is the default behavior).

Figure A.6 displays the result of rendering `TextOnQBezierPath1.svg` that renders a text string along the path of a quadratic Bézier curve.

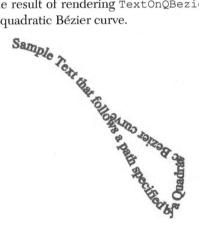

FIGURE A.6 SVG text on a quadratic Bézier.

SVG TRANSFORMS

Earlier in this appendix you saw some examples of SVG transform effects. In addition to the SVG functions `scale()`, `translate()`, and `rotate()`, SVG provides the `skew()` function to create skew effects.

Listing A.7 displays the contents of `TransformEffects1.svg` that illustrates how to apply transforms to rectangles and circles in SVG.

LISTING A.7: TransformEffects1.svg

```
<?xml version="1.0" encoding="iso-8859-1"?>
<!DOCTYPE svg PUBLIC "-//W3C//DTD SVG 20001102//EN"
 "http://www.w3.org/TR/2000/CR-SVG-20001102/DTD/svg-20001102.dtd">

<svg xmlns="http://www.w3.org/2000/svg"
     xmlns:xlink="http://www.w3.org/1999/xlink"
     width="100%" height="100%">
<defs>
  <linearGradient id="gradientDefinition1"
     x1="0" y1="0" x2="200" y2="0"
     gradientUnits="userSpaceOnUse">
     <stop offset="0%"   style="stop-color:#FF0000"/>
     <stop offset="100%" style="stop-color:#440000"/>
  </linearGradient>

  <pattern id="dotPattern" width="8" height="8"
           patternUnits="userSpaceOnUse">

     <circle id="circle1" cx="2" cy="2" r="2"
        style="fill:red;"/>
  </pattern>
</defs>

<!-- full cylinder -->
<g id="largeCylinder" transform="translate(100,20)">
   <ellipse cx="0"   cy="50" rx="20" ry="50"
            stroke="blue" stroke-width="4"
            style="fill:url(#gradientDefinition1)"/>

   <rect x="0" y="0" width="300" height="100"
         style="fill:url(#gradientDefinition1)"/>

   <rect x="0" y="0" width="300" height="100"
         style="fill:url(#dotPattern)"/>

   <ellipse cx="300" cy="50" rx="20"  ry="50"
            stroke="blue" stroke-width="4"
            style="fill:yellow;"/>
</g>

<!-- half-sized cylinder -->
<g transform="translate(100,100) scale(.5)">
   <use xlink:href="#largeCylinder" x="0" y="0"/>
</g>

<!-- skewed cylinder -->
<g transform="translate(100,100) skewX(40) skewY(20)">
   <use xlink:href="#largeCylinder" x="0" y="0"/>
</g>
```

```
<!-- rotated cylinder -->
<g transform="translate(100,100) rotate(40)">
  <use xlink:href="#largeCylinder" x="0" y="0"/>
</g>
</svg>
```

The SVG `<defs>` element in Listing A.7 contains a `<linearGradient>` element that defines a linear gradient followed by an SVG `<pattern>` element that defines a custom pattern, which is shown here:

```
<pattern id="dotPattern" width="8" height="8"
         patternUnits="userSpaceOnUse">

    <circle id="circle1" cx="2" cy="2" r="2"
       style="fill:red;"/>
</pattern>
```

As you can see, the SVG `<pattern>` element contains an SVG `<circle>` element that is repeated in a grid-like fashion inside an 8*8 pixels rectangle (note the values of the `width` attribute and the `height` attribute). The SVG `<pattern>` element has an `id` attribute whose value is `dotPattern` because (as you will see) this element creates a dotted effect.

Listing A.7 contains four SVG `<g>` elements, each of which renders a cylinder that references the SVG `<pattern>` element that is defined in the SVG `<defs>` element.

The first SVG `<g>` element in Listing A.7 contains two SVG `<ellipse>` elements and two SVG `<rect>` elements. The first `<ellipse>` element renders the left-side cover of the cylinder with the linear gradient that is defined in the SVG `<defs>` element. The first `<rect>` element renders the body of the cylinder with a linear gradient, and the second `<rect>` element renders the dot pattern on the body of the cylinder. Finally, the second `<ellipse>` element renders the right-side cover of the ellipse.

The other three cylinders are easy to create: they simply reference the first cylinder and apply a transformation to change the size, shape, and orientation. Specifically, these three cylinders reference the first cylinder with the code

`<use xlink:href="#largeCylinder" x="0" y="0"/>` and then they apply scale, skew, and rotate functions to render scaled, skewed, and rotated cylinders.

Figure A.7 displays the result of rendering `TransformEffects1.svg`.

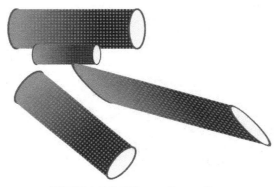

FIGURE A.7 SVG `Transform` effects.

SVG AND HTML

You can use an `<svg>` element in an HTML5 Web page to embed pure SVG code. For example, Listing A.8 renders a red rectangle with a blue border.

LISTING A.8: EmbeddedSVG.html

```
<!DOCTYPE html>
<html lang="en">
<head>
  <meta charset="utf-8" />
  <title>Embedded SVG</title>
</head>

<body>
<svg>
   <rect x="20" y="20" width="200" height="100"
         fill="red" stroke="blue" stroke-width="4"/>
</svg>
</body>
</html>
```

The code in Listing A.8 is straightforward: it consists of HTML5 boilerplate text and an SVG `<rect>` element that you have seen earlier in this appendix.

Figure A.8 displays the graphics image (i.e., a red rectangle) that is rendered by the code in the HTML Web page in Listing A.8.

FIGURE A.8 An SVG Rectangle in an HTML Web Page.

CSS3 AND SVG

CSS3 selectors can reference SVG documents using the CSS3 `url()` function, which means that you can incorporate SVG-based graphics effects (including animation) in your HTML pages. For example, the following code block references the SVG document `Blue3DCircle1.svg` in a CSS selector:

```
#circle1 {
opacity: 0.5; color: red;
width: 250px; height: 250px;
position: absolute; top: 0px; left: 0px;
font-size: 24px;
-webkit-border-radius: 4px;
-moz-border-radius: 4px;
border-radius: 4px;
```

```
-webkit-background: url(Blue3DCircle1.svg) top right;
-moz-background: url(Blue3DCircle1.svg) top right;
background: url(Blue3DCircle1.svg) top right;
}
```

Similarities and Differences Between SVG and CSS3

This section briefly summarizes the features that are common to SVG and CSS3 as well as the features that are unique to each technology. SVG and CSS3 both provide support for the following:

- linear and radial gradients
- 2D graphics and animation effects
- shapes such as rectangles, circles, and ellipses

WAI ARIA (web accessibility initiative—accessible rich internet applications) SVG provides support for the following features that are not available in CSS3:

- Bézier curves
- hierarchical object definitions
- custom glyphs
- rendered text along an arbitrary path
- defined event listeners on SVG objects
- programmatic creation of 2D shapes using JavaScript
- accessibility to XML-based technologies and tools

CSS3 provides support for the following features that are not available in SVG:

- 3D graphics and animation effects
- multicolumn rendering of text
- WebGL-oriented functionality (e.g., CSS shaders)

Note that SVG filters and CSS filters will become one and the same at some point in the not-too-distant future.

In general, SVG is better suited than CSS3 for large data sets that will be used for data visualization, and you can reference the SVG document (which might render some type of chart) in a CSS3 selector using the CSS3 url() function. You have already seen such an example in appendix three, where the SVG document contains the layout for a bar chart. In general, there might be additional processing involved where data is retrieved or aggregated from one or more sources (such as databases and web services) and then manipulated using some programming language (such as XSLT [eXxtensible Stylesheet Language Transformations], Java, or JavaScript) to programmatically create an SVG document or perhaps create SVG elements in a browser session.

INTRODUCTION TO D3

The second part of this appendix introduces you to D3 and provides a collection of short code samples that illustrate how to use some useful D3 application programming interfaces (API).

This appendix moves quickly, so even if you are already familiar with D3 it's worth your while to read (or at least skim through) the material in this appendix.

The first part provides a brief description of the D3 toolkit, and the second shows you how to use some basic D3 methods by rendering simple two-dimensional (2D) shapes. In addition, you will learn how to create linear gradients and radial gradients.

NOTE   *Be sure to launch the HTML Web pages in a browser as you read code samples in this book because this will show you what the code actually does, and it will also save you time.*

WHAT IS D3?

Mike Bostock created the open-source toolkit Protovis, and then he created the D3 toolkit, which is a JavaScript-based open-source project for creating very appealing data visualization. D3 is an acronym for "data-driven documents," and its home page is here:

http://mbostock.github.com/d3/d3

Although D3 can be used for practically any type of data visualization, common-use cases include rendering maps, geographic-related data, economic data (such as employment figures) in conjunction with various locales, and medical data (diabetes seems to be very popular).

In December of 2011, D3 was named the data-visualization project of the year (by Flowing Data!), which is not surprising when you see the functionality that is available in D3.

D3 provides a layer of abstraction that generates underlying scalable vector graphics (SVG) code. D3 enables you to create a surprisingly rich variety of data visualizations. If you need to generate graphics-oriented Web pages, and you prefer to work with JavaScript instead of working with raw SVG, then you definitely ought to consider using D3. Two key aspects of D3 involve tools for reading data in multiple formats and the ability to transform the data and render the data in many forms. D3 supports the following features:

- creation of SVG-based 2D shapes
- 2D graphics and animation effects
- method chaining

D3 has an extensive collection of "helper methods," such as select(), append(), data(), and attr(), among others. Read the online documentation about these and other D3 methods.

D3 BOILERPLATE

If you have worked with HTML5, you are probably familiar with various boilerplate toolkits that are available. In a similar spirit, you can download a D3 boilerplate toolkit (d3.js-boilerplate) here:

https://github.com/zmaril/d3.js-boilerplate

This concludes the brief introduction to D3. The next section of this appendix introduces you to the concept of method chaining to facilitate the discussion of subsequent code samples.

METHOD CHAINING IN D3

Practically every code sample in this book (and almost all the online code samples in various forums) use method chaining, so it's worth your time to understand method chaining before delving into the code samples.

The key idea to remember is that a D3 search actually returns a result set that is the set of elements that match the selection criteria. You can then apply an action to that set of elements. For example, you can find all the paragraphs in an HTML Web page and then set their text in red. Here is an example (taken from Listing A.1) that uses the d3.selectAll() method to select all the HTML <p> elements in an HTML Web page and then invokes the style() method to set the color of the text in those paragraphs to red:

```
d3.selectAll("p").style("color", "red");
```

Returning to our previous discussion, after applying an action to a set of elements, a new set of elements is returned. In fact, you can apply a second action to that modified set, which returns yet another set. This process of applying multiple methods to a set is called method chaining, and the good news is that you can chain together as many function invocations as you wish. Method chaining enables you to write very compact yet powerful code, as you will see in the code examples in this appendix.

THE D3 METHODS SELECT() AND SELECTALL()

D3 supports various selection-based methods that return arrays of arrays of elements to maintain the hierarchical structure of subselections. D3 also binds additional methods to the array of selected elements thereby enabling you to perform operations on those elements.

D3 provides the method selectAll() that you saw in the previous section and the method select(). Both methods accept selector strings, and both are used for selecting elements. *The select() method selects only the first matching element, whereas the selectAll() method selects all matching elements (in document traversal order).* Due to space constraints, this appendix covers a modest subset of the D3 selection-based methods, but you can find a complete list of methods here:

https://github.com/mbostock/d3/wiki/Selections

SPECIFYING UTF-8 IN HTML5 WEB PAGES WITH D3

All versions of D3 require UTF-8, and failing to specify UTF-8 can cause HTML5 Web pages to behave unpredictably (depending on the browser). You can ensure that your HTML5 Web pages with D3 code will work correctly by including the following snippet immediately after the <head> element:

```
<meta charset="utf-8" />
```

In particular, the preceding tag will ensure that your HTML5 Web pages with D3 and Unicode characters will work correctly.

CREATING NEW HTML ELEMENTS

The code sample in this section uses method chaining, the D3 .select() method, and the d3.append() method to modify an HTML Web page. This simple example shows you how to use these two useful D3 methods.

Listing A.9 displays the contents of AppendElement1.html that illustrates how to add an HTML <p> element to an HTML Web page.

LISTING A.9: AppendElement1.html

```
<!DOCTYPE html>
<html>
 <head>
   <meta charset="utf-8" />
   <title>Append Elements</title>
   <script src="d3.js"></script>
 </head>

<body>
   <script>
     d3.select("body").append("p").text("Hello1 D3");
     d3.select("body").append("p").text("Hello2 D3");
     d3.select("body").append("p").text("Hello3 D3");
     d3.select("body").append("p").text("Hello4 D3");

     d3.selectAll("p").style("color", "red");
   </script>
 </body>
</html>
```

Listing A.9 starts by referencing the D3 JavaScript file d3.js. Next, the <script> element appends four HTML <p> elements to the <body> element using the d3.select() method. Finally, Listing A.9 changes the color of all four HTML <p> elements to red with this code snippet:

```
d3.selectAll("p").style("color", "red");
```

Incidentally, if you want to alternate the colors in the four HTML <p> elements, insert the following code in Listing A.1:

```
d3.selectAll("p").style("color", function(d, i) {
  return i % 2 ? "#f00" : "#eee";
});
```

The preceding code snippet uses a ternary operator to return the color #f00 for even-numbered HTML <p> elements and #eee for odd-numbered HTML <p> elements.

Some older browsers run JavaScript code before the Document Object Model (DOM) is available, in which case you can either use `window.onload()` *to ensure that this does not happen, or you can insert an empty* `<div></div>` *element immediately after the* `<body>` *element and change the occurrences of* `d3.select("body")` *to* `d3.select("div")`. *Figure A.9 displays the graphics image that is rendered by the code in the* HTML *Web page in Listing A.9.*

Hello1 D3

Hello2 D3

Hello3 D3

Hello4 D3

FIGURE A.9 Dynamically appending <p> elements using D3.

THE MOST COMMON IDIOM IN D3

The most common idiom in D3 (TMCIID3) for programmatically creating new DOM elements uses the following type of construct (which, of course, involves method chaining):

```
var theData = [1,2,3,4,5];

var paras = d3.select("body")
              .selectAll("p")
              .data(theData)
              .enter()
              .append("p")
              .text("D3 ");
```

Here is how to read the code in the preceding code block, starting from the definition of the `paras` variable:

- Step 1: Start by selecting the `<body>` element of the current HTML Web page (using the `select()` method).
- Step 2: Return the result set of all the child `<p>` elements using the `selectAll()` method. (If there are no child `<p>` elements, the returned set is a set of length zero).
- Step 3: Iterate or loop through the numbers in the JavaScript array `theData` to create a new HTML `<p>` element whose text value is the string D3.
- Step 4: After each iteration in Step 3, append the newly created `<p>` element to the result set in Step 2.

The `d3.selectAll()` *method always returns a result set, which can be an empty set (and therefore, this method never returns a null or undefined value).*

When the preceding code snippet has completed, the JavaScript variable `paras` will consist of five new HTML `<p>` elements. If you understand this sequence of events, you are ready for the code sample in the next section. If you do not understand, then continue to the next section and launch the HTML Web page in a browser to confirm that the preceding explanation is correct.

The acronym TMCIID3 is a convenient way to refer to the D3 code snippet that was discussed in this section, and you will see this acronym used in the code samples throughout this book.

BINDING DATA TO DOCUMENT-OBJECT-MODEL ELEMENTS

Now that you understand method chaining and how to use the most common idiom in D3, you are ready to see how to perform both in an HTML Web page.

Listing A.10 displays the contents of `Binding1.html` that illustrates how to combine JavaScript variables with the D3 methods `.data()` and `.text()` to append a set of HTML `<p>` elements to an HTML Web page.

LISTING A.10: Binding1.html

```
<!DOCTYPE html>
<html>
 <head>
   <meta charset="utf-8" />
   <title>Appending Sets of Elements</title>
   <script src="d3.js"></script>
 </head>

 <body>
   <script>
     var theData = [1,2,3,4,5];

     var paras = d3.select("body")
                   .selectAll("p")
                   .data(theData)
                   .enter()
                   .append("p")
                   .text("D3 ");

     d3.select("body").append("paras");
   </script>
 </body>
</html>
```

Listing A.10 starts by referencing the D3 JavaScript file; the code in the `<script>` element has already been discussed in the preceding section. The only new code in Listing A.10 is the following code snippet:

```
d3.select("body").append("paras");
```

The preceding code snippet appends the contents of the `paras` variable, which consists of five new HTML `<p>` elements, to the existing HTML `<p>` elements (if there are any) that are child elements of the `<body>` element.

NOTE *Since every* HTML *Web page in this book starts with the same boilerplate code in the* HTML <head> *element, we will omit this duplicated description for the rest of the book.*

Figure A.10 displays the result of rendering the HTML Web page in Listing A.10 in a Web browser.

D3

D3

D3

D3

D3

FIGURE A.10 Using TMCIID3 to generate <p> elements in a Web page.

GENERATING TEXT STRINGS

The code sample in the previous section simply generated a set of text strings with the same text. In this section you will see how to generate a set of text strings that contain the numbers in a JavaScript array.

Listing A.11 displays the contents of `GenerateText1.html` that illustrate how to iterate through a JavaScript array (containing numbers) and render text strings with the values in the array.

LISTING A.11: GenerateText1.html

```
<!DOCTYPE html>
<html>
 <head>
   <meta charset="utf-8">
   <title>Iterating Through Arrays</title>
   <script src="d3.min.js"></script>
 </head>

 <body>
  <script>
    var dataValues1 = [50, 100, 250, 150, 300];

    d3.select("body")
        .selectAll("p")
        .data(dataValues1)
        .enter()
        .append("p")
        .text(function(d) { return "Paragraph Number: "+d; })
        .style("font-size", "16px")
        .style("color", "blue");
   </script>
 </body>
</html>
```

Listing A.11 contains a `<script>` element that initializes a JavaScript variable, `dataValues1`, followed by TMCIID3 to create and append a set of new HTML `<p>` elements to the existing HTML Web page. The only new construct is the use of a function, as shown in the following code snippet:

```
.text(function(d) { return "Paragraph Number: "+d; })
```

When you define a function in TMCIID3, D3 understands that it must populate the variable `d` with the value of the current iteration through the numbers in the JavaScript array `dataValues1`.

You can use any legitimate name that you want in the preceding function, but perhaps it helps to think of the variable `d` as datum, or a single piece of data (such as a number in an array). Later, you will see functions that specify a datum and an index using the following syntax:

```
.text(function(d, i) { return d[i]; })
```

Figure A.11 displays the result of rendering the HTML Web page in Listing A.11 in a Web browser.

Paragraph Number: 50

Paragraph Number: 100

Paragraph Number: 250

Paragraph Number: 150

Paragraph Number: 300

FIGURE A.11 Generate `<p>` elements with styling effects.

The next section shows you how to leverage what you have learned about D3 to render various 2D shapes in an HTML Web page.

CREATING SIMPLE TWO-DIMENSIONAL SHAPES

This section contains a code sample that shows you how to create simple 2D shapes in D3. The D3 code specifies attributes that are the same as the SVG-based attributes for each 2D shape. For example, an ellipse is defined in terms of its center point (`cx, cy`), its major axis `rx`, and its minor axis `ry`. Similar comments apply for creating a rectangle (`x, y, width`, and `height` attributes) and for creating a line segment (`(x1,y1)` and `(x2,y2)` as the coordinates of the two endpoints of the line segment). In fact, Listing A.4 is nothing more than using TMCIID3 and the D3 `.attr()` method to set the attributes of various 2D shapes.

Listing A.12 displays the contents of `SimpleShapes1.html` that illustrates how to create a circle, an ellipse, a rectangle, and a line segment in D3.

LISTING A.12: SimpleShapes1.html

```
<!DOCTYPE html>
<html>
 <head>
```

```
  <meta charset="utf-8" />
  <title>Create Simple 2D Shapes</title>
  <script src="d3.min.js"></script>
</head>

<body>
 <script>
   var width = 600, height = 400;

   // circle and ellipse attributes
   var cx = 50,   cy = 80,   radius1 = 40,
       ex = 250,  ey = 80,   radius2 = 80;

   // rectangle attributes
   var rectX = 20, rectY = 200;
   var rWidth = 100, rHeight = 50;

   // line segment attributes
   var x1=150,y1=150,x2=300,y2=250,lineWidth=4;

   var colors = ["red", "blue", "green"];

   // create an SVG element
   var svg = d3.select("body")
               .append("svg")
               .attr("width",  width)
               .attr("height", height);

   // append a circle
   svg.append("circle")
      .attr("cx", cx)
      .attr("cy", cy)
      .attr("r",  radius1)
      .attr("fill", colors[0]);

   // append an ellipse
   svg.append("ellipse")
      .attr("cx", ex)
      .attr("cy", ey)
      .attr("rx", radius2)
      .attr("ry", radius1)
      .attr("fill", colors[1]);

   // append a rectangle
   svg.append("rect")
      .attr("x",  rectX)
      .attr("y",  rectY)
      .attr("width",  rWidth)
      .attr("height", rHeight)
      .attr("fill", colors[2]);

   // append a line segment
   svg.append("line")
      .attr("x1", x1)
```

```
            .attr("y1", y1)
            .attr("x2", x2)
            .attr("y2", y2)
            .attr("stroke-width", lineWidth)
            .attr("stroke", colors[0]);
    </script>
  </body>
</html>
```

Listing A.12 contains a `<script>` element that creates multiple SVG elements and uses the D3 `.attr()` method to set the value of the attributes of each SVG element. When you launch the HTML Web page in Listing A.12, D3 appends the following code block to the existing HTML Web page:

```
<svg width="600" height="400">
  <circle cx="50" cy="80" r="40" fill="red"></circle>
  <ellipse cx="250" cy="80" rx="80" ry="40" fill="blue"></ellipse>
  <rect x="20" y="200" width="100" height="50" fill="green"></rect>
  <line x1="150" y1="150" x2="300" y2="250"
        stroke-width="4" stroke="red"></line>
</svg>
```

Compare the code in Listing A.12 with the preceding code block to verify that the preceding SVG elements correspond to the code in Listing A.12. You can use an alternate coding style that defines multiple JavaScript variables, as shown in the following code block:

```
var theBody = d3.select("body");

var theSVG = theBody.append("svg")
      .attr("width",  100)
      .attr("height", 100);

var circleSelection = theSVG.append("circle")
      .attr("cx", 50)
      .attr("cy", 50)
      .attr("r", 30)
      .style("fill", "red");
```

Figure A.12 displays the graphics image that is rendered by the code in the HTML Web page in Listing A.12.

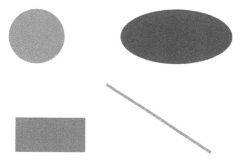

FIGURE A.12 D3 code for a circle, ellipse, rectangle, and a line segment.

BÉZIER CURVES AND TEXT

Listing A.13 displays the contents of `BezierCurvesAndText1.html` that illustrates how to use D3 to render a quadratic Bézier curve, a cubic Bézier curve, and text strings that follow the path of the Bézier curves.

LISTING A.13: BezierCurvesAndText1.html

```
<!DOCTYPE html>
<html>
 <head>
   <meta charset="utf-8" />
   <title>Bezier Curves and Text</title>
   <script src="d3.min.js"></script>
 </head>

<body>
   <script>
     var width = 600, height = 400, opacity=0.5;
     var cubicPath  = "M20,20 C300,200 100,500 400,100";
     var quadPath   = "M200,20 Q100,300 500,100";

     var cValues    = "M20,20 C300,200 100,500 400,100";
     var qValues    = "M200,20 Q100,300 500,100";

     var fontSizeC  = "24";
     var fontSizeQ  = "18";

     var textC =
       "Sample Text that follows a path of a cubic Bezier curve";

     var textQ =
       "Sample Text that follows a path of a quadratic Bezier curve";

     var fillColors = ["red", "blue", "green", "yellow"];

     // create an SVG container...
     var svgContainer = d3.select("body").append("svg")
                          .attr("width",  width)
                          .attr("height", height);

     var defs      = svgContainer
                        .append("svg:defs");

     var patternC = defs.append("svg:path")
                        .attr("id", "pathInfoC")
                        .attr("d",  cValues);

     var patternQ = defs.append("svg:path")
                        .attr("id", "pathInfoQ")
                        .attr("d",  qValues);
```

```
      // now add the 'g' element...
      var g1 = svgContainer.append("svg:g");

      // create a cubic Bezier curve...
      var bezierC = g1.append("path")
                      .attr("d", cubicPath)
                      .attr("fill",   fillColors[0])
                      .attr("stroke", "blue")
                      .attr("stroke-width", 2);

      // text following a cubic Bezier curve...
      var textC  = g1.append("text")
                      .attr("id", "textStyleC")
                      .attr("stroke", "blue")
                      .attr("fill",   fillColors[1])
                      .attr("stroke-width", 2)
                        .append("textPath")
                        .attr("font-size", fontSizeC)
                        .attr("xlink:href", "#pathInfoC")
                        .text(textC);

      // create a quadratic Bezier curve...
      var bezierQ = g1.append("path")
                      .attr("d", quadPath)
                      .attr("fill",   fillColors[1])
                      .attr("opacity", opacity)
                      .attr("stroke", "blue")
                      .attr("stroke-width", 2);

      // text following a cubic Bezier curve...
      var textQ  = g1.append("text")
                      .attr("id", "textStyleQ")
                      .attr("stroke", fillColors[3])
                      .attr("stroke-width", 2)
                        .append("textPath")
                        .attr("font-size", fontSizeQ)
                        .attr("xlink:href", "#pathInfoQ")
                        .text(textQ);
   </script>
 </body>
</html>
```

Listing A.13 contains the usual boilerplate code and a <script> element that defines a quadratic Bézier curve and a cubic Bézier curve. The JavaScript variables bezierC, bezierQ, textC, and textQ are set to the values for a cubic Bézier curve, a quadratic Bézier curve, the text for the cubic Bézier curve, and the text for the quadratic Bézier curve, respectively. These variables are used in the D3 code that creates a <path> element, which is how you specify quadratic and cubic Bézier curves in SVG.

As you can see, most of the code in Listing A.13 does two things: it creates SVG elements with the D3 .append() method and it then sets the required attributes with the D3 .attr() method.

Moreover, the definitions for the cubic Bézier curve and the quadratic Bézier curve consist of a string of values, as shown here:

```
var cubicPath = "M20,20 C300,200 100,500 400,100";
var quadPath  = "M200,20 Q100,300 500,100";
```

In fact, if you want to use standard SVG code instead of D3, you could literally copy and paste the preceding strings as the value for the d attribute in the SVG <path> element. Figure A.13 displays the graphics image that is rendered by the code in the HTML Web page in Listing A.13.

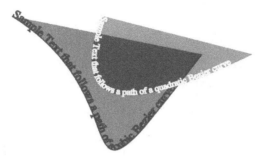

FIGURE A.13 Generating text along two Bézier curves in D3.

A DIGRESSION: SCALING ARRAYS OF NUMBERS TO DIFFERENT RANGES

This section covers the d3.range() method for determining the range of a set of numbers followed by the d3.scale() function for scaling a set of numbers. The rationale for including this section here is that the d3.range() method is used in the gradient-related code samples that you will see later in this appendix. This method is both easy to use and straightforward to understand, and you will see this method in many code samples in this book.

When you work with D3 functions that scale the values in an array, keep in mind that the domain specifies the input values that you provide, and the range refers to the target values that are calculated based on the domain values.

The simplest use of the d3.range() method is to generate a list of integers. For example, d3.range(15) generates the integers between 0 and 14. You can verify this fact by including the following code snippet in a D3-based HTML Web page:

```
console.log("range from 0 to 14: "+d3.range(15))
```

When you open the web Inspector or equivalent, which depends on the particular browser that you use (search online for browser-specific instructions), you will see the following:

```
Numbers from 0 to 14: 0,1,2,3,4,5,6,7,8,9,10,11,12,13,14
```

Another use for the d3.range() method enables you to scale the values in a JavaScript array by mapping them to a different range of values. This functionality is very useful whenever you need to scale the elements in a bar chart or graph, so the graphics output (such as the individual bar elements) fits the dimensions of the screen where you are rendering the chart or graph.

Suppose you have the following set of numbers in a JavaScript array:

```
var dataValues = [10, 20, 30, 40, 50];
```

You can scale them to the range `[0,10]` with the following code snippet:

```
x = d3.scale.linear().domain([10,50]).range([0,10]);
```

Although the preceding code snippet is correct, there are two limitations. First, the minimum and maximum values of the JavaScript array `dataValues` are hard-coded with the values 10 and 50. Second, the range of values is also hard-coded in the code.

The following code snippet is a better way to scale a set of numbers:

```
var dataValues = [10, 20, 30, 40, 50], left=0, right=10;
var xScale = d3.scale.linear()
            .domain([d3.min(dataValues), d3.max(dataValues)])
            .range([left, right]);
```

Notice that all the hard-coded values have been replaced by JavaScript variables. Although we have not discussed the `d3.min()` and `d3.max()` methods, they return the minimum and maximum values, respectively, in a JavaScript array of numbers.

The advantage of the preceding code block is that it works correctly for *any* JavaScript array of numbers. However, you do need to make a manual change to the range values if you want to use a different range.

NOTE *You will probably indent the range of values so there is padding on the left and right of your charts and graphs to avoid inadvertently clipping portions of data from the visual display.*

For example, if you want to render a scatter plot in the horizontal range of `[0,600]`, and you also want to indent by 20 on the left and on the right of the chart, you can use something like the following code snippet:

```
var pad=20;
xScale = d3.scale.linear()
          .domain([d3.min(dataValues), d3.max(dataValues)])
          .range([left+pad, right-pad]);
```

The preceding code block is for scaling numbers along the horizontal axis, and the same type of code works for scaling numbers along the vertical axis, as shown here:

```
yScale = d3.scale.linear()
          .domain([d3.min(dataValues), d3.max(dataValues)])
          .range([pad, height-pad]);
```

NOTE *The vertical axis is positive in the top-to-bottom direction, and if you want to reverse the polarity of the vertical axis, simply reverse the two numbers in the `d3.range()` method in the preceding definition for `yScale`.*

Other convenient array-related functions are also available in D3. For example, if you want to reverse the order of the integers between 1 and 4 inclusive, you can use this code snippet:

```
var range1 = d3.range(1,5).reverse();
```

The next appendix shows more examples of JavaScript arrays in D3 in greater detail.

TWEENING IN D3

The term *tweening* refers to the process of calculating the numbers between a start value and an end value. The tweened values have the same type as the start and end values (tweening a pair of numbers produces a set of numbers, and tweening a pair of colors produces a set of colors). There are different formulas for different tweening effects. By way of analogy, think of accelerating in a car: a smooth acceleration from 0 to 50 is one type of tweening effect that produces a smooth experience. On the other hand, a rollercoaster has one or more intervals involving slow-fast-slow acceleration, which provides another type of tweening effect.

D3 provides support for three tweening methods: `styleTween()`, `attrTween()`, and `tween()`. An example of using `styleTween()` is here:

```
d3.select("body").transition()
   .styleTween("color", function() {
       return d3.interpolate("green", "red");
   });
```

Tip: You can use colors in addition to numbers in the `d3.range()` function. For example, the following code snippet is valid in D3:

```
var colorScale = d3.scale.linear()
                   .domain([0,100])
                   .range(['red', 'blue']);
...
.attr('fill', function(d) {
   return colorScale[d];
})
...
```

The preceding code block sets the color of a shape (not shown here) to a value that is a linear interpolation between `red` and `blue`. Moreover, you can specify hexadecimal values, `(R, G, B)` values, and `HSL` values, in addition to common color names, which is a very nice feature of D3.

You will see many code samples in this book that use this type of code, so you will have plenty of opportunity to become more comfortable with this coding technique in D3.

FORMATTING NUMBERS

D3 supports various formats for numbers. As a simple example, you can insert a comma "," in a number. For example, if you want to render `1234000` as `1,234,000` you can use the following code snippet:

```
var x1 = 1234000;
var x2 = d3.format(",")(x1)
d3.format(".3s");
```

If you want to display `1234000` as `1.234M`, use the following code snippet:

```
var x1 = 1234000;
var x3 = d3.format(".4s")(x1);
```

More information about D3 formatting is here:

https://github.com/mbostock/d3/wiki/Formatting#wiki-d3_format

WORKING WITH GRADIENTS

SVG supports linear gradients and radial gradients, and therefore, you can also render both of these gradients in D3. The next two code samples show you how to render 2D shapes with linear gradients and radial gradients in D3.

Linear Gradients

D3 enables you to define linear gradients in a straightforward manner. The definition of a linear gradient is shown in the following code block:

```
var gradient = svg.append("svg:defs")
        .append("svg:linearGradient")
            .attr("id", "gradient")
            .attr("x1", "0%")
            .attr("y1", "0%")
            .attr("x2", "100%")
            .attr("y2", "100%")
            .attr("spreadMethod", "pad");

gradient.append("svg:stop")
            .attr("offset", "0%")
            .attr("stop-color", "#0c0")
            .attr("stop-opacity", 1);

gradient.append("svg:stop")
            .attr("offset", "100%")
            .attr("stop-color", "#c00")
            .attr("stop-opacity", 1);
```

The preceding code block starts with a code snippet by creating an SVG `<defs>` element that is appended to an SVG `<svg>` element (not shown here). The next two code snippets define a so-called stop color that specifies the attributes of the color to render in the linear gradient.

Radial Gradients

In addition to linear gradients, D3 enables you to define radial gradients. The HTML Web page `RadialGradient1.html` illustrates how to create radial gradients in D3. The definition of a radial gradient is very similar to a linear gradient, and the difference is shown in the following code block:

```
    var gradient = svg.append("svg:defs")
        .append("svg:radialGradient")
```

```
        .attr("id", "gradient")
        .attr("x1", "0%")
        .attr("y1", "0%")
        .attr("x2", "100%")
        .attr("y2", "100%");

    gradient.append("svg:stop")
        .attr("offset", "0%")
        .attr("stop-color", "#f00")
        .attr("stop-opacity", 1.0);
    // add other stop colors as needed
```

ADDING HTML `<div>` ELEMENTS WITH GRADIENT EFFECTS

If you have worked with CSS3 graphics, the CSS3 selectors in Listing A.6 will be familiar to you. If you are new to CSS3, this code sample gives you a preview of how easily you can combine CSS3 with D3 in an HTML Web page.

Listing A.14 displays the contents of GenerateGradientDivs1.html that illustrates how to iterate through an array and render text strings that are displayed with CSS3 gradients.

LISTING A.14: GenerateGradientDivs1.html

```html
<!DOCTYPE html>
<html>
 <head>
   <meta charset="utf-8">
   <title>Creating Gradients </title>
   <script src="d3.min.js"></script>

   <style>
     .gradient {
       display: inline-block;
       top:    20px;
       width:  100px;
       height: 100px;

       background-image: -webkit-gradient(linear,
                     100% 0%, 0% 100%,
                     from(#f00), to(#00f));
       background-image: -gradient(linear,
                     100% 0%, 0% 100%,
                     from(#f00), to(#00f));

       border-radius: 8px;
     }
   </style>
 </head>

<body>
  <script>
    var dataValues1 = [0, 150, 300, 450, 600];

    d3.select("body")
```

```
      .selectAll("p")
      .data(dataValues1)
        .enter()
        .append("div")
        .attr("left", function(d) {
            return d+"px";
        })
        .attr("class", "gradient");
    </script>
  </body>
</html>
```

Listing A.14 contains the usual boilerplate code, and the <script> element uses TMCIID3 to create and append a set of HTML <div> elements to the existing HTML Web page. There are two new things to notice about this code. First, there is a function definition that uses the D3 .attr() method, as shown here:

```
.attr("left", function(d) {
   return d+"px";
})
```

The preceding code block uses each and every value in the JavaScript array dataValues1 (remember that D3 is iterating through an array behind the scenes) to set the pixel value of the CSS left property of each new HTML <div> element. Second, the following code snippet sets the CSS class property to .gradient (which is defined as a selector in the <style> element near the top of Listing A.6):

```
.attr("class", "gradient");
```

Launch the code in Listing A.14 and view the source code to verify the previous statements and to familiarize yourself with this technique for using D3 to create gradient effects in HTML Web pages. Figure A.14 displays the graphics image that is rendered by the code in the HTML Web page in Listing A.14.

FIGURE A.14 Applying gradients to <div> elements in D3.

OTHER D3 GRAPHICS SAMPLES

There are many charts and graphs that can be generated with D3 that you can find online. An open-source project with more than 1,000 D3-based code samples (many of which are similar variants) using various polar equations is here:

https://github.com/ocampesato/d3-graphics

As an example, Figure A.15 displays the graphics image displayed by the D3-based code sample CardioidEllipses1Grad2.html that is included in the preceding link.

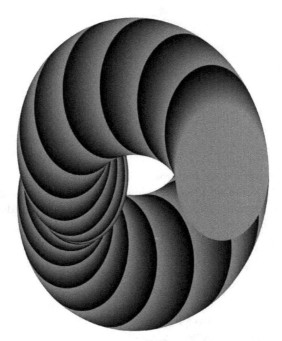

FIGURE A.15 A cardioid-based graphics effect in D3.

D3 APPLICATION PROGRAMMING INTERFACE REFERENCE

If you are impatient and you want to dive into the D3 APIs, they are listed here:

https://github.com/mbostock/d3/wiki/API-Reference

The D3 APIs are listed in various categories, including: Ajax, arrays, axes, chord, cluster, colors, force, geography, hierarchy, histogram, ordinals, pie, projections, scales, shapes (SVG), selections, stack, string formatting, time, transitions, tree, and treemap. In addition, known issues for D3 are listed here:

https://github.com/mbostock/d3/issues?page=1&state=open

OTHER FEATURES OF D3

In addition to the functionality that you have seen in this appendix, D3 and SVG support other useful functionality, such as animation effects as well as 2D transforms. In particular, D3 provides support for four 2D transforms: rotate, scale, skew, and translate. You can apply these transforms to 2D shapes using the D3 .attr() method, as shown in the following code snippets:

```
.attr("transform", "translate("+transX+","+transY+")");
.attr("transform", "rotate("+rotateX+")");
.attr("transform", "scale("+scaleX+","+scaleY+")");
.attr("transform", "skewX("+skewX+")");
```

Perform an online search for complete D3 and SVG code samples that illustrate how to perform animation effects and 2D transforms.

SUMMARY

The first half of this appendix introduced you to SVG, along with examples of how to create the following shapes in SVG:

- line segments
- rectangles
- circles, ellipses, and arcs
- Bézier curves

The second half of this appendix introduced you to D3, followed by examples of using D3 methods to render simple 2D shapes, such as circles, line segments, and rectangles. The supplemental files also include code samples for rendering polygons, ellipses, elliptic arcs, and Bézier curves. In addition, you learned about TMCIID3, which is an extremely useful code construct that is ubiquitous in HTML Web pages that use D3. In particular, you learned about the following D3 methods:

- select()
- selectAll()
- append()
- enter()
- domain()
- range()
- styleTween()

Finally, you learned the syntax for rendering linear gradients and radial gradients in D3.

INDEX

www.ingramcontent.com/pod-product-compliance
Lightning Source LLC
Chambersburg PA
CBHW060524060326
40690CB00017B/3378